Globalisation, Migration and International Relations

Globalisation, Migration and International Relations

G.K. Pagare

CYBER TECH PUBLICATIONS
4264/3, Ansari Road, Daryaganj, New Delhi-110002 (India)
Ph.: 011-23244078, 011-43559448 Fax: 011-23280028
E-Mail: cyberpublicationsdelhi@yahoo.com
Website: www.cybertechpublications.com

GLOBALISATION, MIGRATION AND INTERNATIONAL RELATIONS

G.K. Pagare

First Edition 2010

Published by :

G.S. Rawat for **Cyber Tech Publications**
4264/3, Ansari Road, Daryaganj, New Delhi-110002 (India)
Ph.: 011-23244078, 011-43559448 Fax: 011-23280028
E-Mail: cyberpublicationsdelhi@yahoo.com
Website: www.cybertechpublications.com

Printed at: Asian Offset Printers, Delhi-53

Preface

The global economy as a worldwide economic system began ca. 1500 with the rise and spread of commercialism and has evolved into an expanding system of industrial capitalism. The primary driver of globalization is rapid technological change in core countries and their ability to dominate production of consumer goods to the rest of the world.

It involves the increasing interdependence of national economies, financial markets, trade, corporations, production, distribution, and consumer marketing. By its very nature, globalization draws attention to the economic and technological aspects of life, and to change at the level of culture or identity.

Globalization draws attention to the role of transnational corporations in creating a global market and system of production; to capital markets in creating an integrated financial system; and to bodies such as the International Monetary Fund (IMF) in disseminating a particular view of the state's role within the international economy.

The idea of globalization is the object of controversy. Some of the more dramatic and simplistic versions of the globalization thesis have been challenged by scholars and journalists who are skeptical about the actual extent of transnationalized economic activity.

The hyperglobalist perspective contends that history and economics have come together to create a new order of relations in which states are either converging economically and politically, or are being made irrelevant by the activities of transnational business.

Economic policies are determined more by markets than by governments and, in the economically developed portions of the world, the telecommunications media have facilitated the spread of global mass culture. According to the hyperglobalist perspective, key production factors such as capital technology and even labor are globally mobile and the notions of national products, national industries and national corporations have become redundant, as have the nation-state and its strategies.

—*Author*

CONTENTS

1

INTRODUCTION

Politics is the process by which groups make decisions. Although the term is generally applied to behavior within governments, politics is observed in all human (and many non-human) group interactions, including corporate, academic, and religious institutions. In general, politics can be considered the art of navigating through tensions among multiple "I"s and the "we" to achieve collectively desired ends.

The study of politics originated in Greek political philosophy. For the Greek philosophers, politics was the means by which philosophy came into practicality. Political philosophy concerned the life of man in the polis (Greek roughly meaning "city").

Today, Political Philosophy is the study of what politics is and what the best regime is. Political science (also political studies) is the study of political behavior and examines the acquisition and application of power. Government may refer to the study of particular political regimes and practices, though "government" is sometimes used as a synonym for political science. In practice, political philosophy, politics as a social science and/or practical concerns may be integrated in various kinds of political studies.

A NATURAL STATE

There are many debates as to who was the first person to study politics, many credit Socrates with the first study of politics, while others credit Aristotle. One of the first works concerning politics was Plato's. In Plato's concept, the polis was the way in which man became virtuous. His student and successor Aristotle went on to right the Politics (book) Politics, where he asserts that the city is, by nature, and that man is, by nature, a political animal. Though he does not define it in this manner, Aristotle's assertions point to the natural state of man as being in the city. Only through the city can man become totally self sufficient and thus truly human. These two positions held supreme until the dawn of Modernity (a reaction to the Classical and Scholastic view of philosophy). Machiavelli was among the first political philosophers of Modernity. His most famous work was the Prince (book) Princewhere he discusses the nature of principalities. The idea of "ends justify the means" came from this book, along with the idea of harsh politics. Many people misunderstand Machiavelli's most well known work, believing him to be a fan of strong princes with absolute control. In fact, Machiavelli was a well known republican (one who believes in republican government) and praises it in his Discourses on Livy (book) Discourses on Livy. Modernity thinkers (Enlightenment thinkers), believed that man by nature was not born into a polis, separating from the classical view of Plato and Aristotle. The idea of politics changed from what can the state do for you to what can you do for the state. It became man's job to perfect nature. In 1651, Thomas Hobbes published his most famous work, Leviathan, in which he proposed a model of early human development to justify the creation of a government.

Hobbes described an ideal state of nature wherein every person had equal right to every resource in nature and was free to use any means to acquire those resources. He claimed that such an arrangement created a "war of all against all" (bellum omnium contra omnes). Further, he noted that men would enter into a social contract and would give up absolute rights in exchange for certain protections. Hobbes' During the latter half of the 1600's and into the 1700's an Englishman named John Locke wrote his first and second Treatises on Government (book) first and second Treatises on Government. In the first, Locke argues against the idea of divine right monarchy. He goes to great lengths to prove that no man is by nature placed over another man. In the second treatise (much more well known), Locke asserts that the state of nature consists of every man being equal to every other and all of nature was in common for every one else.

Unlike Hobbes, this state of nature did not mean a state of war. Locke believed that man by nature possesses reason (which he calls the Law of Nature) and only when he separates from that reason does he enter a state of war. Man leaves the state of nature, according to Locke, because in nature there are no general laws, no common judge, and no one to enforce the laws. By the end of the 1700's the Enlightenment was ending and on the cusp of Post-Modernity sat Jean-Jacque Rousseau. Rousseau asserted that man by nature was utterly free to do what he wished, and is not a social animal. When man leaves the state of nature and enters civil society he becomes sort of a slave to the state. While each era of political thought changed the state of nature, man must leave nature and enter into societies. Politics then is the study of how humans interact with each other and cooperate to become self sufficient.

DEFINITIONS

- Power Max Weber defined power as the ability to impose one's will upon another, while Hannah Arendt states that "political power corresponds to the human ability not just to act but to act in concert."
- Authority is the ability to enforce laws, to exact obedience, to command, to determine, or to judge.
- A government is the body that has the authority to make and enforce rules or laws.
- Legitimacy is an attribute of government gained through the acquisition and application of power in accordance with recognized or accepted standards or principles.
- Sovereignty is the ability of a government to exert control over its territory free from outside influence.

CLASSIFICATION OF POLITICAL IDEOLOGIES

Pragmatic View of Power

Samuel Gompers' maxim, often paraphrased as,"Reward your friends and punish your enemies," hints at two of the five types of power recognized by social psychologists: incentive power (the power to reward) and coercive power (the power to punish). Arguably the other three grow out of these two.

Legitimate power, the power of the policeman or the referee, is the power given to an individual by a recognized authority to enforce standards of behavior. Legitimate power is similar to coercive power in that unacceptable behavior is punished by fine or penalty.

Referent power is bestowed upon individuals by virtue of accomplishment or attitude. Fulfillment of the desire to feel similar to a celebrity or a hero is the reward for obedience.

Expert power springs from education or experience. Following the lead of an experienced coach is often rewarded with success. Expert power is conditional to the circumstances. A brain surgeon is no help when your pipes are leaking.

GOVERNMENT

A government is a body that has the authority to make and the power to enforce laws within a civil, corporate, religious, academic, or other organization or group. In its broadest sense, "to govern" means to administer or supervise, whether over a state, a set group of people, or a collection of assets.

The word government is ultimately derived from the Greek kybernan, which means "to steer" or "to control".

Typically, "the government" refers to the executive function of the state. In many countries (particularly those having parliamentary systems), the government refers to the executive branch of government or a specifically named executive, such as the Blair government (compare to the administration as in the Bush administration in U.S. usage). In countries using the Westminster system, the party in government will also usually control the legislature.

FORMS OF GOVERNMENT

Governments are often classified according to the number of people who hold political power.

- In Autocracies one individual holds all the power. This category includes absolute monarchies as well as dictatorships with an all-powerful president or other central figure.
- In Oligarchies political power is held by a small group of individuals who share interests. For example a plutocracy is composed of the wealthiest members of society.
- Democracies are governments where the people as a whole hold political power. It may be exercised by them (direct democracy), or through representatives chosen by them (representative democracy).

The lines between some of the above forms of government can sometimes be ambiguous. For example, during the 19th century, most self-proclaimed "democracies" restricted voting rights to a minority of the population (e.g. property-owning males). This could qualify them as oligarchies rather than democracies. On the other hand, the voting minority was often quite large (20-30% of the population) and its members did not form the compact group with common interests that is the hallmark of most oligarchies. Thus, this form of government occupied a space between democracy and oligarchy as they are understood today.

Ideas about the Origin of Government

There are a wide range of theories about the reasons for establishing governments. The four major ones are briefly described below. Note that they do not always fully oppose each other -it is possible for a person to subscribe to a combination of ideas from two or more of these theories.

Force Theory

Many political philosophies that are opposed to the existence of a government (such as Anarchism, Nihilism, and to a lesser extent Marxism), as well as others, emphasize the historical roots of governments -the fact that governments, along with private property, originated from the authority of warlords and petty despots who took, by force, certain patches of land as their own (and began exercising authority over the people living on that land). Thus, it is argued that governments exist to enforce the will of the strong and oppress the weak, maintaining and protecting the privilege of a ruling class. It states that the government emerged when all the people of an area were brought under the authority of one person or group!

Order and Tradition

The various forms of conservatism, by contrast, generally see the government as a positive force that brings order out of chaos, establishes laws to end the "war of all against all", encourages moral virtue while punishing vice, and respects tradition. Sometimes, in this view, the government is seen as something ordained by a higher power, as in the divine right of kings, which human beings have a duty to obey.

Natural Rights

Natural rights are the basis for the theory of government shared by most branches of liberalism (including libertarianism). In this view, human beings are born with certain natural rights, and governments are established strictly for the purpose of protecting those rights. What the natural rights actually are is a matter of dispute among liberals; indeed, each branch of liberalism has its own set of rights that it considers to be natural, and these rights are sometimes mutually exclusive with the rights supported by other liberals. As a result, there is some debate between natural rights theorists, ranging from modern writers such as Tibor Machan to Enlightenment thinkers such as Locke, Kant, or Jefferson.

Social Contract

One of the most influential theories of government in the past two hundred years has been the social contract, on which modern democracy and most forms of socialism are founded. The social contract theory holds that governments are created by the people in order to provide for collective needs (such as safety from crime, poverty, illiteracy) that cannot be properly satisfied using purely individual means. Governments thus exist for the purpose of serving the needs and wishes of the people, and their relationship with the people is clearly stipulated in a "social contract" (a constitution and a set of laws) which both the government and the people must abide by. If a majority is unhappy, it may change the social contract. If a minority is unhappy, it may persuade the majority to change the contract, or it may opt out of it by emigration or secession. This theory is based on the idea that all men live in a state of nature which is not ideal to perfect harmony. It is also an agreement among the members of an organized society or between the governed and the government defining and limiting the rights and duties of each. Thomas Hobbes, John Locke, Jean-Jacques Rousseau are three of the most famous philosophers of contractarianism. Today, natural rights are the basis for many issues involving the constitution and ones right to privacy under the government.

Governmental Operations

Governments concern themselves with regulating and administering many areas of human activity, such as trade, education, or medicine. Governments also employ different methods to maintain the established order, such as secrecy, censorship, police and military forces (particularly under despotism, see also police state), making agreements with other states, and maintaining support within the state. Typical methods of maintaining support and legitimacy include providing the infrastructure for administration, justice, transport, communication, social welfare, etc.; claiming support from deities; providing benefits to elites; providing shops for important posts within the state; limiting the power of the state through laws and constitutions; and appealing to nationalism. Different political ideologies hold different ideas on what the government should or should not do. The modern standard unit of territory is a country.

In addition to the meaning used above, the word state can refer either to a government or to its territory. Within a territory, subnational entities may have local governments which do not have the full power of a national government (for example, they will generally lack the authority to declare war or carry out diplomacy).

Size of Government

The scale to which government should exist and operate in the world is a matter of debate. Government spending in developed countries varies considerably but generally makes up between about 30% and 70% of their GDP. One major exception is the United States, where central government spending takes up less than 20% of GDP.

World Government

Some speculate that technological changes such as the Internet and the global English language would bring a World Government into existence. Some consider some governments such as the European Commission as trends towards such a system; however, others do not see this as possible.

CONSTITUTION

A constitution is a system, often codified as a written document, that establishes the rules and principles whereby an organization or political entity is governed. In the case of countries, this term refers specifically to a national constitution defining the fundamental political principles, and establishing the power and duties, of each government. Most national constitutions also guarantee certain rights to the people. Historically, before the evolution of modern-style, codified national constitutions, the term constitution could be applied to any important law that governed the functioning of a government. Constitutions are found in many organizations. They are found extensively in government, at supranational (e.g. United Nations Charter), national (e.g. Constitution of Japan), and sub-national or provincial (e.g. Constitution of Maryland) levels. They are found in many political groups, such as political parties and pressure groups, including trade unions (labour unions). There are many non-political groups and entities that may have constitutions of a sort such as companies and voluntary organisations.

Etymology

The term constitution comes from Latin, referring to issuing any important law, usually by the Roman emperor. Later, the term was widely used in canon law to indicate certain relevant decisions, mainly from the pope.

General Features

Generally, all constitutions confer specific powers to an organization on the condition that it abides by this constitution or charter limitation. The Latin term ultra vires describes activities that fall outside an organisation's or legislative body's legal or constitutional authority.

For example, a students' union may be prohibited as an organization from engaging in activities not concerning students; if the union becomes involved in non-student activities these activities are considered ultra vires of the union's charter. An example from the constitutional law of nation-states would be a provincial government in a federal state trying to legislate in an area exclusively enumerated to the federal government in the constitution.

For example, in the United States, any attempt by a state legislature to ratify a treaty with a foreign nation would be considered ultra vires of Congress' constitutional authority, being contrary to the constitution. In both cases, "ultra vires" gives a legal justification for the forced cessation of such action, which would be enforced by the judiciary in government.

Governmental Constitutions

Most commonly, the term constitution refers to a set of rules and principles that define the nature and extent of government. Most constitutions seek to regulate the relationship between institutions of the state, in a basic sense the relationship between the executive, legislature and the judiciary, but also the relationship of institutions within those branches.

For example, executive branches can be divided into a head of government, government departments/ministries, executive agencies and a civil service/bureaucracy. Most constitutions also attempt to define the relationship between individuals and the state, and to establish the broad rights of individual citizens. It is thus the most basic law of a territory from which all the other laws and rules are hierarchically derived; in some territories it is in fact called "Basic Law".

KEY FEATURES

The following are features of democratic constitutions which have been identified by political scientists to exist, in one form or another, in virtually all national constitutions.

Codification

A fundamental classification is codification or lack of codification. A codified constitution is one that is contained in a single document, which is the single source of constitutional law in a state. The classic example of this is the Constitution of the United States. An uncodified constitution is one that is not contained in a single document, consisting of several different sources, which may be written or unwritten. The Constitution of Australia is an example of a constitution in which constitutional law mainly derives from a single written document, but other written documents are also considered part of the constitution. The Constitution of the United Kingdom is an example of an uncodified constitution which consists of both written and unwritten sources and has no single written fundamental document.

The term written constitution is used to describe a constitution that is entirely written, which by definition includes every codified constitution. However, some constitutions are entirely written but, strictly speaking, not entirely codified. For example, in the Constitution of Australia, most of its fundamental political principles and regulations concerning the relationship between branches of government, and concerning the government and the individual are codified in a single document, the Constitution of the Commonwealth of Australia. However, the presence of statutes with constitutional significance, namely the Statute of Westminster, as adopted by the Commonwealth in the Statute of Westminster Adoption Act 1942, and the Australia Act 1986 means that Australia's constitution is not contained in a single constitutional document. The Constitution of Canada, which evolved from the British North America Acts until severed from nominal British control by the Canada Act 1982 (analogous to the Australia Act 1986), is a similar example.

The term written constitution is often used interchangeably with codified constitution, and similarly unwritten constitution is used interchangeably with uncodified constitution. As shown above, this usage with respect to written and codified constitutions can be inaccurate. Strictly speaking, unwritten constitution is never an accurate synonym for uncodified constitution, because all modern democratic constitutions consist of some written sources, even if they have no different technical status than ordinary statutes. Another term used is formal (written) constitution, for example in the following context: "The United Kingdom has no formal constitution". This usage is correct, but it should be construed to mean that the United Kingdom does not have a written constitution, not that the UK has no constitution of any kind, which would not be correct.

Codified Constitution

Most states in the world have a codified constitution. Only three nations, Israel, New Zealand and the United Kingdom, have uncodified constitutions as of October 2006. Codified constitutions -unlike uncodified constitutions, which are the product of an "evolution" of laws and conventions over centuries -are usually the product of dramatic political change, such as a revolution. For example, the US constitution was written and subsequently ratified less than 25 years after the American Revolution. The process by which a country adopts a constitution is closely tied to the historical and political context driving this fundamental change. This becomes evident when one compares the elaborate convention method adopted in the United States with the MacArthur inspired post war constitution foisted on Japan. Arguably the legitimacy (and often the longevity) of codified constitutions are tied to the process by which they are initially adopted.

The most obvious advantage of a codified constitution is the coherent and easily understood body of rules. A codified constitution at the least is simple to read, being a single document. Although (entrenched) codified constitutions are relatively rigid, codified constitutions still yield a potentially wide range of interpretations by constitutional courts.

States that have codified constitutions normally give them supremacy over ordinary statute law. That is, if there is a conflict between a legal statute and the codified constitution, all or part of the statute can be declared ultra vires by a court and struck down as unconstitutional. Second, an extraordinary procedure is required for constitutional amendments that may involve obtaining ? majorities in the national legislature, the consent of regional legislatures, a referendum process or some other procedure that makes obtaining a constitutional amendment more difficult than passing a simple law.

Uncodified Constitution

By contrast, in the Westminster tradition which originated in England, uncodified constitutions include written sources: e.g. constitutional statutes enacted by the Parliament (House of Commons Disqualification Act 1975, Northern Ireland Act 1998, Scotland Act 1998, Government of Wales Act 1998, European Communities Act 1972 and Human Rights Act 1998); and also unwritten sources: constitutional conventions, observation of precedents, royal prerogatives, custom and tradition, such as always holding the General Election on Thursdays; together these constitute the British constitutional law. In the days of the British Empire, the Judicial Committee of the Privy Council acted as the constitutional court for many of the British colonies such as Canada and Australia which had federal constitutions. In states using uncodified constitutions, the difference between constitutional law and statutory law (i.e. law applying to any area of governance) in legal terms is nil. Both can be altered or repealed by a simple majority in Parliament. In practice, democratic governments do not use this opportunity to abolish all civil rights, which in theory they could do, but the distinction between regular and constitutional law is still somewhat arbitrary, usually depending on the traditional devotion of popular opinion to historical principles embodied in important past legislation. For example, several Acts of Parliament such as the Bill of Rights, Human Rights Act and, prior to the creation of Parliament, Magna Carta are regarded as granting fundamental rights and principles which are treated as almost constitutional.

Entrenchment

The presence or lack of entrenchment is a fundamental feature of constitutions. Entrenchment refers to whether the constitution is legally protected from modification without a procedure of constitutional amendment. Entrenchment is an inherent feature in most written constitutions. The US constitution is an example of an entrenched constitution, and the UK constitution is an example of a constitution that is not entrenched.

The procedure for modifying a constitution is often called amending. Amending an entrenched constitution requires more than the approval of the national legislature, it requires wider acceptance. Sometimes, the reason for this is that the constitution is considered supreme law, such as according to the supremacy clause in the US constitution. Regardless of whether a constitution has this technical status, all states with an entrenched constitution recognise the difference between constitutional law and ordinary statutory law. Procedures for ratification of constitutional amendments vary between states. In a federal system of government, the approval of a majority of state/provincial legislatures may be required. Alternatively, a national referendum may be required in some states, such as in Australia. In constitutions that are not entrenched, no special procedure is required for modification. In the small number of countries with un-entrenched constitutions, the lack of entrenchment is because the constitution is not recognised with any higher legal status than ordinary statutes. In the UK, for example, passing laws which modify sources of the constitution, whether they are written or unwritten, are passed on a simple majority in Parliament. The concept of "amendment" does not apply, as the constitution can be altered as easily in terms of procedure as any national law.

Distribution of Sovereignty

Constitutions also establish where sovereignty is located in the state. There are three basic types of distribution of sovereignty: federal, unitary and confederal. A federal system of government will inevitably have a constitution that recognizes the division of sovereignty between the centre and peripheral/provincial regions of the state. The Canadian Constitution is an example of this, dividing power between the federal government and the provinces. A unitary constitution recognises that sovereignty resides only in the centre of the state. In the UK, the constitutional doctrine of Parliamentary sovereignty dictates than sovereignty is ultimately contained at the centre. Confederal constitutions are rare, and there is often dispute to whether so-called "confederal" states are actually federal. In a confederacy, sovereignty is located in peripheral regions/provinces and only limited power is granted to the centre. A historical example of a confederal constitution is the Swiss Federal Constitution.

Separation of Powers

Constitutions vary extensively as to the degree of separation of powers, usually meaning the constitutional separation of the executive, legislative and judicial branches of government. The United States constitution has a full separation of powers, with each branch having particular enumerated powers. For instance, Congress, the US legislature, has the power of impeachment, which cannot be exercised by another branch.

Lines of Accountability

Lines of accountability are a common feature in all democratic constitutions. In presidential systems of government, such as the United States, and semi-presidential systems, such as France, department secretaries/ministers are accountable to the president, who has patronage powers to appoint and dismiss ministers. The president is accountable to the people in an election. In parliamentary systems, such as the United Kingdom and Australia, ministers are accountable to Parliament, but it is the prime minister who appoints and dismisses them (in Westminster systems this power derives from the monarch, a component of Parliament). There is the concept of a vote of no confidence in many countries with parliamentary systems, which means that if a majority of the legislature vote for a no confidence motion, then the government must resign, and a new one will be formed, or parliament will be dissolved and a general election called.

Facade Constitutions

Italian political theorist Giovanni Sartori noted the existence of national constitutions which are a façade for authoritarian sources of power. While such documents may express respect for human rights or establish an independent judiciary, they may be ignored when the government feels threatened or entirely dishonoured in practice. An extreme example was the Constitution of the Soviet Union that on paper supported freedom of assembly or freedom of speech; however, citizens who acted accordingly were summarily imprisoned. The example demonstrates that the protections and benefits of a constitution are provided less through its written terms, but more through deference by government and society to its principles.

Constitutional Courts

The constitution is often protected by a certain legal body in each country with various names, such as supreme, constitutional or high court. This court judges the compatibility of legislation with the provisions and principles of the constitution, which is termed "constitutionality". Especially important is the court's responsibility to protect constitutionally established rights and freedoms. In constitutions without the concept of supreme law, such as the United Kingdom constitution, the concept of "constitutionality" has little meaning, and constitutional courts do not exist.

A "constitutional violation" is an action or legislative act that is judged by a constitutional court to be contrary to the constitution, that is, "unconstitutional". An example of constitutional violation by the executive could be a politician who abuses the powers of his constitutionally-established office. An example of constitutional violation by the legislature is an attempt to pass a law that would contradict the constitution, without first going through the proper constitutional amendment process.

A constitutional court is normally the court of last resort, the highest judicial body in the government. The process of judicial review is then integrated into the system of courts of appeal. This is the case, for example, with the Supreme Court of the United States. Cases must normally be heard in lower courts before being brought before the Supreme Court, except cases for which the Supreme Court has original jurisdiction. Some other countries dedicate a special court solely to the protection of the constitution, as with the German Constitutional Court.

Most constitutional courts are powerful instruments of judicial review, with the power to declare laws "unconstitutional", that is, incompatible with the constitution. The effect of this ruling varies between governments, but it is common for the courts' action to rule a law unenforceable, as is the case in the United States. However, many courts have the problem of relying on the legislative and executive branches' cooperation to properly enforce their decisions.

For example, in the United States, the Supreme Court's ruling overturning the "separate but equal" doctrine in the 1950s depended on individual states cooperation to enforce. Some failed to do so, prompting the federal government to intervene. Other countries, such as France, have a Constitutional Council of France which may only judge the constitutionality of laws before the ratification process.

Some countries, mainly those with uncodified constitutions, have no such courts at all -for example, as the United Kingdom traditionally functions under the principle of parliamentary sovereignty: the legislature has the power to enact any law it wishes.

However, through its membership in the European Union, the UK is now subject to the jurisdiction of European Community law and the European Court of Justice; similarly, by acceding to the Council of Europe's European Convention on Human Rights, it is subject to the European Court of Human Rights. In effect, these bodies are constitutional courts that can invalidate or interpret UK legislation, first established as a principle by the Factortame case.

History and Development

Excavations in modern-day Iraq by Ernest de Sarzec in 1877 found evidence of the earliest known code of justice, issued by the Sumerian king Urukagina of Lagash ca. 2300 BC. Perhaps the earliest prototype for a law of government, this document itself has not yet been discovered; however it is known that it allowed some rights to his citizens.

For example, it is known that it relieved tax for widows and orphans, and protected the poor from the usury of the rich.

After that, many governments ruled by special codes of written laws. The oldest such document still known to exist seems to be that of Ur-Nammu of Ur (ca. 2050 BC). Some of the more well known among these include the code of Hammurabi of Babylonia, the Hittite code, the Assyrian code, Mosaic law, and likewise the commandments of Cyrus the Great of Persia.

In 621 BC, a scribe named Draco wrote the laws of the city-state of Athens; and being quite cruel, this code prescribed the death penalty for any offense. In 594 BC, Solon, the ruler of Athens, created the new Solonian Constitution. It eased the burden of the workers, however it made the ruling class to be determined by wealth, rather than by birth. Cleisthenes again reformed the Athenian constitution and set it on a democratic footing in 508 BC.

Aristotle (c. 350 BC) was one of the first in recorded history to make a formal distinction between law and constitutional law, establishing ideas of constitution and constitutionalism, and attempting to classify different forms of constitutional government. The most basic definition he used to describe a constitution in general terms was "the arrangement of the offices in a state".

In his works Constitution of Athens, Politics, and Nicomachean Ethics he explored different forms of constitutions. He classified both what he regarded as good and bad constitutions, and came to the conclusion that the best constitution was a mixed system, including monarchic, aristocratic, and democratic elements. He also distinguished between citizens, who had the exclusive opportunity to participate in the state, and non-citizens and slaves who did not. The Romans first codified their constitution in 449 BC as the Twelve Tables. They operated under a series of laws that were added from time to time, but Roman law was never reorganised into a single code until the Codex Theodosianus (AD 438); later, in the Eastern Empire the Codex Justinianus (534) was highly influential throughout Europe. This was followed in the east by the Ecloga of Leo III the Isaurian (740) and the Basilica of Basil I (878).

Many of the Germanic peoples that filled the power vacuum left by the Western Roman Empire in the Early Middle Ages codified their laws. One of the first of these Germanic law codes to be written was the Visigothic Code of Euric (471).

This was followed by the Lex Burgundionum, applying separate codes for Germans and for Romans; the Pactus Alamannorum; and the Salic Law of the Franks, all written soon after 500. In 506, the Breviarum or "Lex Romana" of Alaric II, king of the Visigoths, adopted and consolidated the Codex Theodosianus together with assorted earlier Roman laws. Systems that appeared somewhat later include the Edictum Rothari of the Lombards (643), the Lex Visigothorum (654), the Lex Alamannorum (730) and the Lex Frisionum (c. 785).

Japan's Seventeen-article constitution written in 604, reportedly by Prince Shotoku, is an early example of a constitution in Asian political history. Influenced by Buddhist teachings, the document focuses more on social morality than institutions of government per se and remains a notable early attempt at a government constitution. Another is the Constitution of Medina, drafted by the prophet of Islam, Muhammad, in 622.

The Gayanashagowa, or 'oral' constitution of the Iroquois nation, has been estimated to date from between 1090 and 1150, and is also thought by some to have provided a partial inspiration for the US Constitution.

In England, King Henry I's proclamation of the Charter of Liberties in 1100 bound the king for the first time in his treatment of the clergy and the nobility. This idea was extended and refined by the English barony when they forced John to sign the Magna Carta in 1215. The most important single article of the Magna Carta, related to "habeas corpus", provided that the king was not permitted to imprison, outlaw, exile or kill anyone at a whim --there must be due process of law first. This article, Article 39, of the Magna Carta read:

No free man shall be arrested, or imprisoned, or deprived of his property, or outlawed, or exiled, or in any way destroyed, nor shall we go against him or send against him, unless by legal judgement of his peers, or by the law of the land.

This provision became the cornerstone of English liberty after that point. The social contract in the original case was between the king and the nobility, but was gradually extended to all of the people. It led to the system of Constitutional Monarchy, with further reforms shifting the balance of power from the monarchy and nobility to the House of Commons.

Between 1220 and 1230, a Saxon administrator, Eike von Repgow, composed the Sachsenspiegel, which became the supreme law used in parts of Germany as late as 1900. In 1236, Sundiata Keita presented an oral constitution federating the Mali Empire, called the Kouroukan Fouga. Meanwhile, around 1240, the Coptic Egyptian Christian writer, 'Abul Fada'il Ibn al-'Assal, wrote the Fetha Negest in Arabic. 'Ibn al-Assal took his laws partly from apostolic writings and Mosaic law, and partly from the former Byzantine codes. There are a few historical records claiming that this law code was translated into Ge'ez and entered Ethiopia around 1450 in the reign of Zara Yaqob. Even so, its first recorded use in the function of a constitution (supreme law of the land) is with Sarsa Dengel beginning in 1563. The Fetha Negest remained the supreme law in Ethiopia until 1931, when a modern-style Constitution was first granted by Emperor Haile Selassie I.

The earliest written constitution still governing a sovereign nation today may be that of San Marino. The Leges Statutae Republicae Sancti Marini was written in Latin and consists of six books. The first book, with 62 articles, establishes councils, courts, various executive officers and the powers assigned to them. The remaining books cover criminal and civil law, judicial procedures and remedies. Written in 1600, the document was based upon the Statuti Comunali (Town Statute) of 1300, itself influenced by the Codex Justinianus, and it remains in force today. In 1639, the Colony of Connecticut adopted the Fundamental Orders, which is considered the first North American constitution, and is the basis for every new Connecticut constitution since, and is also the reason for Connecticut's nickname, the Constitution State.

The Commonwealth of Massachusetts adopted its constitution in 1780, before the ratification of the Articles of Confederation and the United States Constitution. It is probably the oldest still-functioning nominal constitution, that is, where the document specifically declares itself to be a constitution. The United States Constitution, ratified 1789, was influenced by the British constitutional system and the political system of the United Provinces, plus the writings of Polybius, Locke, Montesquieu, and others. The document became a benchmark for republican and codified constitutions written thereafter and is commonly believed to be the oldest modern, national, codified constitution in the world.

2

Political Concept of Democracy

Democracy (literally "rule by the people", from the Greek demos, "people," and kratos, "rule") is a form of government. Today, the term democracy is often used to refer to liberal democracy, but there is no necessity that democracies be liberal (i.e. respectful of individual liberty and property) and in some cases may be illiberal democracies. There are many other varieties and the methods used to govern differ. While the term democracy is typically used in the context of a political state, the principles are also applicable to other bodies such as intergovernmental organizations, non-governmental organizations, grassroot organizations, labor unions, industry trade groups, professional bodies, and learned societies.

VARIETIES

The definition of democracy is made complex by the varied concepts used at different periods of history in different contexts. Political systems, or proposed political systems, claiming or claimed to be democratic have ranged very broadly.

Aristotle

Aristotle contrasted rule by the many (democracy/polity), with rule by the few (oligarchy/aristocracy), and with rule by a single person (tyranny/monarchy or today autocracy). He also thought that there was a good and a bad variant of each system (he considered democracy to be degenerate counterpart to polity)..

Sortition

Sortition/Allotment have formed the basis of systems randomly selecting officers from the population: For example, Aristotle described the law courts in Athens which were selected by lot as democratic and described elections as oligarchic.

TRIBAL DEMOCRACY

Certain tribes organised themselves using forms of participatory democracy.

Consensus: Consensus democracy and deliberative democracy seek consensus among the people.

Direct

Direct democracy is largely referred to as a political system where the citizens vote on all major policy decisions. It is called direct because, in the classical forms, there are no intermediaries or representatives. All direct democracies to date have been relatively small communities, usually city-states. Although, some see the extensive use of referenda, as in California, as akin to direct democracy in a very large polity with over 20 million potential voters. Today, a limited direct democracy exists in some Swiss cantons. Other current examples include many small civic organizations (like college faculties) and town meetings in New England (usually in towns under 10,000 population). Direct democracy obviously becomes difficult when the electorate is large. Modern direct democracy tries to accommodate this and sees a role for strictly controlled representatives. It is characterized by three pillars; referendums (initiated by governments or legislatures or by citizens responding to legislation), initiatives (initiated by citizens) and recall elections (on holders of public office).

Representative

Representative democracy is so named because the people select representatives to a governing body. Representatives may be chosen by the electorate as a whole (as in many proportional systems) or represent a particular district (or constituency), with some systems using a combination of the two. Some representative democracies also incorporate some elements of direct democracy, such as referenda.

Liberal Democracy

Liberal democracy is a representative democracy (with free and fair elections) along with the protection of minorities, the rule of law, a separation of powers, and protection of liberties (thus the name liberal) of speech, assembly, religion, and property. Conversely, an illiberal democracy is one where the protections that form a liberal democracy are either nonexistent, or not enforced. The experience in some post-Soviet states drew attention to the phenomenon, although it is not of recent origin. Napoleon III for example used plebiscites to ratify his imperial decisions.

Socialist

Socialism is a broad movement and has several different views on democracy. Social democracy, democratic socialism, Soviet democracy, and the dictatorship of the proletariat are some examples.

Anarchist

Some anarchists oppose democracy while others favor it. Pierre-Joseph Proudhon argued that the only acceptable form of direct democracy is one in which it is recognized that majority decisions are not binding on the minority. However, anarcho-communist Murray Bookchin criticizes individualist anarchists for opposing democracy, and says "majority rule" is consistent with anarchism, There are also some anarchists who expect society to operate by consensus. The notion of direct democracy, or participatory democracy, is very common to many anarchist movements, especially in libertarian communism, as a form of organizing and management based upon consensus, collective action, freedom and responsibility. This goes with the fundamental anarchist principle of denying authoritarian or alienating organizational structures.

HISTORY

Ancient Origins

The word democracy was coined in ancient Greece and used interchangeably with isonomia (equality of political rights). Although Athenian democracy is today considered by many to have been a form of direct democracy, originally it had two distinguishing features: firstly the allotment (selection by lot) of ordinary citizens to government offices and courts, and secondarily the assembly of all the citizens. In theory, all the Athenian citizens were eligible to speak and vote in the Assembly, which set the laws of the city-state, but neither political rights, nor citizenship, were granted to women, slaves, or metics. Of the 250,000 inhabitants only some 30,000 on average were citizens. Of those 30,000 perhaps 5,000 might regularly attend one or more meetings of the popular Assembly. Most of the officers & magistrates of Athenian government were allotted; only the generals (strategoi) and a few other officers were elected.

The seeds of representative democracy were arguably sown in the Roman Republic. Democratic principles and elements have also been argued for the Mahajanapadas of ancient India, and also in the local Sanghas, Ganas and Panchayats that existed throughout the centuries in India. However, political rights were to some extent a representative of social class and in particular the caste system. In these republics, power was typically vested in the hands of an elite class, and so the system would perhaps be better classified as an oligarchy. In the case of the village panchayats, the picture is somewhat more democratic. A panchayat in essence is a meeting of townspeople mediated by a group of village elders, and so it is an example of a direct democracy.

Democracy was also seen to a certain extent in bands and tribes such as the Iroquois Confederacy. However, in the Iroquois Confederacy only the males of certain clans could be leaders and some clans were excluded. Only the oldest females from the same clans could choose and remove the leaders. This excluded most of the population. An interesting detail is that there should be consensus among the leaders, not majority support decided by voting, when making decisions.

Middle Ages

During the Middle Ages, there were various systems involving elections or assemblies, although often only involving a minority of the population, such as the election of Gopala in Bengal, the Polish-Lithuanian Commonwealth, the Althing in Iceland, certain medieval Italian city-states such as Venice, the tuatha system in early medieval Ireland, the Veche in Slavic countries, and Scandinavian Things and Nayashu in Venice like autonomous merchant city of Sakai in the 16th century in Japan. Most regions during the middle-ages were ruled by clergy or feudal lords.

The Parliament of England had its roots in the restrictions on the power of kings written into Magna Carta. The first elected parliament was De Montfort's Parliament in England in 1265. However only a small minority actually had a voice; Parliament was elected by only a few percent of the population (less than 3% in 1780.), and the system had problematic features such as rotten boroughs. The power to call parliament was at the pleasure of the monarch. After the Glorious Revolution of 1688, the English Bill of Rights was enacted in 1689, which codified certain rights and increased the influence of the Parliament. The franchise was slowly increased and the Parliament gradually gained more power until the monarch became entirely a figurehead.

18th and 19th centuries

Although not described as a democracy by the founding fathers, the United States can be seen as the first liberal democracy. The United States Constitution, adopted in 1788, provided for an elected government and protected civil rights and liberties. Already in the colonial period before 1776 most adult white men could vote; there were still property requirements but most men owned their own farms and could pass the tests. On the American frontier, democracy became a way of life, with widespread social, economic and political equality. By 1840s almost all property restrictions were ended and nearly all white adult male citizens could vote; and turnout averaged 60-80% in frequent elections for local, state and national officials. The system gradually evolved, from Jeffersonian Democracy to Jacksonian Democracy and beyond. In Reconstruction after the Civil War (late 1860s) the newly freed slaves became citizens and were given the right to vote. Some scholars, Judith Shklar for instance, argue that because America tolerated slavery, it could not be called a democracy until after the adoption of the Reconstruction Amendments at this time. In 1789, Revolutionary France adopted the Declaration of the Rights of Man and of the Citizen and, although short-lived, the National Convention was elected by all males.

Liberal democracies were few and often short-lived before the late nineteenth century. Various nations and territories have claimed to be the first with universal suffrage.

20th Century

20th century transitions to liberal democracy have come in successive "waves of democracy," variously resulting from wars, revolutions, decolonization, and economic circumstances. World War I and the dissolution of the Ottoman and Austro-Hungarian empires resulted in the creation of new nation-states in Europe, most of them nominally democratic. In the 1920s democracy flourished, but the Great Depression brought disenchantment, and most the countries of Europe, Latin America, and Asia turned to strong-man rule or dictatorships. Fascism and dictatorships flourished in Nazi Germany, Italy, Spain and Portugal, as well as nondemocratic regimes in Poland, the Baltics, the Balkans, Brazil, Cuba, China, and Japan, among others. Together with Stalin's regime in the Soviet Union, these made the 1930s the "Age of Dictators".

World War II brought a definitive reversal of this trend in western Europe. The successful democratization of the occupied Germany and the occupied Japan served as a model for the later theory of regime change. However, most of Eastern Europe was forced into the non-democratic Soviet bloc. The war was followed by decolonisation, and again most of the new independent states had nominally democratic constitutions. In the decades following World War II, most western democratic nations had mixed economies and developed a welfare state, reflecting a general consensus among their electorates and political parties. In the 1950s and 1960s, economic growth was high in both the western and Communist countries; it later declined in the state-controlled economies. By 1960, the vast majority of nation-states were nominally democracies, although the majority of the world's populations lived in nations that experienced sham elections, and other forms of subterfuge (particularly in Communist nations and the former colonies.)

A subsequent wave of democratisation brought substantial gains toward true liberal democracy for many nations. Several of the military dictatorships in South America became democratic in the late 1970s and early 1980s. This was followed by nations in East and South Asia by the mid-to late 1980s. Economic malaise in the 1980s, along with resentment of communist oppression, contributed to the collapse of the Soviet Union, the associated end of the Cold War, and the democratization and liberalisation of the former Eastern bloc countries. The most successful of the new democracies were those geographically and culturally closest to western Europe, and they are now members or candidate members of the European Union. The liberal trend spread to some nations in Africa in the 1990s, most prominently in South Africa. Some recent examples include the Indonesian Revolution of 1998, the Bulldozer Revolution in Yugoslavia, the Rose Revolution in Georgia, the Orange Revolution in Ukraine, the Cedar Revolution in Lebanon, and the Tulip Revolution in Kyrgyzstan.

The number of liberal democracies currently stands at an all-time high and has been growing without interruption for some time. As such, it has been speculated that this trend may continue in the future to the point where liberal democratic nation-states become the universal standard form of human society. This prediction forms the core of Francis Fukayama's "End of History" theory.

THEORY

Conceptions

Among political theorists, there are many contending conceptions of democracy.

- Aggregative democracy uses democratic processes to solicit citizens' preferences and then aggregate them together to determine what social policies society should adopt. Therefore, proponents of this view hold that democratic participation should primarily focus on voting, where the policy with the most votes gets implemented. There are different variants of this:
  - o Under minimalism, democracy is a system of government in which citizens give teams of political leaders the right to rule in periodic elections. According to this minimalist conception, citizens cannot and should not "rule" because, for example, on most issues, most of the time, they have no clear views or their views are not well-founded. Joseph Schumpeter articulated this view most famously in his book Capitalism, Socialism, and Democracy. Contemporary proponents of minimalism include William H. Riker, Adam Przeworski, Richard Posner.
  - o Direct democracy, on the other hand, holds that citizens should participate directly, not through their representatives, in making laws and policies. Proponents of direct democracy offer varied reasons to support this view. Political activity can be valuable in itself, it socializes and educates citizens, and popular participation can check powerful elites. Most importantly, citizens do not really rule themselves unless they directly decide laws and policies.
  - o Government should produce laws and policies that are close to the views of the median voter -with half to his left and the other half to his right. Anthony Downs laid

out this view in his 1957 book An Economic Theory of Democracy.

- o Robert A. Dahl argues that the fundamental democratic principle is that, when it comes to binding collective decisions, each person in a political community is entitled to have his/her interests be given equal consideration (not necessarily that all people are equally satisfied by the collective decision). He uses the term Polyarchy to refer to societies in which there exists a certain set of institutions and procedures which are perceived as leading to such democracy. First and foremost among these institutions is the regular occurrence of free and open elections which are used to select representatives who then manage all or most of the public policy of the society. However, these polyarchic procedures may not create a full democracy if, for example, poverty prevents political participation. Some see a problem with the wealthy having more influence and therefore argue for reforms like campaign finance reform. Some may see it as a problem that the majority of the voters decide policy, as opposed to majority rule of the entire population. This can be used as an argument for making political participation mandatory, like compulsory voting.

- Deliberative democracy is based on the notion that democracy is government by discussion. Deliberative democrats contend that laws and policies should be based upon reasons that all citizens can accept. The political arena should be one in which leaders and citizens make arguments, listen, and change their minds. One modern proponents of this form of government are led by Jürgen Habermas.

"Democracy" and "Republic"

In historical usages and especially when considering the works of the Founding Fathers of the United States, the word "democracy" refers solely to direct democracy, while a representative democracy where representatives of the people are elected and whose power to govern is limited by laws enshrined in a constitution is referred to as a constitutional republic. Constitutional Republics are a deliberate attempt to diminish the threat of mobocracy thereby protecting minority groups from the tyranny of the majority by placing checks on the power of the majority of the population. The power of the majority of the people is checked by limiting that power to electing representatives who govern within limits of overarching constitutional law rather than the popular vote having legislative power itself. Moreover, the power of elected representatives is also checked by prohibitions against any single individual having legislative, judicial, and executive powers so that basic constitutional law is extremely difficult to change. John Adams defined a constitutional republic as "a government of laws, and not of men." Using the term "democracy" to refer solely to direct democracy, or to representative democracy without checks on the power of elected officials, retains some popularity in United States conservative and libertarian circles.

The original framers of the United States Constitution were notably cognizant of what they perceived as a danger of majority rule in oppressing freedom and liberty of the individual. For example, James Madison, in Federalist Paper No. 10, advocates a constitutional republic over a democracy to protect the individual from the majority. The framers carefully created the institutions within the Constitution and the United States Bill of Rights. They kept what they believed were the best elements of majority rule. But they were mitigated by a constitution with protections for individual liberty, a separation of powers, and a layered federal structure.

However, in contemporary usage, the term "democracy" refers to a government chosen by the people, whether it is direct or representative. The term "republic" has many different meanings but today often refers to a representative democracy with an elected head of state, such as a President, serving for a limited term, in contrast to states with a hereditary monarch as a head of state, even if these states also are representative democracies with an elected head of government such as a Prime Minister. Therefore, today the term is used by states which are quite different from the earlier use of the term, such as the Islamic Republic of Iran and the former German Democratic Republic.

Republicanism and Liberalism have complex relationships to democracy and republic.

CONSTITUTIONAL MONARCHS AND UPPER CHAMBERS

Initially after the American and French revolutions the question was open whether a democracy, in order to restrain unchecked majority rule, should have an elitist upper chamber, the members perhaps appointed meritorious experts or having lifetime tenures, or should have a constitutional monarch with limited but real powers. Some countries (as Britain, the Netherlands, Belgium, Scandinavian countries and Japan) turned powerful monarchs into constitutional monarchs with limited or, often gradually, merely symbolic roles.

Often the monarchy was abolished along with the aristocratic system (as in the U.S., France, China, Russia, Germany, Austria, Hungary, Italy, Greece and Egypt). Many nations had elite upper houses of legislatures which often had lifetime tenure, but eventually these senates lost power (as in Britain) or else became elective and remained powerful (as in the United States).

Democratic State

Though there remains some philosophical debate as to the applicability and legitimacy of criteria in defining democracy what follows may be a minimum of requirements for a state to be considered democratic (note that for example anarchists may support a form of democracy but not a state):

1. A demos-a group which makes political decisions by some form of collective procedure-must exist. Non-members of the demos do not participate. In modern democracies the demos is the adult portion of the nation, and adult citizenship is usually equivalent to membership.

2. A territory must be present, where the decisions apply, and where the demos is resident. In modern democracies, the territory is the nation-state, and since this corresponds (in theory) with the homeland of the nation, the demos and the reach of the democratic process neatly coincide. Colonies of democracies are not considered democratic by themselves, if they are governed from the colonial motherland: demos and territory do not coincide.
3. A decision-making procedure exists, which is either direct, in instances such as a referendum, or indirect, of which instances include the election of a parliament.
4. The procedure is regarded as legitimate by the demos, implying that its outcome will be accepted. Political legitimacy is the willingness of the population to accept decisions of the state, its government and courts, which go against personal choices or interests.
5. The procedure is effective in the minimal sense that it can be used to change the government, assuming there is sufficient support for that change. Showcase elections, pre-arranged to re-elect the existing regime, are not democratic.
6. In the case of nation-states, the state must be sovereign: democratic elections are pointless if an outside authority can overrule the result.

Advantages and Disadvantages of Liberal Democracy

It has been suggested that this article or section be merged with liberal democracy.

DIRECT DEMOCRACY

Some argue that "liberal democracy" does not respect absolute majority rule (except when electing representatives). The "liberty" of majority rule is restricted by the constitution or precedent decided by previous generations. Also, the real power is actually held by a relatively small representative body. Thus, the argument goes, "liberal democracy" is merely a decoration over an oligarchy. A system of direct democracy would be preferable. New technology, such as E-democracy, may make direct democracy easier to implement. Others would say that only a liberal democracy can guarantee the individual liberties of its citizens and prevent the development into a dictatorship. Unmoderated majority rule could, in this view, lead to an oppression of minorities. Another argument is that the elected leaders may be more interested and able than the average voter. A third that it takes much effort and time if everyone should gather information, discuss, and vote on most issues. Some liberal democracies have elements of direct democracy such as referenda and plebiscite. Switzerland and Uruguay are some examples; likewise several states of the United States. Many other countries have referenda to a lesser degree in their political system.

Democracy and Ethnic and Religious Conflicts

For historical reasons, many states are not culturally and ethnically homogeneous. There may be sharp ethnic, linguistic, religious and cultural divisions. In fact, some groups may be actively hostile to each other. A democracy, which by definition allows mass participation in decision-making theoretically also allows the use of the political process against 'enemy' groups. That may be especially visible during democratization, if the previous non-democratic government oppressed certain groups. It is also visible in established democracies, in the form of anti-immigrant populism. However, arguably the worst repressions have occurred in states without universal suffrage, like formerly apartheid South Africa and Nazi Germany.

Yale Law School professor Amy Chua claims that democratization can increase ethnic conflicts when an ethnic minority is disproportionately wealthy. "When free market democracy is pursued in the presence of a market-dominant minority, the almost invariable result is backlash. This backlash typically takes one of three forms. The first is a backlash against markets, targeting the market-dominant minority's wealth. The second is a backlash against democracy by forces favorable to the market-dominant minority.

The third is violence, sometimes genocidal, directed against the market-dominant minority itself.". Also, "overnight democracy will empower the poor, indigenous majority. What happens is that under those circumstances, democracy doesn't do what we expect it to do --that is, reinforce markets. Instead, democracy leads to the emergence of manipulative politicians and demagogues who find that the best way to get votes is by scapegoating the minorities." Chua also states that she is "big fan of trying to promote markets and democracy globally", but that it should be accompanied by attempts to "redistribute the wealth, whether it's property title and giving poor people property, land reform.... Redistributive mechanisms are tough to have if you have so much corruption."

The collapse of the Soviet Union and the partial democratisation of Soviet bloc states was followed by wars and civil war in the former Yugoslavia, in the Caucasus, and in Moldova. Nevertheless, statistical research shows that the fall of Communism and the increase in the number of democratic states were accompanied by a sudden and dramatic decline in total warfare, interstate wars, ethnic wars, revolutionary wars, and the number of refugees and displaced people.

Bureaucracy

A persistent libertarian and monarchist critique of democracy is the claim that it encourages the elected representatives to change the law without necessity, and in particular to pour forth a flood of new laws. This is seen as pernicious in several ways. New laws constrict the scope of what were previously private liberties. Rapidly changing laws make it difficult for a willing non-specialist to remain law-abiding. This may be an invitation for law-enforcement agencies to misuse power. The claimed continual complication of the law may be contrary to a claimed simple and eternal natural law -although there is no consensus on what this natural law is, even among advocates. Supporters of democracy point to the complex bureaucracy and regulations that has occurred in dictatorships, like many of the former Communist states.

Liberal democracies are also criticized for a claimed slowness and complexity of their decision-making.

Short-term Focus

Modern liberal democracies, by definition, allow for regular changes of government. That has led to a common criticism of their short-term focus. In four or five years the government will face a new election, and it must think of how it will win that election. That would encourage a preference for policies that will bring short term benefits to the electorate (or to self-interested politicians) before the next election, rather than unpopular policy with longer term benefits. This criticism assumes that it is possible to make long term predictions for a society, something Karl Popper has criticized as historicism.

Besides the regular review of governing entities, short-term focus in a democracy could also be the result of collective short-term thinking. For example, consider a campaign for policies aimed at reducing environmental damage while causing temporary increase in unemployment. However, this risk applies also to other political systems. Anarcho-capitalist Hans-Herman Hoppe explained short-termism of the democratic governments by the rational choice of currently ruling group to overexploit temporarily accessible resources, thus deriving maximal economic advantage to the members of this group. (He contrasted this with hereditary monarchy, in which a monarch has an interest in preserving the long-term capital value of his property (i.e. the country he owns) counter-balancing his desire to extract immediate revenue. He argues that the historical record of levels of taxation in certain monarchies (5-8%) and certain liberal democracies (40-60%) seems to confirm this contention. On the other hand, in hereditary autocracies like North Korea the state controls the whole economy while many liberal democratic states that score very high on rankings of economic freedom.

Public Choice Theory

Public choice theory is a branch of economics that studies the decision-making behavior of voters, politicians and government officials from the perspective of economic theory. One studied problem is that each voter has little influence and may therefore have a rational ignorance regarding political issues. This may allow special interest groups to gain subsidies and regulations beneficial to them but harmful to society. However, special interest groups may be equally or more influential in nondemocracies.

Plutocracy

Marxists, socialists and left-wing anarchists, argue that liberal democracy is an integral part of the capitalist system and is class-based and not fully democratic or participatory. It is bourgeois democracy where only the most financially powerful people rule. Because of this it is seen as fundamentally un-egalitarian, existing or operating in a way that facilitates economic exploitation. According to Marx, parliamentary elections are an opportunity citizens of a country get every few years to decide who among the ruling classes will misrepresent them in parliament.

The cost of political campaigning in representative democracies may mean that the system favors the rich, a form of plutocracy who may be a very small minority of the voters. In Athenian democracy, some public offices were randomly allocated to citizens, in order to inhibit the effects of plutocracy. Modern democracy may also be regarded as a dishonest farce used to keep the masses from getting restless, or a conspiracy for making them restless for some political agenda. It may encourage candidates to make deals with wealthy supporters, offering favorable legislation if the candidate is elected -perpetuating conspiracies for monopolization of key areas. Campaign finance reform is an attempt to correct this perceived problem. However, United States economist Steven Levitt claims in his book Freakonomics, that campaign spending is no guarantee of electoral success. He compared electoral success of the same pair of candidates running against one another repeatedly for the same job, as often happens in United States Congressional elections, where spending levels varied. He concludes: "A winning candidate can cut his spending in half and lose only 1 percent of the vote. Meanwhile, a losing candidate who doubles his spending can expect to shift the vote in his favor by only that same 1 percent."

Ownership of the media by the few may lead to more specific distortion of the electoral process, since the media are themselves a vital element of that process. Some critics argue that criticism of the status quo or a particular agenda tends to be suppressed by such media cartels, to protect their own self-interests. Proponents respond that constitutionally protected freedom of speech makes it possible for both for-profit and non-profit organizations to debate the issues. They argue that media coverage in democracies simply reflects public preferences, and does not entail censorship.

Limited Voter Turnout

Some see a problem with limited voter turnout since not all eligible voters participate in the political process. Get out the vote campaigns may increase voter turnout but may be advocated by special interest groups.

Some therefore argue for compulsory voting and several nations have this system. Proponents argue that this increases the legitimacy of the elections and ensure political participation by all those affected by the political process. Also, political parties do not have to spend time and energy convincing voters that they should vote at all. Arguments against include restriction of freedom, economic costs of enforcing this, increased number of invalid and blank votes, and random voting.

Majoritarianism

The "tyranny of the majority" is the fear that a democratic government, reflecting the majority view, can take action that oppresses a particular minority. Theoretically, the majority could only be a majority of those who vote and not a majority of the citizens. In those cases, one minority tyrannizes another minority in the name of the majority. It can apply in both direct democracy or representative democracy. Possible examples include:

- those potentially subject to conscription are a minority.

- several European countries have introduced bans on personal religious symbols in public schools. Opponents see this as a violation of rights to freedom of religion. Supporters see it as following from the separation of state and religious activities.
- prohibition of pornography is typically determined by what the majority is prepared to accept.
- recreational drug use is also typically legalized (or at least tolerated) to the degree that the majority finds acceptable. Users may see themselves as an oppressed minority, victims of unjustifiable criminalisation.
- society's treatment of homosexuals is also cited in this context. Homosexual acts were widely criminalised in democracies until several decades ago; in some democracies they still are, reflecting the religious or sexual mores of the majority.
- the Athenian democracy and the early United States had slavery.
- the majority often taxes the minority who are wealthy at progressively higher rates, with the intention that the wealthy will incur a larger tax burden for social purposes. However, this is generally offset to some degree, by their better access to relevant expert advice (tax consultants and lawyers).
- in prosperous western democracies, the poor form a minority of the population, and may be disadvantaged by a majority who resent transfer taxation. Especially when they form a distinct underclass, the majority may use the democratic process to, in effect, withdraw the protection of the state.
- an often quoted example of the 'tyranny of the majority' is that Adolf Hitler came to power by legitimate democratic procedures. The Nazi party gained the largest share of votes in the democratic Weimar republic in 1933. Some might consider this an example of "tyranny of a minority" since he never gained a majority vote, but it is common for a

plurality to exercise power in democracies, so the rise of Hitler can not be considered irrelevant. However, his regime's large-scale human rights violations took place after the democratic system had been abolished. Also, the Weimar constitution in an "emergency" allowed dictatorial powers and suspension of the essentials of the constitution itself without any vote or election, something not possible in most liberal democracies.

Proponents of democracy make a number of defenses concerning 'tyranny of the majority'. One is to argue that the presence of a constitution protecting the rights of all citizens in many democratic countries acts as a safeguard. Generally, changes in these constitutions require the agreement of a supermajority of the elected representatives, or require a judge and jury to agree that evidentiary and procedural standards have been fulfilled by the state, or two different votes by the representatives separated by an election, or, sometimes, a referendum. These requirements are often combined. The separation of powers into legislative branch, executive branch, judicial branch also makes it more difficult for a small majority to impose their will. This means a majority can still legitimately coerce a minority (which is still ethically questionable), but such a minority would be very small and, as a practical matter, it is harder to get a larger proportion of the people to agree to such actions. Another argument is that majorities and minorities can take a markedly different shape on different issues. People often agree with the majority view on some issues and agree with a minority view on other issues. One's view may also change. Thus, the members of a majority may limit oppression of a minority since they may well in the future themselves be in a minority.

A third common argument is that, despite the risks, majority rule is preferable to other systems, and the tyranny of the majority is in any case an improvement on a tyranny of a minority. All the possible problems mentioned above can also occur in nondemocracies with the added problem that a minority can oppress the majority. Proponents of democracy argue that empirical statistical evidence strongly shows that more democracy leads to less internal violence and mass murder by the government.. This is sometimes formulated as Rummel's Law, which states that the less democratic freedom a people have, the more likely their rulers are to murder them.

POLITICAL STABILITY

One argument for democracy is that by creating a system where the public can remove administrations, without changing the legal basis for government, democracy aims at reducing political uncertainty and instability, and assuring citizens that however much they may disagree with present policies, they will be given a regular chance to change those who are in power, or change policies with which they disagree. This is preferable to a system where political change takes place through violence. Some think that political stability may be considered as excessive when the group in power remains the same for an extended period of time. On the other hand, this is more common in nondemocracies. One notable feature of liberal democracies is that their opponents (those groups who wish to abolish liberal democracy) rarely win elections. Advocates use this as an argument to support their view that liberal democracy is inherently stable and can usually only be overthrown by external force, while opponents argue that the system is inherently stacked against them despite its claims to impartiality. In the past, it was feared that democracy could be easily exploited by leaders with dictatorial aspirations, who could get themselves elected into power. However, the actual number of liberal democracies that have elected dictators into power is low. When it has occurred, it is usually after a major crisis have caused many people to doubt the system or in young/poorly functioning democracies. Some possible examples include Adolf Hitler during the Great Depression and Napoleon III who become first President of the young Second French Republic and later Emperor.

Effective Response in Wartime

A liberal democracy, by definition, implies that power is not concentrated. One criticism is that this could be a disadvantage for a state in wartime, when a fast and unified response is necessary. The legislature usually must give consent before the start of an offensive military operation, although sometimes the executive can do this on its own while keeping the legislature informed. If the democracy is attacked, then no consent is usually required for defensive operations. The people may vote against a conscription army. Monarchies and dictatorships can in theory act immediately and forcefully.

However, actual research shows that democracies are more likely to win wars than non-democracies. One explanation attributes this primarily to "the transparency of the polities, and the stability of their preferences, once determined, democracies are better able to cooperate with their partners in the conduct of wars". Other research attributes this to superior mobilization of resources or selection of wars that the democratic states have a high chance of winning.

Stam and Reiter (2002, p. 64-70) also note that the emphasis on individuality within democratic societies means that their soldiers fight with greater initiative and superior leadership. Officers in dictatorships are often selected for political loyalty rather than ability. They may be exclusively selected from a small class or religious/ ethnic group that support the regime. Also this may also exclude many able officers. The leaders in nondemocracies may respond violently to any perceived criticisms or disobedience. This may make the soldiers and officers afraid to raise any objections or do anything without explicit authorisation. The lack of initiative may be particularly detrimental in modern warfare. Enemy soldiers may more easily surrender to democracies since they can expect comparatively good treatment. Nazi Germany killed almost 2/3 of the captured Soviet soldiers. 38% of the American soldiers captured by North Korea in the Korean War were killed.

Better Information on and Corrections of Problems

A democratic system may provide better information for policy decisions. Undesirable information may more easily be ignored in dictatorships, even if this undesirable or contrarian information provides early warning of problems. The democratic system also provides a way to replace inefficient leaders and policies. Thus, problems may continue longer and crises of all kinds may be more common in autocracies.

Corruption

Research by the World Bank suggests that political institutions are extremely important in determining the prevalence of corruption: democracy, parliamentary systems, political stability, and freedom of the press are all associated with lower corruption. Freedom of information legislation is important for accountability and transparency. The Indian Right to Information Act "has already engendered mass movements in the country that is bringing the lethargic, often corrupt bureaucracy to its knees and changing power equations completely."

Terrorism

Several studies have concluded that terrorism is most common in nations with intermediate political freedom. The nations with the least terrorism are the most democratic nations. However, critics of Western democracy such as Noam Chomsky have argued that, according to official definitions of terrorism, liberal democratic states have committed many acts of terrorism against other nations.

Economic Growth and Financial Crises

Statistically, more democracy correlates with a higher gross domestic product (GDP) per capita. However, there is disagreement regarding how much credit the democratic system can take for this. One observation is that democracy became widespread only after the industrial revolution and the introduction of capitalism. On the other hand, the industrial revolution started in England which was one of the most democratic nations for its time within its own borders. (But this democracy was very limited and did not apply to the colonies which contributed significantly to the wealth.)

Several statistical studies support the theory that more capitalism, measured for example with one the several Indices of Economic Freedom which has been used in hundreds of studies by independent researchers, increases economic growth and that this in turn increases general prosperity, reduces poverty, and causes democratization. This is a statistical tendency, and there are individual exceptions like India, which is democratic but arguably not prosperous, or Brunei, which has a high GDP but has never been democratic. There are also other studies suggesting that more democracy increases economic freedom although a few find no or even a small negative effect. One objection might be that nations like Sweden and Canada today score just below nations like Chile and Estonia on economic freedom but that Sweden and Canada today have a higher GDP per capita. However, this is a misunderstanding, the studies indicate effect on economic growth and thus that future GDP per capita will be higher with higher economic freedom. It should also be noted that according to the index Sweden and Canada are among the world's most capitalist nations, due to factors such as strong rule of law, strong property rights, and few restrictions against free trade. Critics might argue that the Index of Economic Freedom and other methods used does not measure the degree of capitalism, preferring some other definition.

Some argue that economic growth due to its empowerment of citizens, will ensure a transition to democracy in countries such as China. However, other dispute this. Even if economic growth has caused democratization in the past, it may not do so in the future. Dictators may now have learned how to have economic growth without this causing more political freedom.

A high degree of oil or mineral exports is strongly associated with nondemocratic rule. This effect applies worldwide and not only to the Middle East. Dictators who have this form of wealth can spend more on their security apparatus and provide benefits which lessen public unrest. Also, such wealth is not followed by the social and cultural changes that may transform societies with ordinary economic growth.

A recent meta-analysis finds that democracy has no direct effect on economic growth. However, it has a strong and significant indirect effects which contribute to growth. Democracy is associated with higher human capital accumulation, lower inflation, lower political instability, and higher economic freedom. There is also some evidence that it is associated with larger governments and more restrictions on international trade. If leaving out East Asia, then during the last forty-five years poor democracies have grown their economies 50% more rapidly than nondemocracies. Poor democracies such as the Baltic countries, Botswana, Costa Rica, Ghana, and Senegal have grown more rapidly than nondemocracies such as Angola, Syria, Uzbekistan, and Zimbabwe.

Of the eighty worst financial catastrophes during the last four decades, only five were in democracies. Similarly, poor democracies are half likely as non-democracies to experience a 10 percent decline in GDP per capita over the course of a single year.

Famines and Refugees

A prominent economist, Amartya Sen, has noted that no functioning democracy has ever suffered a large scale famine. This includes democracies that have not been very prosperous historically, like India, which had its last great famine in 1943 and many other large scale famines before that in the late nineteenth century, all under British rule. However, some others ascribe the Bengal famine of 1943 to the effects of World War II. The government of India had been becoming progressively more democratic for years. Provincial government had been entirely so since the Government of India Act of 1935.

Refugee crises almost always occur in non-democracies. Looking at the volume of refugee flows for the last twenty years, the first eighty-seven cases occurred in autocracies.

Human Development

Democracy correlates with a higher score on the human development index and a lower score on the human poverty index.

Poor democracies have better education, longer life expectancy, lower infant mortality, access to drinking water, and better health care than poor dictatorships. This is not due to higher levels of foreign assistance or spending a larger percentage of GDP on health and education. Instead, the available resources are managed better. Several health indicators (life expectancy and infant and maternal mortality) have a stronger and more significant association with democracy than they have with GDP per capita, size of the public sector, or income inequality. In the post-Communist nations, after an initial decline, those most democratic have achieved the greatest gains in life expectancy.

DEMOCRATIC PEACE THEORY

Numerous studies using many different kinds of data, definitions, and statistical analyzes have found support for the democratic peace theory. The original finding was that liberal democracies have never made war with one another. More recent research has extended the theory and finds that democracies have few Militarized Interstate Disputes causing less than 1000 battle deaths with one another, that those MIDs that have occurred between democracies have caused few deaths, and that democracies have few civil wars. There are various criticisms of the theory, including specific historic wars and that correlation is not causation.

Mass Murder by Government

Research shows that the more democratic nations have much less democide or murder by government. Similarly, they have less genocide and politicide.

Freedoms and Rights: The freedoms and rights of the citizens in liberal democracies are usually seen as beneficial.

Happiness: Democracies are more often associated with a higher average self-reported happiness in a nation.

Criticism: Some far right, theocratic, anarchist, and monarchist groups oppose all forms of democracy.

Beyond the Public Level

While this article deals mainly with democracy as a system to rule countries, voting and representation have been used to govern many other kinds of communities and organizations.

- Many non-governmental organisations decide policy and leadership by voting.
- In business, corporations elect their boards by votes weighed by the number of shares held by each owner.
- Trade unions sometimes choose their leadership through democratic elections. In the U.S. democratic elections were rare before Congress required them in the 1950s.
- Cooperatives are enterprises owned and democratically controlled by their customers or workers.

FEDERATION

A federation (Latin: foedus, covenant) is a union comprising a number of partially self-governing states or regions united by a central ("federal") government. In a federation, the self-governing status of the component states is typically constitutionally entrenched and may not be altered by a unilateral decision of the central government. The form of government or constitutional structure found in a federation is known as federalism (see also federalism as a political philosophy). It can be considered the opposite of another system, the unitary state. Federations may be multi-ethnic, or cover a large area of territory, although neither is necessarily the case. Federations are often founded on an original agreement between a number of sovereign states.

Federations and other Forms of State

In a federation the component states are regarded as in some sense sovereign, in so far as certain powers are reserved to them that may not be exercised by the central government. However a federation is more than a mere loose alliance of independent states. The component states of a federation usually possess no powers in relation to foreign policy and so they enjoy no independent status under international law.

Federations usually exhibit a single, two-tier structure of government across an entire jurisdiction. Exceptions may occur in which certain parts of the federation are under more direct control of the federal government, as is the case with the autonomous 'territories' of Canada and Australia, with Union Territories in India and with the United States District of Columbia. However it is not characteristic in a federation for small peripheral regions to be self-governing, while a central, much larger 'metropolis' region remains under the direct control of the central government.

Some federations are called assymmetric because some states have more autonomy than others, although they have the same constitutional status.

A federation often emerges from an initial agreement between a number of separate states to come together in order to solve mutual problems, or provide for mutual defence. This was the case with the United States, Switzerland, Canada and Australia. In other cases, like Brazil, the federation comes after a unitary state, as a new model in order to decentralize powers and functions.

Unitary States

A unitary state is sometimes one with only a single, centralised, national tier of government. However unitary states often also include one or more self-governing regions. The difference between a federation and this kind of unitary state is that in a unitary state the autonomous status of self-governing regions exists by the sufferance of the central government, and may be unilaterally revoked. While it is common for a federation to be brought into being by agreement between a number of formally independent states, in a unitary state self-governing regions are often created through a process of devolution, where a formerly centralised state agrees to grant autonomy to a region that was previously entirely subordinate. Thus federations are often established voluntarily from 'below' whereas devolution grants self-government from 'above'.

It is often part of the philosophy of a unitary state that, regardless of the actual status of any of its parts, its entire territory constitutes a single sovereign entity or nation-state, and that by virtue of this the central government exercises sovereignty over the whole territory as of right. In a federation, on the other hand, sovereignty is often regarded as residing notionally in the component states, or as being shared between these states and the central government.

DE FACTO FEDERATIONS

The distinction between a federation and a unitary state is often quite ambiguous. A unitary state may closely resemble a federation in structure and, while a central government may possess the theoretical right to revoke the autonomy of a self-governing region, it may be politically difficult for it to do so in practice. The self-governing regions of some unitary states also often enjoy greater autonomy than those of some federations. For these reasons, it is sometimes argued that some modern unitary states are de facto federations.

Spain is suggested as one possible de facto federation as it grants more self-government to its autonomous communities than most federations allow their constituent parts. For the Spanish parliament to revoke the autonomy of regions such as Galicia, Catalonia or the Basque Country, or for the United Kingdom government unilaterally to abolish the legislatures of Wales or Scotland, would be a near political impossibility. Additionally, some regions such as Navarra or the Basque Country have full control over taxation and spending, transferring a small payment to the central government for the common services (army, foreign relations, macroeconomic policy).

In the People's Republic of China, a form of de facto federation has evolved without formal legislation. This has occurred as largely informal grants of power to the provinces, to handle economic affairs and implement national policies. This has resulted in a system some have termed "de facto federalism with Chinese characteristics".

Constitutionally, the power vested in the special administrative regions of the People's Republic is granted from the Central People's Government, through decision by the National People's Congress. Special administrative regions are not constitutionally stated to be administrative divisions. It is also not stated that special administrative regions are incorporated territories.

OTHER FORMS OF STATE

While distinct from a unitary state, a federation is also to be distinguished from a confederation. By connotation, a confederation is similar in structure to a federation but with a weaker central government. Over time these terms acquired distinct connotations leading to the present difference in definition. An example of this is the United States under the Articles of Confederation. The Articles established a national government under what today would be defined as a federal system (albeit with a comparatively weaker federal government).

Empire

An empire is a multi-ethnic state or group of nations with a central government established usually through coercion (on the model of the Roman Empire). An empire will often include self-governing regions but these will possess autonomy only at the sufferance of the central government. The term empire, except where used metaphorically, is usually reserved for an entity headed by an emperor, although his or her constitutional role may be purely ceremonial. An empire may, in some cases, also consist of multiple kingdoms organised together with a high king designated as an emperor. One example of this was Imperial Germany.

European Union

The European Union (EU) possesses some of the attributes of a federal state. However, its central government is far weaker than that of most federations so it is usually characterised as an unprecedented form of supra-national union or confederation. The

EU has responsibility for important areas such as trade and monetary union, and today around sixty per cent of the legislation in member-states originates in the institutions of the Union. Nonetheless, EU member-states retain the right to act independently in matters of foreign policy and defence, and also enjoy a near monopoly over other major policy areas such as criminal justice and taxation. Furthermore, member-states are separate, sovereign entities under international law and, currently at least, possess a de facto if not explicit de jure right of secession. The proposed Constitutional Treaty would codify the Member States' right to leave the Union, but would at the same time also provide the European Union with more powers in some areas. Whether or not this would move the European Union closer to a federal state than an international organisation is currently the subject of heated political debate.

Russian Federation

An interesting example is provided by the Russian Federation. It has inherited its structure from the Russian Soviet Federative Socialist Republic that was one of the 15 republics of the Soviet Union and itself was considered a federation. The RSFSR, however, consisted of "autonomous republics" which had a certain degree of autonomy, at least de jure, and of other types of administrative units (mostly oblasts and krays) whose status was the same as that of oblasts in other -unitary -Soviet republics. In today's Russia, republics, oblasts and krays, as well as one "autonomous oblast" and "autonomous districts" are equal in legal terms, save some symbolic features of a republic (constitution, president, citizenship, national language). Some regions have concluded agreements with the Federation so as to modify the degree of their autonomy. It is also to be noted that several "autonomous districts" are part of the territory of a kray, a complicated system that is now being gradually abolished through referendums on merging certain regions.

Since 2004, governors of each region, who were previously elected by popular vote, have been directly appointed by the President of Russia. Local parliaments theoretically have authority to veto an appointment, but if this occurs the parliament must be dissolved and new elections held. This lets some argue that the Russian Federation is not a federation in the strictest sense.

Soviet Union (USSR)

The constitution of the 1922-1991 Soviet Union (USSR) theoretically provided for a voluntary federation or confederation of 'soviet socialist republics'. Each was notionally governed by its own supreme council and had the right to secede. Furthermore, some republics themselves possessed further nominally self-governing units. Two of them, Belarus and Ukraine, were even members of the United Nations, some other republics had their own foreign ministries. In practice, the system of one-party government found in the USSR meant that governance of the Union was highly centralised, with important decisions taken by the leaders of the Communist Party in Moscow and merely 'rubber stamped' by local institutions. Nonetheless, with the introduction of free, competitive elections in the final days of the USSR, the Union's theoretically federal structure became a reality in practice; this occurred only for a brief interim period, as the elected governments of many republics demanded their right to secede and became independent states. Thus the USSR's de jure federal structure played a key role in its dissolution.

Myanmar

Myanmar (formerly Burma) is claimed to have adopted federation status (the country's official name is "Union of Myanmar"). However, after General Ne Win seized power Burma in 1962 and abolished the Constitution of the Union of Burma, the country adopted a unitary system under his military dictatorship.

3

THE CONSTITUTIONAL STRUCTURE

DIVISION OF POWERS

In a federation, the division of power between federal and regional governments is usually outlined in the constitution. It is in this way that the right to self-government of the component states is usually constitutionally entrenched. Component states often also possess their own constitutions which they may amend as they see fit, although in the event of conflict the federal constitution usually takes precedence.

In almost all federations the central government enjoys the powers of foreign policy and national defence. Were this not the case a federation would not be a single sovereign state. Beyond this the precise division of power varies from one nation to another. The United States Constitution provides that all powers not specifically granted to the federal government are retained by the states. The Constitution of Canada, on the other hand, provides the opposite: that powers not explicitly granted to the provincial governments are retained by the centre. In Germany, the division of powers is less one of content than of administration: the federal government often merely issues broad directives to the Länder (self-governing regions), which then have broad discretion as to how to implement them. In the People's Republic of China, regarded by some as a de facto although not de jure federation, the central government sets up general economic policy and goals, and leaves the implementation to provincial governments. Much like the Canadian system, the Australian Division of Powers serperates some powers which were considered too difficult for the states to manage so that the Federal Government takes on that responsibility.

Where every component state of a federation possesses the same powers, we are said to find 'symmetric federalism'. Asymmetric federalism exists where states are granted different powers, or some possess greater autonomy than others do. This is often done in recognition of the existence of a distinct culture in a particular region or regions. In Spain, "historical communities" such as Navarre, Galicia, Catalonia, and the Basque Country have more powers than other autonomous communities, partly to deal with their distinctness and to appease nationalist leanings, partly out of respect of privileges granted earlier in history.

It is common that during the historical evolution of a federation there is a gradual movement of power from the component states to the centre, as the federal government acquires additional powers, sometimes to deal with unforeseen circumstances. The acquisition of new powers by a federal government may occur through formal constitutional amendment or simply through a broadening of the interpretation of a government's existing constitutional powers given by the courts.

Usually, a federation is formed at two levels: the central government and the regions (states, provinces, territories). Brazil is an exception, because the 1988's Constitution has included the municipalities as autonomous political entities making the federation tripartite: encompassing the Union, the States, and the municipalities. Each state is divided into municipalities (municípios) with their own legislative council (câmara de vereadores) and a mayor (prefeito), which are autonomous and hierarchically independent from both Federal and State Government. Each municipality has a "little constitution", called "organic law" (lei orgânica).

Federations often employ the paradox of being a union of states, while still being states (or having aspects of statehood) in themselves. For example, James Madison (author of the US Constitution) wrote in Federalist Paper No. 39 that the US Constitution "is in strictness neither a national nor a federal constitution; but a composition of both. In its foundation, it is federal, not national; in the sources from which the ordinary powers of the Government are drawn, it is partly federal, and partly national...." This paradox stems from the fact that states in a federation maintain all sovereignty that they do not yield to the federation by their own consent. The sharing of sovereignty between a federation and its constituent states sometimes makes it difficult to differentiate between a sovereign state and a non-sovereign state.

ORGANS OF GOVERNMENT

The structures of most federal governments incorporate mechanisms to protect the rights of component states. One method, known as 'intrastate federalism', is to directly represent the governments of component states in federal political institutions. Where a federation has a bicameral legislature the upper house is often used to represent the component states while the lower house represents the people of the nation as a whole. A federal upper house may be based on a special scheme of apportionment, as is the case in the senates of the United States and Australia, where each state is represented by an equal number of senators irrespective of the size of its population.

Alternatively, or in addition to this practice, the members of an upper house may be indirectly elected by the government or legislature of the component states, as occurred in the United States prior to 1913, or be actual members or delegates of the state governments, as, for example, is the case in the German Bundesrat. The lower house of a federal legislature is usually directly elected, with apportionment in proportion to population, although states may sometimes still be guaranteed a certain minimum number of seats. In Canada, the provincial governments represent regional interests and negotiate directly with the central government. A First Ministers conference of the prime minister and the provincial premiers is the de facto highest political forum in the land, although it is not mentioned in the constitution.

Federations often have special procedures for amendment of the federal constitution. As well as reflecting the federal structure of the state this may guarantee that the self-governing status of the component states cannot be abolished without their consent. An amendment to the constitution of the United States must be ratified by three-quarters of either the state legislatures, or of constitutional conventions specially elected in each of the states, before it can come into effect. In referenda to amend the constitutions of Australia and Switzerland it is required that a proposal be endorsed not just by an overall majority of the electorate in the nation as a whole, but also by separate majorities in each of a majority of the states or cantons. In Australia, this latter requirement is known as a double majority.

Some federal constitutions also provide that certain constitutional amendments cannot occur without the unanimous consent of all states or of a particular state. The US constitution provides that no state may be deprived of equal representation in the senate without its consent. In Australia, if a proposed amendment will specifically impact one or more states than it must be endorsed in the referendum held in each of those states. Any amendment to the Canadian constitution that would modify the role of the monarchy would require unanimous consent of the provinces. The German Basic Law provides that no amendment is admissible at all that would completely abolish the federal system.

OTHER TECHNICAL TERMS

- Fiscal federalism -federalism involving the transfer of funds between different levels of government.
- Formal federalism (or 'constitutional federalism') -the delineation of powers is specified in a written constitution.
- Executive federalism (also known as 'administrative federalism').

Federalism as a Political Philosophy

The meaning of federalism, as a political movement, and of what constitutes a 'federalist', varies with country and historical context. Movements associated with the establishment or development of federations can be either centralising or decentralising. For example, at the time those nations were being established, 'federalists' in the United States and Australia were those who advocated the creation of strong central government. Similarly, in European Union politics, federalists are mostly those who seek greater EU integration. In contrast, in Spain and post-war Germany, federal movements have sought decentralisation: the transfer of power from central authorities to local units. In Canada, where Quebec separatism has been a political force for several decades, the 'federalist' force is dedicated to keeping the federation intact and adapting the federal structure to better suit Quebec interests.

Internal Controversy and Conflict

Certain forms of political and constitutional dispute are common to federations. One issue is that the exact division of power and responsibility between federal and regional governments is often a source of controversy. Often, as is the case with the United States, such conflicts are resolved through the judicial system, which delimits the powers of federal and local governments. The relationship between federal and local courts varies from nation to nation and can be a controversial and complex issue in itself.

Another common issue in federal systems is the conflict between regional and national interests, or between the interests and aspirations of different ethnic groups. In some federations the entire jurisdiction is relatively homogeneous and each constituent state resembles a miniature version of the whole; this is known as 'congruent federalism'. On the other hand, incongruent federalism exists where different states or regions possess distinct ethnic groups.

The ability of a federal government to create national institutions that can mediate differences that arise because of linguistic, ethnic, religious, or other regional differences is an important challenge. The inability to meet this challenge may lead to the secession of parts of a federation or to civil war, as occurred in United States and Switzerland. In case of Malaysia, Singapore was expelled from the federation because of rising racial tension. In some cases internal conflict may lead a federation to collapse entirely, as occurred in Nigeria, the Federation of Rhodesia and Nyasaland, the United Provinces of Central America and the West Indies Federation.

POLITICAL POWER

Political power (imperium in Latin) is a type of power held by a person or group in a society. There are many ways to hold such power. Officially, political power is held by the holders of the sovereignty. Political powers are not limited to heads of states, however, and the extent to which a person or group holds such power is related to the amount of societal influence they can wield, formally or informally. In many cases this influence is not contained within a single state and it refers to international power.

Political scientists have frequently defined power as "the ability to influence the behaviour of others" with or without resistance.

For analytical reasons, MacMillan separates the concepts power

Power is the capacity to restructure actual situations.

—I.C. Macmillan

and influence

Influence is the capacity to control and modify the perceptions of others.

—I.C. Macmillan

Abuse of Power

Throughout history there have been many examples of the destructive or senseless use of political power. This has happened most frequently when too much power has been concentrated in too few hands, without enough room for political debate, public criticism, and other types of correctives. Examples of such regimes are despotism, tyranny, and dictatorship. To counter these potential problems, people have devised and practised different solutions, most of them related to the sharing of power (as in democracy), the placing of limitations on the extent of power one individual or group can have, and the creation of protective rights for individuals through legislation or charters (such as human rights).

Separation of Powers

Charles de Montesquieu claimed that without following a principle of containing and balancing legislative, executive and judiciary powers, there is no freedom and no protection against abuse of power. This is the separation of powers principle.

Division of Power

A similar concept, termed Division of Power, also consists of differentiated legislative, executive and judiciary powers. However, while Separation of Power prohibits one branch from interfering with another, Division of Power permits such interference. For example, in Indonesia, the President (who wields executive power) can introduce a new bill, but the People's Consultative Assembly (holding legislative power) chooses to either legalize or reject the bill.

POLITICAL SCIENCE PERSPECTIVES

Within normative political analysis, there are also various levels of power as described by academics that add depth into the understanding of the notion of power and its political implications. Robert Dahl, a prominent American political scientist, first ascribed to political power the trait of decision-making as the source and main indicator of power. Later, two other political scientists, Peter Bachrach and Morton Baratz, decided that simply ascribing decision-making as the basis of power was too simplistic and they added what they termed a 2nd dimension of power, agenda-setting by elites who worked in the backrooms and away from public scrutiny in order to exert their power upon society. Lastly, British academic Steven Lukes added a 3rd dimension of power, preference-shaping, which he claimed was another important aspect of normative power in politics which entails theoretical views similar to notions of cultural hegemony. These 3 dimensions of power are today often considered defining aspects of political power by political researchers.

A radical alternative view of the source of political power follows the formula: information plus authority permits the exercise of power. Political power is intimately related to information. Sir Francis Bacon's statement: "Nam et ipsa scientia potestas est" for knowledge itself is power, assumed authority as given. Many will know that unless someone with authority listens and acts, there is no political power. It is said democracy is the best method of informing those entrusted with authority. They are best able to use authority without ignorance to maximize political power. Those who exercise authority in ignorance are not powerful, because they do not realize their intentions and have little control over the effects of using their authority.

Post-modernism has debated over how to define political power. Perhaps, the best known definition comes from the late Michel Foucault, whose work in Discipline and Punish (and other writings) conveys a view of power that is organic within society. This view holds that political power is more subtle and is part of a series of societal controls and 'normalizing' influences through historical institutions and definitions of normal vs. abnormal. Foucault once characterized power as "an action over actions" (une action sur des actions), arguing that power was essentially a relation between several dots, in continuous transformation as in Nietzsche's philosophy. His view of power lent credence to the view that power in human society was part of a training process in which everyone, from a Prime Minister to a homeless person, played their role within the power structure of society. Jürgen Habermas opposed himself to Foucault's conception of discourse as a battlefield for power relations, arguing that it should be possible to achieve consensus on the fundamentals rules of discourse, in order to establish a transparent and democratic dialogue.

Thenceforth, he argued against Foucault and Althusser that power was not immanent to discourse, and that philosophy could be completely distinguished from ideology. More recently, there has been a move among academics to differentiate power from a new concept of luck. Under some conditions (particularly the when examining the third dimension of power) it becomes necessary to determine who obtains a favourable result through the wielding of genuine power and who is simply "lucky". An example might be an ethnic minority who receive favourable treatment while not intentionally seeking it. A person promoted through positive discrimination would be considered "lucky" rather than "powerful". The eventual aim of such discrimination would be to eventually convert some (or all) of that luck into power. Some groups remain serially lucky without ever obtaining power.

ANARCHY IN INTERNATIONAL RELATIONS

Anarchy in international relations posits that the world system is leaderless: there is no universal sovereign or worldwide government. There is thus no hierarchically superior, coercive power that can resolve disputes or order the system. Political scientists do not use the term "anarchy" to signify a world in chaos, in disorder, or in conflict. It simply reflects the order of the international system: independent states with no central authority above them. The concept of anarchy is the foundation for realist, liberal, neorealist, and neoliberal international relations theories. Constructivist theory disputes that anarchy is a fundamental condition of the international system, saying that "anarchy is what states make of it" (Alexander Wendt).

REALISM AND INTERNATIONAL RELATIONS

Realism, also known as political realism, in the context of international relations, encompasses a variety of theories and approaches, all of which share a belief that states are primarily motivated by the desire for military and economic power or security, rather than ideals or ethics. This term is often synonymous with power politics. The term realism can, instead of referring to the broad family of realist theories, refer specifically to classical realism, the common ancestor and original form of realism.

Common Assumptions

Realist theories share the following key assumptions:

- The international system is anarchic. There is no authority above states capable of regulating their interactions; states must arrive at relations with other states on their own, rather than it being dictated to them by some higher controlling entity (that is, no true authoritative world government exists).
- Sovereign states are the principal actors in the international system. International institutions, non-governmental organizations, multinational corporations and other sub-state or trans-state actors are viewed as having little independent influence.
- States are rational unitary actors each moving towards their own national interest. There is a general distrust of long-term cooperation or alliance.
- The overriding 'national interest' of each state is its national security and survival.
- In pursuit of national security, states strive to amass resources.
- Relations between states are determined by their comparative level of power derived primarily from their military and economic capabilities.

In summary, realists believe that mankind is not inherently benevolent but rather self-centered and competitive. This Hobbesian perspective contrasts with the liberalism approach to international relations which views human nature as selfish and conflictual unless given appropriate conditions under which to cooperate. Further, they believe that states are inherently aggressive (offensive realism) and/or obsessed with security (defensive realism); and that territorial expansion is only constrained by opposing power(s). This aggressive build-up, however, leads to a security dilemma where increasing one's own security can bring along greater instability as the opponent(s) builds up its own arms. Thus, security is a zero-sum game where only relative gains can be made.

HISTORY AND BRANCHES

Historic Antecedents

While Realism as a formal discipline in international relations didn't arrive until World War II, its primary assumptions have been expressed in earlier writings:

- Sun Tzu (or Sunzi), an ancient Chinese military strategist who wrote the Art of War.
- Chanakya early Indian statesman, and writer on the Arthashastra.
- Thucydides, an ancient Greek historian who wrote the History of the Peloponnesian War and is also cited as an intellectual forebearer of realpolitik.
- Hanfeizi, Chinese scholar who theorised Legalism (or Legism) and who served in the court of the King of Qin -later unifier of China ending the Warring States Period. His writings include The Two Handles (about punishments and rewards as tools of governance). He theorised about a neutral, manipulative ruler who would act as Head of State while secretly controlling the executive through his ministers -the ones to take real responsibility for any policy.
- Niccolò Machiavelli, a Florentine political philosopher, who wrote II Principe (The Prince) in which he held that the sole aim of a prince (politician) was to seek power, regardless of religious or ethical considerations.
- Thomas Hobbes, an English philosopher who wrote Leviathan in which he stated that in anarchy there is a "war of all against all".
- Otto von Bismarck, a Prussian statesman coined the term balance of power. Balancing power meant keeping the peace and careful realpolitik practitioners tried to avoid arms races.
- Carl von Clausewitz was a 19th century Prussian general and military theorist who wrote Vom Kriege (On War).

"Classical Realism"

Modern realism began as a serious field of research in the United States during and after World War II. This evolution was partly fueled by European war migrants like Hans Morgenthau who had a negative view of human nature, thought by some to be due to their experiences in war.

Prominent classical realists:

- George F. Kennan -Containment
- Nicholas Spykman -Geostrategy, Containment
- Herman Kahn -Nuclear strategy
- E. H. Carr
- Reinhold Niebuhr
- Hans Morgenthau
- Arnold Wolfers
- Charles Beard
- Walter Lippmann

"Liberal Realism" or the "English School" or "Rationalism"

The English School holds that while the international system is anarchical, order can be promoted through diplomacy, international law and society. This school thus gives credence to establishing IGOs such as the United Nations.

Prominent liberal realists:

- Hedley Bull -Liberal realism (sometimes called the "English School" or "Rationalism")

Hedley Bull argued for both the existence of international society of states and its perseverance even in times of great systemic upheaval, meaning regional or so-called "world wars."

- Martin Wight

This section is a stub. You can help by expanding it.

"Neorealism" or "Structural Realism"

Neorealism derives from classical realism except that instead of human nature, its focus is predominantly on the international system. While states remain the principal actors, greater attention is given to the forces above and below the states through a levels of analysis or structure-agency debate. The international system is seen as a structure acting on the state with individuals below the level of the state acting as agency on the state as a whole.

While neorealism shares a focus on the international system with the English School, neorealism differs in the emphasis it places on the permanence of conflict. To ensure state security, states must be on constant preparation for conflict through economic and military build-up.

Prominent neorealists:

- Robert Jervis -Defensive realism
- Kenneth Waltz -Defensive realism
- Stephen Walt -Defensive realism
- John Mearsheimer -Offensive realism
- Robert Gilpin -Hegemonic theory

"Neoclassical Realism"

Neoclassical Realism can be seen as the third generation of realism, coming after the classical authors of the first wave (Thucydides, Machiavelli, Hobbes, Morgenthau), and the neorealists (esp. Kenneth Waltz). Its designation of "neoclassical", then, has a double meaning: 1) It offers the classics a renaissance; 2) It is a synthesis of the neorealist and the classical realist approaches.

Gideon Rose is responsible for coining the term in a book review he wrote.

The primarily motivation underlying the development of neoclassical realism was the fact that neorealism was only useful to explain political outcomes (classified as being 'theories of international politics'), but had nothing to offer about particular states' behavior (or 'theories of foreign policy'). The basic approach, then, was for these authors to "refine, not refute, Kenneth Waltz", by adding domestic intervening variables between systemic incentives and a state's foreign policy decision. Thus, the basic theoretical architecture of Neoclassical Realism is:

Distribution of power in the international system (Independent Variable) >>> Domestic perception of the system and/or domestic incentives (Intervening Variable) >>> Foreign Policy decision (Dependent Variable)

While neoclassical realism has only been used for theories of foreign policy so far, Randall Schweller notes that it could be useful to explain certain types of political outcomes as well..

Neoclassical realism is particularly appealing from a research standpoint because it still retains a lot of the theoretical rigor that Waltz has brought to realism, but at the same time can easily incorporate a content-rich analysis, since its main method for testing theories is the process-tracing of case studies.

NEOREALISM

Neorealism or structural realism is a theory of international relations, outlined by Kenneth Waltz in his 1979 book, Theory of International Politics. Waltz argues in favor of a systemic approach: the international structure acts as a constraint on state behavior, so that different states behave in a similar rational manner, and outcomes fall within an expected range.

Neorealism, developed largely within the American political science tradition, seeks to reformulate the classical realism tradition of E.H. Carr, Hans Morgenthau, and Reinhold Niebuhr into a rigorous and positivistic social science.

Theory

Neorealism shuns classical realism's use of often essentialist concepts such as "human nature" to explain international politics. Instead, neorealist thinkers developed a theory that privileges structural constraints over agents' strategies and motivations. Neorealism holds that the international structure is defined by its ordering principle, anarchy, and by the distribution of capabilities, measured by the number of great powers within the international system. The anarchic ordering principle of the international structure is decentralized, having no formal central authority, and is composed of formally equal sovereign states. These states act according to the logic of self-help--states seek their own interest and will not subordinate their interest to another's.

States are assumed at a minimum to want to ensure their own survival as this is a prerequisite to pursue other goals. This driving force of survival is the primary factor influencing their behaviour and in turn ensures states develop offensive military capabilities, as a means to increase their relative power. Because states can never be certain of other states' future intentions, there is a lack of trust between states which requires states to be on guard against relative losses of power which could enable other states to threaten their survival. This lack of trust, based on uncertainty, is called the security dilemma.

States are deemed similar in terms of needs but not in capabilities for achieving them. The positional placement of states in terms of abilities determines the distribution of capabilities. The structural distribution of capabilities then limits cooperation among states through fears of relative gains made by other states, and the possibility of dependence on other states.

The desire and relative abilities of each state to maximize relative power constrain each other, resulting in a 'balance of power', which shapes international relations. It also gives rise to the 'security dilemma' that all nations face. There are two ways in which states balance power: internal balancing and external balancing. Internal balancing occurs as states grow their own capabilities by increasing economic growth and/or increasing military spending. External balancing occurs as states enter into alliances to check the power of more powerful states or alliances.

Neorealists contend that there are essentially three possible systems according to changes in the distribution of capabilities, defined by the number of great powers within the international system. A unipolar system contains only one great power (this is often referred to as hegemony), a bipolar system contains two great powers, and a multipolar system contains more than two great powers. Neorealists conclude that a bipolar system is more stable (less prone to great power war and systemic change) than a unipolar system because balancing can only occur through internal balancing as there are no extra great powers with which to form alliances. Because there is only internal balancing in a bipolar system, rather than external balancing and internal balancing, there is less opportunity for miscalculations and therefore less chance of great power war.

Neorealists conclude that because war is an effect of the anarchic structure of the international system, it is likely to continue in the future. Indeed, neorealists often argue that the ordering principle of the international system has not fundamentally changed from the time of Thucydides to the advent of nuclear warfare. The view that long-lasting peace is not likely to be achieved is described by other theorists as a largely pessimistic view of international relations. One of the main challenges to neorealist theory is the democratic peace theory and supporting research such as the book Never at War. Neorealists answer this challenge by arguing that democratic peace theorists tend to pick and choose the definition of democracy to get the wanted empirical result. For example, Germany of Kaiser Wilhem II, the Dominican Republic of Juan Bosch, or Chile of Salvador Allende are not considered to be democratic or the conflicts do not qualify as wars according to these theorists. Furthermore they claim several wars between democratic states have been averted only by causes other than ones covered by democratic peace theory.

Criticism

Neorealism has been criticized from the point of view of the philosophy of science. John Vasquez uses the Lakatosian criteria of the Methodology of Scientific Research Programs in an attempt to prove the degenerative nature of the neorealist research program. Thus, Waltz's theory of neorealism explains international behaviour through the balance-of-power concept, according to which states in almost all cases balance each other in order to survive. Stephen Walt, on the other hand, argues that states do not balance power, but there is a so-called balance-of-threat, thus always balancing states which seem to be the most threatening, not necessarily the most powerful. Randall Schweller introduces the concept of balance-of-interests, better known as bandwagoning.

Thomas J. Christensen and Jack Snyder try to correct gaps in Waltz's original theory by using the concepts of buck-passing and chain-ganging. However these similar theories contradict each other, at least partially: for example balancing versus bandwagoning. Vasquez considers them as theory shifts which explain away discrepant evidence. These contradictory hypotheses increase the probability that at least one passes an empirical test, thus the whole neorealist research program showing signs of degeneration.

IDEALISM AND INTERNATIONAL RELATIONS

Idealism in international relations usually refers to the school of thought personified in American diplomatic history by Woodrow Wilson, such that it is sometimes referred to as Wilsonianism. Idealism holds that a state should make its internal political philosophy the goal of its foreign policy. For example, an idealist might believe that ending poverty at home should be coupled with tackling poverty abroad. Wilson's idealism was a precursor to liberal international relations theory, which would arise amongst the "institution-builders" after World War II.

Idealism is also marked by the prominent role played by international law and international organizations in its conception of policy formation. One of the most well-known tenets of modern idealist thinking is democratic peace theory, which holds that states with similar modes of democratic governance do not fight one another. Wilson's idealistic thought was embodied in his Fourteen points speech, and in the creation of the League of Nations.

Idealism transcends the left-right political spectrum. Idealists can include both human rights campaigners (traditionally, but not always, associated with the left) and American neoconservatism which is usually associated with the right.

Idealism may find itself in opposition to Realism, a worldview which argues that a nation's national interest is more important than ethical or moral considerations; however, there need be no conflict between the two. Realist thinkers include Hans Morgenthau, Niccolò Machiavelli, Otto von Bismarck, George F. Kennan and others.

Descendant Theories

Idealism proper was a relatively short lived school of thought, and suffered a crisis of confidence following the failure of the League of Nations and the outbreak of World War II. However, subsequent theories of international relations would draw elements from Wilsonian Idealism when constructing their world views.

Liberalism

Liberalism manifested a tempered version of Wilson's idealism in the wake of World War II. Cognizant of the failures of Idealism to prevent renewed isolationism following World War I, and its inability to manage the balance of power in Europe to prevent the outbreak of a new war, liberal thinkers devised a set of international institutions based on rule of law and regularized interaction. These international regimes, such as the United Nations, NATO, the Bretton Woods system, and the GATT, were calculated both to maintain a balance of power as well as regularize cooperation between nations.

Neoconservatism

Neoconservatism drew from Liberalism its intense focus on the promotion of "universal values", in this case democracy, human rights, free trade, women's rights and minority protections. However, it differs in that instead of building institutions or negotiating treaties, neoconservatism is less wedded to the importance of preserving international institutions and treaties while pursuing assertive or aggressive stances which it deems morally worthy, and is willing to use force or the threat of force, unilaterally if necessary, to push for its goals.

IDEALISM

Idealism is a class of positions in ontology and epistemology. Idealism as an epistemological position asserts that everything we experience is of a mental nature. That is, we can only have direct, immediate knowledge of the contents of our mind. We can never directly know or experience an external object itself. As an ontological position Idealism asserts either that only minds and the objects of mind exist, or that everything is composed of mental realities (e.g., thoughts, feelings, perceptions, ideas, or will). As a foundation for cosmology, or an approach to understanding the nature of existence, idealism is often contrasted with materialism, both belonging to the class of monist as opposed to dualist or pluralist ontologies. (Note that this contrast between idealism and materialism is approximately as to whether the substance of the world is at base mental or physical -it has nothing to do with thinking that things should be idealized, or with coveting goods.) Subjective Idealists and Phenomenalists (such as George Berkeley) hold that minds and their experiences constitute existence. Objective Idealists hold either that all of reality is included in a Universal Thought or Experience (Absolute Idealism), or hold that the world is composed of mental realities. Panpsychists (such as Leibniz) hold that all objects of experience are also subjects.

That is, plants and minerals have subjective experiences--though very different from the consciousness of animals. Most Idealists tend to reject representationalist views of experience and instead hold that the world of experience is the same as the world of reality. The approach to idealism by Western philosophers has been different from that of Eastern thinkers. In much of Western thought (though not in such major Western thinkers as Plato and Hegel) the ideal relates to direct knowledge of subjective mental ideas, or images. It is then usually juxtaposed with realism in which the real is said to have absolute existence prior to and independent of our knowledge. Epistemological idealists (such as Kant) might insist that the only things which can be directly known for certain are ideas. In Eastern thought, as reflected in Hindu idealism, the concept of idealism takes on the meaning of consciousness, essentially the living consciousness of an all-pervading God, as the basis of all phenomena. A type of Asian idealism is Buddhist idealism.

History

Idealism names a number of philosophical positions with quite different tendencies and implications.

Idealism in the East

Several Hindu traditions and schools of Buddhism can be accurately characterized as idealist. Some of the Buddhist schools are called "Consciousness-only" schools as they focus on consciousness without an omnipotent deity or soul.

Idealism in the West

In his chief work Truth, Antiphon wrote: "Time is a thought or a measure, not a substance". This presents time as an ideational, internal, mental operation, rather than a real, external object.

Plato

Plato proposed an idealist theory as a solution to the problem of universals. A universal is that which all things share in virtue of having some particular property. So for example the wall, the moon and a blank sheet of paper are all white; white is the universal that all white things share. Plato argued that it is universals, The Forms, or Platonic Ideals that are real, not specific individual things. Confusingly, because this idea asserts that these mental entities are real, it is also called Platonic realism; in this sense realism contrasts with nominalism, the notion that mental abstractions are merely names without an independent existence. Nevertheless, it is a form of idealism because it asserts the primacy of the idea of universals over material things.

Plato's Allegory of the Cave relates to epistemological idealism. The mental images, or ideas, that are immediately and directly known are not the same as the exterior objects in the real world.

This world that appears to the senses has no true being, but only a ceaseless becoming; it is, and it also is not; and its comprehension is not so much a knowledge as an illusion. This is what he expresses in a myth at the beginning of the seventh book of the Republic, the most important passage in all his works .... He says that men, firmly chained in a dark cave, see neither the genuine original light nor actual things, but only the inadequate light of the fire in the cave, and the shadows of actual things passing by the fire behind their backs. Yet they imagine that the shadows are the reality, and that determining the succession of these shadows is true wisdom. -Schopenhauer, The World as Will and Representation, Vol. I, Appendix

Plotinus

Schopenhauer wrote of this Neoplatonist philosopher: "With Plotinus there even appears, probably for the first time in Western philosophy, idealism that had long been current in the East even at that time, for it taught (Enneads, iii, lib. vii, c.10) that the soul has made the world by stepping from eternity into time, with the explanation: 'For there is for this universe no other place than the soul or mind' (neque est alter hujus universi locus quam anima), indeed the ideality of time is expressed in the words: 'We should not accept time outside the soul or mind' (oportet autem nequaquam extra animam tempus accipere)." (Parerga and Paralipomena, Volume I, "Fragments for the History of Philosophy."

Descartes

Writing about Descartes, Schopenhauer claimed, "... he was the first to bring to our consciousness the problem whereon all philosophy has since mainly turned, namely that of the ideal and the real. This is the question concerning what in our knowledge is objective and what subjective, and hence what eventually is to be ascribed by us to things different from us and what is to be attributed to ourselves." (Parerga and Paralipomena, Vol. I, "Sketch of a History of the Doctrine of the Ideal and the Real") According to Descartes, we really know only what is in our own consciousnesses. We are immediately and directly aware of only our own states of mind. The whole external world is merely an idea or picture in our minds. Therefore, it is possible to doubt the reality of the external world as consisting of real objects. "I think, therefore I am" is the only assertion that can't be doubted. This is because self-consciousness and thinking are the only things that are unconditionally experienced for certain as being real. In this way, Descartes clearly presented the main problem of philosophical idealism, which is awareness of the difference between the world as an ideational mental picture and the world as a system of external objects.

Malebranche

Malebranche a student of the Cartesian School of Rationalism disagreed that if the only things that we know for certain are the ideas within our mind, then the existence of the external world would be dubious and known only indirectly. He declared instead that the real external world is actually God. All activity only appears to occur in the external world. In actuality, it is the activity of God. For Malebranche, we directly know internally the ideas in our mind. Externally, we directly know God's operations. This kind of idealism led to the pantheism of Spinoza.

Leibniz

Leibniz expressed a form of Idealism known as Panpsychism in his theory of monads, as exposited in his Monadologie. He held Monads are the true atoms of the universe, and are also entities having sensation. The monads are "substantial forms of being" They are indecomposable, individual, subject to their own laws, un-interacting, and each reflecting the entire universe. Monads are centers of force; substance is force, while space, matter, and motion are phenomenal. For Leibniz, there is an exact pre-established harmony or parallel between the world in the minds of the alert monads and the external world of objects. God, who is the central monad, established this harmony and the resulting world is an idea of the monads' perception. In this way, the external world is ideal in that it is a spiritual phenomenon whose motion is the result of a dynamic force. Space and time are ideal or phenomenal and their form and existence is dependent on the simple and immaterial monads. Leibniz's cosmology, with its central monad, embraced a traditional Christian Theism and was more of a Personalism than the naturalistic Pantheism of Spinoza.

George Berkeley

Bishop Berkeley, in seeking to find out what we could know with certainty, decided that our knowledge must be based on our perceptions. This led him to conclude that there was indeed no "real" knowable object behind one's perception, that what was "real" was the perception itself. This is characterised by Berkeley's slogan: "Their esse est aut percipi aut percipere" or "To be is to be perceived or to perceive", meaning that something only exists, in the particular way that it is seen to exist, when it is being perceived (seen, felt etc.) by an observing subject. This subjective idealism or dogmatic idealism led to his placing the full weight of justification on our perceptions. This left Berkeley with the problem, common to other forms of idealism, of explaining how it is that each of us apparently has much the same sort of perceptions of an object. He solved this problem by having God intercede, as the immediate cause of all of our perceptions. Schopenhauer wrote: "Berkeley was, therefore, the first to treat the subjective starting-point really seriously and to demonstrate irrefutably its absolute necessity. He is the father of idealism...." (Parerga and Paralipomena, Vol. I, "Fragments for the History of Philosophy," § 12)

Arthur Collier

Arthur Collier published the same assertions that were made by Berkeley. However, there seemed to have been no influence between the two contemporary writers. Collier claimed that the represented image of an external object is the only knowable reality. Matter, as a cause of the representative image, is unthinkable and therefore nothing to us. An external world, as absolute matter, unrelated to an observer, does not exist for human perceivers. As an appearance in a mind, the universe cannot exist as it appears if there is no perceiving mind.

Collier was influenced by John Norris's (1701) An Essay Towards the Theory of the Ideal or Intelligible World. The idealist statements by Collier were generally dismissed by readers who were not able to reflect on the distinction between a mental idea or image and the object that it represents.

Jonathan Edwards

Jonathan Edwards, an American theologian, went to Yale University in 1716 at the age of thirteen. After reading Locke's doctrine of ideas, he kept a notebook entitled "Mind." In it, he wrote, at the age of fourteen, that the only things that are real are minds. He contended that matter exists only as an idea in a mind. Due to his theological manner of thinking, he asserted that space is God, due to its infinity. After adolescence, he never elaborated on these early idealistic notes.

Immanuel Kant

Immanuel Kant held that the mind shapes the world as we perceive it to take the form of space-and-time. Kant focused on the idea drawn from British empiricism (and its philosophers such as Locke, Berkeley, and Hume) that all we can know is the mental impressions, or phenomena, that an outside world which may or may not exist independently creates in our minds; our minds can never perceive that outside world directly.

... if I remove the thinking subject, the whole material world must at once vanish because it is nothing but a phenomenal appearance in the sensibility of ourselves as a subject, and a manner or species of representation. –Critique of Pure Reason A383

Kant's postscript to this added that the mind is not a blank slate (contra John Locke), but rather comes equipped with categories for organising our sense impressions. This Kantian sort of idealism opens up a world of abstractions (i.e., the universal categories minds use to understand phenomena) to be explored by reason, but in sharp contrast to Plato's, confirms uncertainties about a (un)knowable world outside our own minds. We cannot approach the noumenon, the "Thing in Itself" (German: Ding an Sich) outside our own mental world. (Kant's idealism goes by the counterintuitive name of transcendental idealism.)

Kant distinguished his transcendental or critical idealism from previous varieties: The dictum of all genuine idealists, from the Eleatic school to Bishop Berkeley, is contained in this formula: "All knowledge through the senses and experience is nothing but sheer illusion, and only in the ideas of the pure understanding and reason is there truth." The principle that throughout dominates and determines my idealism is, on the contrary,: "All knowledge of things merely from pure understanding or pure reason is nothing but sheer illusion, and only in experience is there truth." — Prolegomena, 374

Fichte

Johann Fichte denied Kant's noumenon, and made the claim that consciousness made its own foundation, that the mental ego of the self relied on no external, and that an external of any kind would be the same as admitting a real material. He was the first to make the attempt at a presuppositionless theory of knowledge, wherein nothing outside of thinking would be assumed to exist outside the initial analysis of concept.

So that conception could be solely grounded in itself, and assume nothing without deduction from there first, what he called a Wissenschaftslehre. (This stand is very similar to Giovanni Gentile's Actual Idealism, except that Gentile's theory goes further by denying a ground for even an ego or self made from thinking.)

Hegel

Hegel, another philosopher whose system has been called idealism, argued in his Science of Logic (1812-1814) that finite qualities are not fully "real," because they depend on other finite qualities to determine them. Qualitative infinity, on the other hand, would be more self-determining, and hence would have a better claim to be called fully real. Similarly, finite natural things are less "real"--because they're less self-determining--than spiritual things like morally responsible people, ethical communities, and God. So any doctrine, such as materialism, that asserts that finite qualities or merely natural objects are fully real, is mistaken. Hegel called his philosophy absolute idealism, in contrast to the "subjective idealism" of Berkeley and the "transcendental idealism" of Kant and Fichte, which were not based (like Hegel's idealism) on a critique of the finite. The "idealists" listed above whose philosophy Hegel's philosophy most closely resembles are Plato and Plotinus. None of these three thinkers associates their idealism with the epistemological thesis that what we know are "ideas" in our minds.

Schopenhauer

In the first volume of his Parerga and Paralipomena, Schopenhauer wrote his "Sketch of a History of the Doctrine of the Ideal and the Real". He defined the ideal as being mental pictures that constitute subjective knowledge. The ideal, for him, is what can be attributed to our own minds. The images in our head are what comprise the ideal. Schopenhauer emphasized that we are restricted to our own consciousness. The world that appears there is only a representation or mental picture of objects. We directly and immediately know only representations. All objects that are external to the mind are known indirectly through the mediation of our mind. Schopenhauer's history is an account of the concept of the "ideal" in its meaning as "ideas in a subject's mind." In this sense, "ideal" means "ideational" or "existing in the mind as an image." He does not refer to the other meaning of "ideal" as being qualities of the highest perfection and excellence. In his On the Freedom of the Will, Schopenhauer noted the ambiguity of the word "idealism" by calling it a "term with multiple meanings."

True philosophy must at all costs be idealistic; indeed, it must be so merely to be honest. For nothing is more certain than that no one ever came out of himself in order to identify himself immediately with things different from him; but everything of which he has certain, sure, and therefore immediate knowledge, lies within his consciousness. Beyond this consciousness, therefore, there can be no immediate certainty .... There can never be an existence that is objective absolutely and in itself; such an existence, indeed, is positively inconceivable. For the objective, as such, always and essentially has its existence in the consciousness of a subject; it is therefore the subject's representation, and consequently is conditioned by the subject, and moreover by the subject's forms of representation, which belong to the subject and not to the object.-The World as Will and Representation, Vol. II, Ch. 1

British Idealism

British idealism enjoyed ascendancy in English-speaking philosophy in the later part of the 19th century. F. H. Bradley of Merton College, Oxford, saw reality as a monistic whole, which is apprehended through "feeling", a state in which there is no distinction between the perception and the thing perceived. Bradley was the apparent target of G. E. Moore's radical rejection of idealism.

J. M. E. McTaggart of Cambridge University, argued that minds alone exist, and that they only relate to each other through love. Space, time and material objects are for McTaggart unreal. He argued, for instance, in The Unreality of Time that it was not possible to produce a coherent account of a sequence of events in time, and that therefore time is an illusion. American philosopher Josiah Royce described himself as an objective idealist.

Karl Pearson

In The Grammar of Science, Preface to the 2nd Edition, 1900, Karl Pearson wrote, "There are many signs that a sound idealism is surely replacing, as a basis for natural philosophy, the crude materialism of the older physicists." This book influenced Einstein's regard for the importance of the observer in scientific measurements. In § 5 of that book, Pearson asserted that "...science is in reality a classification and analysis of the contents of the mind...." Also, "...the field of science is much more consciousness than an external world."

CRITICISM OF IDEALISM

Immanuel Kant

In the 1st edition (1781) of his Critique of Pure Reason, Kant described Idealism as such.

We are perfectly justified in maintaining that only what is within ourselves can be immediately and directly perceived, and that only my own existence can be the object of a mere perception. Thus the existence of a real object outside me can never be given immediately and directly in perception, but can only be added in thought to the perception, which is a modification of the internal sense, and thus inferred as its external cause .... In the true sense of the word, therefore, I can never perceive external things, but I can only infer their existence from my own internal perception, regarding the perception as an effect of something external that must be the proximate cause .... It must not be supposed, therefore, that an idealist is someone who denies the existence of external objects of the senses; all he does is to deny that they are known by immediate and direct perception .... —Critique of Pure Reason, A367 f.

In the 2nd edition (1787) of his Critique of Pure Reason, he wrote a section called Refutation of Idealism to distinguish his transcendental idealism from Descartes's Sceptical Idealism and Berkeley's Dogmatic Idealism. In addition to this refutation in both the 1781 & 1787 editions the section "Paralogisms of Pure Reason" is an implicit critique of Descartes Problematic Idealism, namely the Cogito. He says that just from "the spontaneity of thought" (cf. Descartes' Cogito) it is not possible to infer the 'I' as an object.

Søren Kierkegaard

Kierkegaard attacked Hegel's idealist philosophy in several of his works, but most succinctly in Concluding Unscientific Postscript (1846). In the Postscript, Kierkegaard, as the pseudonymous philosopher Johannes Climacus, argues that a logical system is possible but an existential system is impossible. Hegel argues that once one has reached an ultimate understanding of the logical structure of the world, one has also reached an understanding of the logical structure of God's mind. Climacus claims Hegel's absolute idealism mistakenly blurs the distinction between existence and thought. Climacus also argues that our mortal nature places limits on our understanding of reality. As Climacus argues: "So-called systems have often been characterized and challenged in the assertion that they abrogate the distinction between good and evil, and destroy freedom. Perhaps one would express oneself quite as definitely, if one said that every such system fantastically dissipates the concept existence.... Being an individual man is a thing that has been abolished, and every speculative philosopher confuses himself with humanity at large; whereby he becomes something infinitely great, and at the same time nothing at all."

Friedrich Nietzsche

Friedrich Nietzsche was the first to mount a logically serious criticism of Idealism that has been popularised by David Stove. He pre-empts Stove's GEM by arguing that Kant's argument for his transcendental idealism rests on a tautology and/or begging the question, and therefore is an invalid, improper argument.

In his book Beyond Good and Evil, Part 1 On the Prejudice of Philosophers Section 11, he ridicules Kant for admiring himself because he had undertaken and (thought he) succeeded in tackling "the most difficult thing that could ever be undertaken on behalf of metaphysics."

Quoting Nietzsche's prose: "But let us reflect; it is high time to do so. 'How are synthetic judgements a priori possible?' Kant asked himself-and what really is his answer? 'By virtue of a faculty'

-but unfortunately not in five words,...The honeymoon of German philosophy arrived. All the young theologians of the Tübingen seminary went into the bushes all looking for 'faculties.'...'By virtue of a faculty' -he had said, or at least meant. But is that an answer? An explanation? Or is it not rather merely a repetition of the question? How does opium induce sleep? 'By virtue of a faculty,' namely the virtus dormitiva, replies the doctor in Moliére."

In addition to the Idealism of Kant, Nietzsche in the same book attacks the idealism of Schopenhauer and Descartes via a similar argument to Kant's original critique of Descartes. Quoting Nietzsche: There are still harmless self-observers who believe that there are "immediate certainties"; for example, "I think," or as the superstition of Schopenhauer put it, "I will"; as though knowledge here got hold of its objects purely and nakedly as "the thing in itself," without any falsification on the part of either the subject or the object. But that "immediate certainty," as well as "absolute knowledge" and the "thing in itself," involved a contradictio in adjecto, (contradiction between the noun and the adjective) I shall repeat a hundred times; we really ought to free ourselves from the seduction of words!

G. E. Moore

The first criticism of Idealism that falls within the analytic philosophical framework is by one of its cofounders Moore. This 1903 seminal article, The Refutation of Idealism. This one of the first demonstrations of Moore's commitment to analysis as the proper philosophical method.

Moore proceeds by examining the Berkeleian aphorism esse est percipi: "to be is to be perceived". He examines in detail each of the three terms in the aphorism, finding that it must mean that the object and the subject are necessarily connected. So, he argues, for the idealist, "yellow" and "the sensation of yellow" are necessarily identical -to be yellow is necessarily to be experienced as yellow. But, in a move similar to the open question argument, it also seems clear that there is a difference between "yellow" and "the sensation of yellow". For Moore, the idealist is in error because "that esse is held to be percipi, solely because what is experienced is held to be identical with the experience of it".

Though this refutation of idealism was the first strong statement by analytic philosophy against its idealist predecessors this argument did not show that the GEM is logically invalid. Arguments advanced by Nietzsche (prior to Moore), Russell (just after Moore) & 80 years later Stove put a nail in the coffin for the "master" argument supporting idealism.

Bertrand Russell

Despite his hugely popular book The Problems of Philosophy (this book was in its 17th printing by 1943) which was written for a general audience rather than academia; few ever mention Russell's critique even though he completely anticipates David Stove's GEM both in form and content. In chapter 4 (Idealism) highlights Berkeley's tautological premise for advancing idealism.

Quoting Russell's prose (1912:42-43): "If we say that the things known must be in the mind, we are either un-duly limiting the mind's power of knowing, or we are uttering a mere tautology. We are uttering a mere tautology if we mean by 'in the mind' the same as by 'before the mind', i.e. if we mean merely being apprehended by the mind. But if we mean this, we shall have to admit that what, in this sense, is in the mind, may nevertheless be not mental. Thus when we realize the nature of knowledge, Berkeley's argument is seen to be wrong in substance as well as in form, and his grounds for supposing that 'idea'-i.e. the objects apprehended-must be mental, are found to have no validity whatever. Hence his grounds in favour of the idealism may be dismissed."

A.C. Ewing

Published in 1933 A.C. Ewing according to David Stove mounted the first full length book critique of Idealism, entitled Idealism; a critical survey. Stove does not mention that Ewing anticipated his GEM.

David Stove

The Australian philosopher David Stove argued in typically acerbic style that idealism rested on what he called "the worst argument in the world". His critique of Idealism is perhaps the most devastating critique of subjective idealism in philosophy. From a logical point of view his critique is no different from Russell or Nietzsche's but Stove has been more widely cited and most clearly highlighted the mistake of idealist proponents.

He named the form of this argument -invented by Berkeley "the GEM". Berkeley claimed that "[the mind] is deluded to think it can and does conceive of bodies existing unthought of, or without the mind, though at the same time they are apprehended by, or exist in, itself". Stove argued that this claim proceeds from the tautology that nothing can be thought of without its being thought of, to the conclusion that nothing can exist without its being thought of.

The following is Stove's homely version of Berkeley's GEM (1991:139):

(1) You cannot have trees-without-the-mind in mind, without having them in mind.

(2) Therefore, you cannot have trees-without-the-mind in mind.

(i) Is a tautology (self-referential statement); therefore the premise of this argument is trivially true.

(ii) Is not a trivially true conclusion. The logic flowing from 1) to 2) is valid (as this premise cannot lead to a false conclusion), but unsound because tautological premises can bring only tautological conclusions.

Refer to Stove's 1991 book The Plato Cult & Other Philosophical Follies chapter 6 Idealism: A Victorian Horror Story for numerous elucidations and numerous GEM's quoted from the history of philosophy and GEM's reconstructed in syllogistic form.

For readers familiar with Nietzsche, Russell and Stove's criticism of Idealism it is clear that Stove's GEM merely repackages Russell's precise points and borrowing Nietzsche's polemics against idealism.

John Searle

In The Construction of Social Reality John Searle offers an attack on some versions of idealism. Searle conveniently summarises two important arguments for idealism. The first is based on our perception of reality:

1. All we have access to in perception are the contents of our own experiences
2. The only epistemic basis we can have for claims about the external world are our perceptual experiences therefore,
3. the only reality we can meaningfully speak of is the reality of perceptual experiences (The Construction of Social Reality p. 172)

Whilst agreeing with (2), Searle argues that (1) is false, and points out that (3) does not follow from (1) and (2).

The second argument for idealism runs as follows:

Premise: Any cognitive state occurs as part of a set of cognitive states and within a cognitive system

Conclusion 1: It is impossible to get outside of all cognitive states and systems to survey the relationships between them and the reality they are used to cognize

Conclusion 2: No cognition is ever of a reality that exists independently of cognition (The Construction of Social Reality p. 174)

Searle goes on to point out that conclusion 2 simply does not follow from its precedents.

Alan Musgrave

Alan Musgrave in an article titled Realism and Antirealism in R. Klee (ed), Scientific Inquiry: Readings in the Philosophy of Science, Oxford, 1998, 344-352 -later re-titled to Conceptual Idealism and Stove's GEM in A. Musgrave, Essays on Realism and Rationalism, Rodopi, 1999 also in M.L. Dalla Chiara et. al. (eds), Language, Quantum, Music, Kluwer, 1999, 25-35 -Alan Musgrave argues in addition to Stove's GEM, Conceptual Idealists compound their mistakes with use/mention confusions and proliferation of unnecessary hyphenated entities.

Stock examples of use/mention confusions:

Santa Claus (the person) does not exist.

'Santa Claus' (the name/concept/fairy tale) does exist; because adults tell children this every Christmas season.

The distinction in philosophical circles is highlighted by putting quotations around the word when we want to refer only to the name and not the object.

Stock examples of hyphenated entities:

things-in-itself (Immanuel Kant)

things-as-interacted-by-us (Arthur Fine)

Table-of-commonsense (Sir Arthur Eddington)

Table-of-physics (sir Arthur Eddington)

Moon-in-itself

Moon-as-howled-by-wolves

Moon-as-conceived-by-Aristotelians

Moon-as-conceived-by-Galileans

Hyphenated entities are "warning signs" for conceptual idealism according to Musgrave is because they over emphasis the epistemic (ways on how people come to learn about the world) activities and will more likely commit errors in use/mention. These entities do not exist (strictly speaking and are ersatz entities) but highlight the numerous ways in which people come to know the world.

In Sir Arthur Eddington's case use/mention confusions compounded his problem when he thought he was sitting at two different tables in his study (table-of-commonsense and table-of-physics). In fact Eddington was sitting at one table but had two different perspectives or ways of knowing about that one table. Richard Rorty and Postmodernist Philosophy in general have been attacked by Musgrave for committing use/mention confusions.

Musgrave argues that these confusions help proliferate GEM's in our thinking and serious thought should avoid GEM's.

Philip J. Neujahr

"Although it would be hard to legislate about such matters, it would perhaps be well to restrict the idealist label to theories which hold that the world, or its material aspects, are dependent upon the specifically cognitive activities of the mind or Mind in perceiving or thinking about (or 'experiencing') the object of its awareness." (Kant's Idealism, Ch. 1)

Idealism in Religious Thought

A broad enough definition of idealism could include most religious viewpoints. The belief that personal beings (e.g., God and the angels) preceded the existence of insentient matter seems to suggest that an experiencing subject is a necessary reality. Also, the existence of an omniscient God suggests, regardless of the actual nature of matter, that all of nature is the object of at least one consciousness. Materialism sees no incoherence in a scenario of there being a cosmos where no sentient subject ever develops; a wholly unknown universe where neither any subject, nor any object of a subject's experience ever exists. Historically, Mechanistic Materialism has been the favorite viewpoint of Atheist philosophers. Still, idealistic viewpoints that have not included God, supernatural beings, or a post-mortem existence have sometimes been advanced.

While many religious philosophies are indeed specifically idealist, for example, some Hindu denominations view regarding the nature of Brahman, souls, and the world are idealistic, some have favored a form of substance dualism. Mahayana Buddhist denominations have usually embraced some form of idealism, while some Christian theologians have held idealist views, substance dualism has been the more common view of Christian authors, especially with the strong influence of the philosophy of Aristotle among the Scholastics. Several modern religious movements, for example the organizations within the New Thought Movement and the Unity Church, may be said to have a particularly idealist orientation. The theology of Christian Science includes a form of subjective idealism: it teaches that all that exists is God and God's ideas; that the world as it appears to the senses is a distortion of the underlying spiritual reality.

To meet Wikipedia's quality standards, this section may require cleanup.

Please discuss this issue on the talk page, and/or replace this tag with a more specific message. Editing help is available.

This section has been tagged since September 2006.

A Course in Miracles, a spiritual self-study course published in 1976, represents an explicitly idealist, pure non-dualistic thought system. In the Course, only God and His Creation, which is Spirit and has nothing to do with the world, are real. The physical universe is an illusion and does not exist. The Course compares the world of perception with a dream. It arises from the projection of the dreamer, i.e. the mind ("projection makes perception," T-21.in.1:5), according to its wishes (perception "is the outward picture of a wish; an image that you wanted to be true," T-24.VII.8:10). The purpose of the perceptual world is to ensure our separate, individual existence apart from God but avoid the responsibility and project the guilt onto others. As we learn to give the world another purpose and recognize our perceptual errors, we also learn to look past them or "forgive," as a way to awaken gradually from the dream and finally remember our true Identity in God. The Course's non-dualistic metaphysics is similar to Advaita Vedanta. What A Course in Miracles adds, is that it gives a motivation for the seeming though illusory existence of the perceptual world.

The West is inundated with physicalistic monism. There is widespread belief that everything will be explained in terms of matter/energy by science. Since we are constantly taught this it may make the idea of mentalistic monism hard to grasp. One way to begin to grasp the idea is through analogy. One analogy is the movie screen. If we next consider "Star Trek's holodeck" it takes us a step further as what appear to be physical objects are not. Next consider the movie "The Matrix". In "The Matrix" even people's bodies and identities are projected. Then replace the machine with a vast and powerful mind. A last analogy is our dreams at night. We seem to be in a world filled with other objects and other people and yet nothing of it is real. Although this is not a strict philosophical argument it does allow us to begin to think along these lines.

Idealism is based on the root word "Ideal," meaning a perfect form of, and is also described as a belief in perfect forms of virtue, truth, and the absolute. (i.e., Webster's Dictionary says "conforming exactly to an ideal, law, or standard: perfect."). idealism in comparison to pragmatism

OTHER USES

In general parlance, "idealism" or "idealist" is also used to describe a person having high ideals, sometimes with the connotation that those ideals are unrealisable or at odds with "practical" life.

The word "ideal" is commonly used as an adjective to designate qualities of perfection, desirability, and excellence. This is foreign to the epistemological use of the word "idealism" which pertains to internal mental representations. These internal ideas represent objects that are assumed to exist outside of the mind.

HUMAN RIGHTS

Human rights refers to inherent, universal rights of human beings regardless of jurisdiction or other factors, such as ethnicity, nationality, or sex.

The idea of human rights descended from the philosophical idea of natural rights; some recognize no difference between the two and regard both as labels for the same thing while others choose to keep the terms separate to eliminate association with some features traditionally associated with natural rights.

As is evident in the United Nations Universal Declaration of Human Rights, human rights, at least in the post-war period, are conceptualized as based on inherent human dignity, retaining their universal and inalienable character. The existence, validity and the content of human rights continue to be the subject to debate in philosophy and political science and many other forms. Legally, human rights are defined in international law and covenants, and further, in the domestic laws of many states. However, for many people the doctrine of human rights goes beyond law and forms a fundamental moral basis for regulating the contemporary geo-political order. For them, they are democratic ideals.

Human Rights Legislation

Where it has been adopted, legislation commonly contains:

- security rights that protect people against crimes such as murder, massacre, torture and rape
- liberty rights that protect freedoms in areas such as belief and religion, association, assembling and movement
- political rights that protect the liberty to participate in politics by expressing themselves, protesting, participating in a republic
- due process rights that protect against abuses of the legal system such as imprisonment without trial, secret trials and excessive punishments
- equality rights that guarantee equal citizenship, equality before the law and nondiscrimination
- welfare rights (also known as economic rights) that require the provision of education and protections against severe poverty and starvation
- group rights that provide protection for groups against ethnic genocide and for the ownership by countries of their national territories and resources

History

Appalled by the barbarism of the Second World War, the United Nations General Assembly adopted the Universal Declaration of Human Rights in 1948. While not legally binding, it urged member nations to promote a number of human, civil, economic and social rights, asserting these rights are part of the "foundation of freedom, justice and peace in the world". The declaration was the first international legal effort to limit the behavior of states and press upon them duties to their citizens following the model of the rights-duty duality.

Many states wanted to go beyond the declaration of rights and create legal covenants which would put greater pressure on states to follow human rights norms. Because some states disagreed over whether this international covenant should contain economic and social rights (which usually require a greater effort to fulfill on the part of individual states), two treaties were prepared.

In 1966 and 1976 respectively, the International Covenant on Civil and Political Rights and the International Covenant on Economic, Social and Cultural Rights came into force. With the Universal Declaration of Human Rights these documents form the International bill of rights.

- ...recognition of the inherent dignity and of the equal and inalienable rights of all members of the human family is the foundation of freedom, justice and peace in the world" - Preamble to the Universal Declaration of Human Rights, 1948

Since then several other pieces of legislation have been introduced at the international level:

- Convention on the Prevention and Punishment of the Crime of Genocide (entry into force: 1951)
- Convention against Torture (entry into force: 1984)
- Convention on the Elimination of All Forms of Racial Discrimination (entry into force: 1969)
- Convention on the Elimination of All Forms of Discrimination Against Women (entry into force: 1981)
- Convention on the Rights of the Child (entry into force: 1989)

- Rome Statute of the International Criminal Court (entry into force: 2002)

With the exception of the non-deformable human rights (the four most important are the right to life, the right to be free from slavery, the right to be free from torture and the right to be free from retroactive application of penal laws), the UN recognises that human rights can be limited or even pushed aside during times of national emergency -although "the emergency must be actual, affect the whole population and the threat must be to the very existence of the nation. The declaration of emergency must also be a last resort and a temporary measure". Conduct in war is governed by International Humanitarian Law.

INTERNATIONAL BODIES

The International Covenant on Civil and Political Rights created an agency, the Human Rights Committee to promote compliance with its norms. The 18 members of the committee express opinions as to whether a particular practice is a human rights violation, although its reports are not legally binding.

A modern interpretation of the original Declaration of Human Rights was made in the Vienna Declaration and Programme of Action adopted by the World Conference on Human Rights in 1993. The degree of unanimity over these conventions, in terms of how many and which countries have ratified them varies, as does the degree to which they are respected by various states. The UN has set up a number of bodies to monitor and study human rights, under the leadership of the UN High Commissioner for Human Rights (UNHCHR).

Regional Legislation

There are also many regional agreements and organisations governing human rights including the European Court of Human Rights, which is the only international court with jurisdiction to deal with cases brought by individuals (rather than states); the African Commission on Human and Peoples' Rights; Inter-American

Commission on Human Rights; Cairo Declaration on Human Rights in Islam; Inter-American Court of Human Rights; and Iran's Defenders of Human Rights Center.

History of Human Rights

Ur-Nammu, the king of Ur created what was arguably the first legal codex in ca. 2050 BC. Several other sets of laws were created in Mesopotamia including the Code of Hammurabi, (ca. 1780 BC) which is one of the best preserved examples of this type of document. It shows rules and punishments if those rules are broken on a variety of matters including women's rights, children's rights and slave rights.

The Persian Empire (Iran) established unprecedented principles of human rights in the 6th century BC under the reign of Cyrus the Great. After his conquest of Babylon in 539 BC, the king issued the Cyrus Cylinder, discovered in 1879 and recognized by many today as the first human rights document. The cylinder declared that citizens of the empire would be allowed to practice their religious beliefs freely. It also abolished slavery, so all the palaces of the kings of Persia were built by paid workers in an era where slaves typically did such work. These two reforms were reflected in the biblical books of Chronicles and Ezra, which state that Cyrus released the followers of Judaism from slavery and allowed them to migrate back to their land. The cylinder now lies in the British Museum, and a replica is kept at the United Nations headquarters.

Three centuries later, the Mauryan Empire of ancient India established unprecedented principles of civil rights in the 3rd century BC under the reign of Ashoka the Great. After his brutal conquest of Kalinga in circa 265 BC, he felt remorse for what he had done, and as a result, adopted Buddhism. From then, Ashoka, who had been described as "the cruel Ashoka" eventually came to be known as "the pious Ashoka". During his reign, he pursued an official policy of nonviolence (ahimsa). The unnecessary slaughter or mutilation of animals was immediately abolished, such as sport hunting and branding. Ashoka also showed mercy to those imprisoned, allowing them outside one day each year, and offered common citizens free education at universities. He treated his subjects as equals regardless of their religion, politics or caste, and constructed free hospitals for both humans and animals. Ashoka defined the main principles of nonviolence, tolerance of all sects and opinions, obedience to parents, respect for teachers and priests, being liberal towards friends, humane treatment of servants (slavery was non-existent in India at the time), and generosity towards all. These reforms are described in the Edicts of Ashoka.

Elsewhere societies have located the beginnings of human rights in religious documents. The Vedas, the Bible, the Qur'an and the Analects of Confucius are some of the oldest written sources which address questions of people's duties, rights, and responsibilities.

In 1215 King John of England issued the Magna Carta, a document forced upon him by the Pope and English barons, which required him to renounce certain rights, respect certain legal procedures and accept that the will of the king could be bound by law. Although the document did not itself limit the power of the king in the Middle Ages, its later reinterpretation in the Elizabethean and Stuart periods established it as a powerful document on which constitutional law was founded in Britain and elsewhere.

In 1222, the Manden Charter in Mali was a declaration of essential human rights, including the right to life, and opposed the practice of slavery. Several 17th and 18th century European philosophers, most notably John Locke, developed the concept of natural rights, the notion that people possess certain rights by virtue of being human. Though Locke believed natural rights were derived from divinity since humans were creations of God, his ideas were important in the development of the modern notion of rights. Lockean natural rights did not rely on citizenship nor any law of the state, nor were they necessarily limited to one particular ethnic, cultural or religious group.

Two major revolutions occurred that century in the United States (1776) and in France (1789). The United States Declaration of Independence includes concepts of natural rights and famously states "that all men are created equal, that they are endowed by their creator with certain unalienable rights, that among these are life, liberty and the pursuit of happiness." Similarly, the Declaration of the Rights of Man and of the Citizen defines a set of individual and collective rights of the people. These are held to be universal -not only to French citizens but to all men without exception.

Philosophers such as Thomas Paine, John Stuart Mill and Hegel expanded on the theme of universality during the 18th and 19th centuries. In 1831 William Lloyd Garrison wrote in a newspaper called The Liberator that he was trying to enlist his readers in "the great cause of human rights" so the term human rights probably came into use sometime between Paine's The Rights of Man and Garrison's publication. In 1849 a contemporary, Henry David Thoreau, wrote about human rights in his treatise On the Duty of Civil Disobedience which was later influential on human rights and civil rights thinkers. United States Supreme Court Justice Davis Davis, in his 1867 opinion for Ex Parte Milligan, wrote "By the protection of the law, human rights are secured; withdraw that protection and they are at the mercy of wicked rulers or the clamor of an excited people."

Many groups and movements have managed to achieve profound social changes over the course of the 20th century in the name of human rights. In Western Europe and North America, labour unions brought about laws granting workers the right to strike, establishing minimum work conditions and forbidding or regulating child labour. The women's rights movement succeeded in gaining for many women the right to vote. National liberation movements in many countries succeeded in driving out colonial powers. One of the most influential was Mahatma Gandhi's movement to free his native India from British rule. Movements by long-oppressed racial and religious minorities succeeded in many parts of the world, among them the civil rights movement, and more recent diverse identity politics movements, on behalf of women and minorities in the United States.

4

INTERNATIONAL HUMANITARIAN LAWS

INTRODUCTION

The majority of armed conflicts clashed in the latter half of the twentieth century, and the beginning of the twenty-first, some of which are still going on, involve in one way or another armed non-state actors (ANSAs), outside the control of states or governments recognized by the United Nations (UN). State-on-state conflict is no longer the primary approach to war for a long time now. The decolonization period and the subsequent recognition of a people´s right to self-determination changed the constitution of armed conflicts and our belief in what entities in the international arena that can trigger such conflicts. Even the mode of warfare has changed; despite the spectacular combat technology, most armed conflicts are fought on foot using low technology methods of guerrilla warfare. This resulted in the conclusion that civil wars are the concern of both international community and international law. Contemporary conflicts usually involve ANSAs who act autonomously from their or any other recognized government. They have simply become economically self-sufficient. This fact makes these groups and the armed conflicts in which they are involved dangerous, especially when many states are unwilling to apply the international humanitarian law to this kind of warfare.

The traditional instruments, stipulated in the Geneva Conventions of 1949 (the Conventions) and the Two additional

Protocols of 1977 (the Protocols) to protect Human Rights (HR) and restrain humanitarian abuses, were developed to be applicable only to States. Since only States can have diplomatic relations with other states, sign treaties and be parties to international institutions, ANSAs were usually not expected to meet the same standard as states. Their acts of violence were seen as a domestic problem of the state concerned, to be dealt with through legal, political, or military means.

The increased attention due to the recent events made the world change their framework of ANSAs. They came to be fairly recognized as the key players in armed conflicts. The international community are going ahead on holding ANSAs responsible for their actions based on international humanitarian law (IHL). They had to realize that if IHL is not applicable, the humanitarian protection it offers is not available and the consequences of that are and will be horrifying.

Internal conflicts constitute a unique form of conflict, involving both guerrilla and regular army forces that produce many difficult questions and legal problems. The first question to consider is whether IHL is applicable to ANSAs and armed conflicts in which they are parties. However to answer that, I feel the need to address numerous other questions. What are ANSAs? And how does international law recognize them? Regardless of whether these ANSAs are engaged in armed conflicts of an international or non-international character, how does IHL view them? And are individuals involved in or supportive of these armed groups to be regarded as criminals, lawful or unlawful combatants? How can or how do these ANSAs adhere to or abide by the norms of IHL?

PURPOSE

The purpose of this paper is to examine the applicability of IHL (The Hague Convention of 1899 and 1907, the Conventions of 1949, and the Protocols of 1977) to ANSAs and the armed conflicts in which they are involved. Included in this category are rebel groups, irregular armed groups, warlords, insurgents, dissident armed forces, armed opposition groups, guerrillas, militias, liberation movements, resistant movements, freedom fighters and de facto territorial governing bodies. However, due to the limited space I have to discuss this subject, I had to limit this rather broad issue. I deliberately left questions of terrorist groups out of the study. I also avoided addressing the issue of private military forces (mercenaries), especially since international law regards mercenaries as totally illegal; there was no point here to take up the debate. Although even here there are international rules that applies irrespective of the legality of the group.

I have omitted these questions not because I do not find them significant, as it is manifest that they are questions of the greatest importance, but simply because each requires a detailed study which cannot be undertaken here. I have therefore focused on the main question whether IHL is applicable on ANSAs or not. In the process I had to review the relevant provisions of IHL which are applicable to the armed conflicts of such actors in a manner that makes the law clear and readily accessible and to discuss the protection offered thereby to both civilians and combatants.

In the process, I avoided diving in the history of IHL and drowning in too many details as I assumed that my readers have a fair portion of knowledge on the law and its sources, i.e. treaties and customary International law.

SCOPE

The central hypothesis of this paper is that these ANSAs, in particular national liberation movements (NLMS), abide by the same international law as states do. This paper will attempt to find out how these ANSAs been looked upon. In order to do that, I would have to examine the status of ANSAs in international law. First of all I will examine the scope of the first additional protocol and thereby the applicability of the Conventions and the first additional protocol of 1977 (Protocol I) to wars of national liberation and to analyse the application, or lack thereof, of these provisions to conflicts of this kind. Second of all I will examine the scope of a famous provision in the Conventions and the second additional protocol of 1977 (Protocol II) to other internal conflicts. The key question is whether IHL is applicable to ANSAs and all their acts of violence. The main purpose of this study is to bring the applicable instrument under the light and to make an attempt to explain some of the reasons behind the failure of the law´s applicability in theory and practice.

METHOD

The working method chosen was more of a qualitative approach in order to reach an understanding of the current position of ANSAs and of the rules applied to their violent activities. This allowed me to draw my own conclusion based on the written material at the end of this paper. A survey of international documents through the years concerning the subject helped in understanding the conceptualization contours and development of these instruments. This paper is based on scholarly and UN sources on international law, HR law, IHL and internal conflicts. The enormous amount of documents on ICRC´s database and other electronic sources were very useful. In this paper I have generally used the term *"International humanitarian law"* which has become more accepted and frequently used by academics and politicians than either "the law of war" or "the law of armed conflict".

OUTLINE

The paper outlines the debate over the applicability of these instruments, sets forth the relevant provisions, and reviews the positions of the different parties involved on these issues. To do so, I will have to briefly examine their status in international law.

Chapter one begins with a review of the traditional international law approach to ANSAs and their involvement in armed conflicts, focusing on both their status and the protection it offers to those involved in such conflicts. It shows the traditional law´s negligence of NLMS which later received both international and observer status. They can even be included under the "power" notion under the conventions. Chapter two discusses the development of the provisions applicable to ANSAs, beginning with the adoption of the Conventions in 1949 to the adoption of the Protocols in 1977. While an in-depth analysis of the concept of self-determination is beyond the scope of this paper, some discussion of this topic is necessary for a full understanding of the evolutionary process undergone by IHL relating to wars of national liberation. It will also observe the difference between international and non-international conflicts and the recent developments in customary law.

Chapter three examines Protocol I in relation to wars of national liberation currently regarded as an international armed conflict. It highlights the exclusion of many wars of national liberation because they do not fit under the definition of struggle for self-determination. It also examines the protection afforded for members of NLMs.

Chapter four concentrates on Internal conflicts of a non-international character. It examines the applicability of Article 3 common to the Conventions (Common Article 3) and Protocol II to situations of conflict between ANSAs and regular forces of an established government. I would also examine the protection provided by these instruments to unrecognized ANSAs.

Last but not least I would give you a very brief summary in the last chapter. I would also seize the opportunity to highlight the problems and prospects that these instruments provide together with the current development of IHL. Reflecting over the past, present and future, I would leave you with some questions to be answered hopefully in the near future.

ARMED NON-STATE ACTORS

Traditional view

The idea that International Law is exclusively concerned with the rights and duties of States has dominated the international scene for more than three centuries with States being at the core of the international legal system since the Westphalia peace treaties of 1648. But this does not necessarily mean that IHL applies only to

States. However in order for an ANSA to even become a party to a conflict, recognition granted by the State they were fighting against or by a third State was required. Traditional international law only recognizes three different categories of ANSAs that posed a challenge to the established Government.

These challenges along a range of ascending intensity are: rebellion, insurgency and belligerency. An analysis of these different categories and the basic conditions required before they can be categorized as such are of a great significance, since, the rights and obligations of parties to an armed conflict are decided upon the status accorded on these parties. When failed to achieve recognition as belligerents, customary international law had no application to the conduct of the parties of an internal armed conflict. These categories and the traditional view of them are further important to have in mind when reading the next chapters. Although these recognitions procedures were later abandoned, ANSAs are still categorized under the following labels.

Rebels

Rebels are individuals that are typically involved in purely sporadic and isolated acts of violence and hostilities against the established government. Rebels had never been considered to have any international rights or obligations. Their acts of violence were susceptible to standard containment procedures of internal security. Upon capture, these rebels were treated as criminals under domestic law. States had a recognized right to crush rebellion as a part of its inherent sovereignty and in order to preserve its territorial integrity. Indeed, the domestic law of every State prohibited rebellion and applied the most severe penalties to the rebels. The only way for the rebel's legal status to change was to be graduated to insurgents.

The adoption of the Conventions in 1949 did not alter the traditional view and treatment of rebels. Nevertheless they started to welcome international recognition for the designation of their hostilities as armed conflicts. Since such a designation would trigger the application of the very famous Common Article 3 on the armed conflict in which they are involved - internal armed conflicts - even when the threshold for this provisions applicability is not reached.

Insurgents

Insurgents constitute armed groups that become involved in civil disturbances and riots. These hostilities are usually restricted to a limited area of the States territory. Therefore the international rights and obligations they obtain are also limited to the same territory and still fall within the remit of domestic law. Insurgent´s violent acts are viewed as means of revenge against the State in an attempt to draw attention to their situation and to conflicts in their countries in order to address and redress the difficulties and problems of their countries. There is a lot of confusion and divergence in opinions and schools surrounding this category, since traditional international law does not provide an explicit definition of insurgency. Nevertheless, the recognition of insurgency does bring the insurgents out of the domestic sphere and into the international sphere giving them a quasi- international law status. Since insurgents are for the most time organized, they have even been allowed to enter into general agreements and arrange for humanitarian protection through the international Committee of the Red Cross (ICRC).

Recognition of insurgents has later for the most part been replaced by Common Article 3 and in some cases by some ICRC requested unilateral declarations of parties to a conflict. Insurgents might even realize an international legal significance through the effective control of territory and population, i.e. the recognition of an artificial statehood. This recognition is considered as the key factor in determining the formal status of insurgents. Nonetheless, it is questionable whether such recognition on its own is sufficient. Clearly, however, recognition of belligerency would assimilate the insurgents to state actors.

Belligerents

Belligerents are the most organized of them all. The act of belligerency is clearly defined in international law pointing out certain material conditions to be fulfilled first in order for a case of belligerency to be present; (1) the existence of an armed conflict; (2) occupation by the insurgents of a significant part of the national territory;(3) an internal organization exercising sovereignty on that part of territory; (4) the same organization is keen on conducting the armed conflict in accordance with IHL; and (5) circumstances which make it necessary for outside States to define their attitude by means of recognition of belligerency.

Recognition of belligerency confers international rights and obligations on belligerents analogous to those of States. This was comprehensible considering the fact that belligerents are more organized than both rebels and insurgents and as a result belligerency is of a more serious nature. And since a state of belligerency can only be recognized if the conflict takes on the characteristics of war, such recognition means simply the recognition of the existence of a war. However, recognition of belligerency rarely took place.

NATIONAL LIBERATION MOVEMENTS

An additional category of ANSAs to be considered in this context is NLMs which in contradiction to the categories, have as their main objective to replace the existing State or form their own state. The essential difference may even lie in NLMs ability to claim international rights, and be subject to international obligations, even in the absence of control of a territory or expressed recognition by the established Government.

Traditional international law lacked recognition for this specific category. Members of NLMs were recognized as rebels and were treated as criminals under domestic law. Although NLMs fulfilled the requirements for belligerency, recognition of such a state has never been made in a war of national liberation. One of the reasons behind such failure is that States often are unwilling to admit that they have a serious conflict over which they have no control is occurring within its borders. Another reason may be State´s reluctance to do anything that might legitimize NLMs position and cause.

Many States opt to recognize NLMs, allowing them to establish official representation in their territory, providing them with moral and material assistance as well. Many States also concede to treating captives in an internal armed conflict as prisoners of war (POW), even when they do not recognize them as such. However, this was simply viewed as a matter of courtesy, not a legal obligation on the States part. Accordingly it was not always bestowed. In some cases, governments moderated their positions, when they realized that the armed conflict is stretched over a long period of time, with the intention to merely provide some protection or basic needs to both civilians caught up in the conflict.

Still, NLMs have the special undertaking to represent the territory under their control and the people whose right to self-determination is being denied. This representative character of NLMs came to be recognized in Article 96 of Protocol I, wherein it refers to NLMs as the authority representing a people engaged against a State Party to Protocol I in a war of national liberation. Nevertheless, already in the Conventions, articles are found prepared to recognize other forms of power than the State. The first provision is found in the articles regarding the accession to the Conventions. These provide that the Conventions shall be open to any "Power" to accede to this Convention. The second provision is Common Article 2 (3) to the Conventions. This article states:

Although one of the powers in conflict may not be a party to the present Convention, the Powers who are parties thereto shall remain bound by the Convention in relation to the said Power, if the latter accepts and applies the provisions thereof.

Although the term 'Power' usually signifies a State, it has occasionally been used in broader sense to include other entities; such as de facto and interims governments. Accordingly, this could be liberally interpreted to include even NLMs.

The Power Notion

Using the term "power" instead of "State" indicates the recognition of other powers and that these can be granted accession to the Conventions. This could mean that NLMs that exercise power over a certain territory can without any difficulties prove itself to be an authority or a 'Power' within the meaning of the provisions of the Conventions. This could also mean that NLMs compliance to, or their acceptance to be bound by the Conventions will render the entire corpus of the law to be applicable to wars of national liberation. But in order for that to come about, this particular NLM would have to enjoy considerable recognition and the support of the civilian population. Obviously such an interpretation of the provisions would have made the conflicts international and brought them within the scope of the Conventions already in 1949. Undoubtedly, however, such interpretation would have been very compatible with the humanitarian ambition and the purpose and spirit of the Conventions.

Unfortunately when the PLO communicated to the Swiss Federal Political Department in 1969 that they were willing to accede to the Conventions on condition of reciprocity, they were not taken seriously. The Swiss failed to even consider bringing this offer to the State Parties knowledge because they believed that the PLO cannot be viewed as a power and thereby a party, as it did not control its own territory, and had not yet formed its own ad hoc government.

Observer Status

However, NLMs are entitled to represent their people at an international level. This privilege is granted even when they are not yet in control of the territory they claim to represent. They are then only recognized as representatives of their people. Therefore, they are being accorded the status of 'observer' and thereby acquiring international legal personality through the international acknowledgment of their political aspiration of liberation from colonial domination. This can be demonstrated by the cases of PLO and SWAPO that have been permitted to represent their people at an international level, thereby appointed the status of "observer" although it was neither in control of the territory nor the sole representative of their people. This indicates that the legal international personality is not based on a single set of objective or subjective criteria. While the PLO was not allowed to accede to the Conventions, they were accorded an observer status.

Transnationality

The globalized world with the increase of cross-border flows of capital, services, people and information, helped ANSAs to extend their control outside the former limited territory and their mother State. Nevertheless a large group of ANSAs, in particular NLMs receive transnational support and aid and therefore can also be recognized as transnational. But not quite because transnational ANSAs differ from NLMs since they do not pursue international recognition and aim only to displace their mother State. This group although mentioned under this chapter, will not be further discussed.

Rebels, insurgents and belligerents were the main categories of ANSAs under traditional international law. These groups were positioned on a sliding scale according to degrees of control over territory and recognition by States. Rebels were considered to have rights and obligations under international law, only once they upgrade to insurgency. Insurgents were considered to have international rights and obligations with regard to those States that recognize them as having such a status. However even insurgent´s legal status were followed by a lot of confusion as there were still great differences in opinions and a lack of an exact definition in international law. Only when insurgents were recognized by the State which they were fighting against expressly as belligerents, did they become assimilated to a State actor with all the granted rights and obligations. Such recognition almost never occurred. So traditional international law was left incapable of dealing with ANSAs and conflicts in which they were involved.

NLMs, however, were totally ignored by traditional international law leaving their members to be dealt with, under domestic criminal law. Later, they would also come very close to being conceived as a power, providing that they represented the people whose self-determination right has been denied and exercised control over a certain territory. They were granted observer status, although they failed to control their territory, on the premise that they represented their people. These developments bit by bit internationalized wars of national liberation and brought the whole *jus in bello* to apply. Before 1949, in the absence of recognized belligerency accorded to ANSAs, IHL had no application to internal armed conflicts.

INTERNATIONAL DEVELOPMENT

The Adoption of the Geneva Conventions

Before the introduction of the term "armed conflict" to include all spectrums of violence and with the absence of recognized belligerency, internal armed conflicts were outside the scope of IHL; not even the customary law was applicable. Rebellion could not even be considered a violation of IHL, as it fell completely under domestic jurisdiction. The adoption of the Conventions in 1949 and more importantly Common Article 3 altered the way internal armed conflicts were viewed and dealt with. By this provision, recognition of an armed conflict by the established government or a third State is no longer necessary for the applicability of IHL. These recognition procedures (mentioned in the previous Chapter) have been abandoned and replaced by compulsory rules of IHL that start applying as soon as the hostilities reach certain thresholds and the conditions for IHL´s applicability have been fulfilled. IHL´s application is compulsory irrespective of which party took the decision to resort to force. The Conventions confirmed the distinction and the autonomy of *jus in bello* with regard to *jus ad bellum.* This change in international law came about mainly because the old procedures allowed the State to deny ANSAs recognition and prevent the law´s application. Indeed this has been the case and recognition according to the old rules has hardly occurred since World War I.

Already in Common Article 1, the Signatory Parties agree to respect and ensure respect for the instruments established by the Conventions in all circumstances. The adoption of this provision stripped the States of the possibility of using arguments based on the legality of the use of force in order to be released from their obligations under the Conventions. Moreover, Common Article 2 specifies that the Conventions apply to all cases of declared war or of any other armed conflict between two or more of the Signatory Parties. The provision prohibits States from using arguments as being a victim of aggression to justify its refusal to apply IHL to armed conflicts in which ANSAs are involved.

A debate around the Convention´s application to internal conflicts where the people are struggling for their self-determination (wars of national liberation) was virtually absent, during the drafting period of the Conventions. So any suggestions to apply the provisions of the Conventions regarding international conflicts to wars of national liberation was viewed as a liberal approach, and was left to be merely an option that could be considered by both States and ANSAs. For instance, Portugal refused even to apply Common Article 3 to the internal conflicts taking place on its territories of Guinea-Bissau, Angola and Mozambique and they implemented only domestic criminal law to try to quell the conflicts. Still many internal armed conflicts had been of such an intense character that States felt compelled to apply IHL. But States were well determined to make sure that this "act of humanitarianism" is not mistakenly looked onto as a legal obligation on their behalf. NLMs, on the other hand, have been principally more willing to apply and to declare their intention to apply the Conventions than States in an effort to internationalise and legitimise their struggle and their cause. They hoped that their adhesion to IHL would be reciprocated by the States.

In 1956 and 1958, FLN declared its intention to apply the POW Convention to French Prisoners and gave orders to its members to comply with IHL. The French government recognized the applicability of Common Article 3 to the Algerian War already in 1956. However, the French recognition may have taken place partially because the FLN threatened reprisals if executions of captured FLN members continued.

THE DEVELOPMENT OF THE PROTOCOLS

Under the decolonization period, new developments in wars of national liberation proved the insufficiency of Common Article 3 in dealing with this particular kind of confkcts. During this period the international community supported these conflicts through various resolutions. At this point the international community realized the need to develop IHL to improve the way it dealt with this particular kind of armed conflicts. While treaties are the principal instruments of IHL in which States formally establish binding rules, a new treaty which the international community could agree upon was required. ICRC presented a report on the subject of the development of IHL to the 21st International Red Cross Conference in Istanbul in 1969. In 1970 a declaration regarding self-determination was made.

The Conferences of Government Experts of 1971-1972

Due to these developments, ICRC organized two Conferences of Government Experts in 1971 and in 1972 both of which were welcomed by the international community as major events. ICRC sought to update and supplement the Conventions so it proposed that they would formulate an Additional Protocol on Guerrilla Warfare. The protocol would be composed of 5 main principles. The first concerned the status of combatants and POWs following from Article 4 A (2) of the POW Convention. The second principle dealt with the controversial issue of international versus non-international conflicts. The third principle concerned the civilian population and its protection which emphasised the idea of distinction. The fourth principle concerned methods and means of warfare, with the recognition that the right to inflict injury on the enemy is not unlimited, and the reaffirmation of the principles of the 4th Hague Convention. The fifth principle, regarded the important issue of implementation. Furthermore, ICRC demanded to be certified to offer certain support to victims and that both parties to the conflict should allow international observers to confirm alleged violations of the rules.

Regarding the second principle, the Experts proposed the drafting of standard minimum rules which would apply to all armed conflicts but which would have no bearing on the categorisation of the conflict as international or non-international or on the legal status of the parties to the conflict. The rules would be the subject of undertakings by both belligerent parties which would then be made known to the ICRC who would in turn notify the parties to the conflict and also the other signatories of the Conventions.

However, these proposals proved to be too radical for the Conference of Experts which was not willing to allow for a separate Protocol on guerrilla warfare. Most experts did not agree however that there was a need to treat guerrilla warfare in such a specialised manner as to devote a specific protocol to it and believed that the issue of guerrilla warfare would be better dealt with in the context of other forms of armed conflict. The Norwegian Experts, however, proposed that the adoption of one uniform Additional Protocol that would be applicable to conflicts of either an international or a non-international character. They believed that one protocol was the logical approach from the point of view of the victims who suffer equally in international and non-international conflicts. In their opinion, a distinction in the protection afforded to victims of international and non-international conflicts would result in "selective humanitarianism". This proposal did not appeal to the participant States. On the one hand, they were eager to maintain the current structure of the world which in their eyes required keeping a distinction between international and non-international armed conflicts. They were not prepared to deal with ANSAs within their territory as equals to the regular armed forces of enemy States especially when they strive to maintain their sovereignty. So they argued that a uniform protocol would inevitably reduce the level of IHL for international conflicts to that of non-international conflicts.

Evidently, the first Conference declared all these proposals as unacceptable. Two additional protocols were then drafted to be discussed at the next Conference of Experts in 1972. Experts from 77 States were present at this conference. The first draft Protocol concerned international armed conflicts and dealt with aspects of both Geneva and Hague law. The second draft Protocol developed and supplemented Common Article 3 regarding non-international conflicts. However it did not make Common Article 3 excessive for reasons I would explain later in this paper.

In addition to the two protocol drafts, a draft Declaration on the Application of IHL in Armed Struggles for Self-determination was presented, but did not manage to gain any approval. The Declaration sought to have the Conference assert that the Conventions, Protocol I and other rules of armed conflicts should be applied to wars of national liberation. In other cases both Common Article 3 and Protocol II should be applied or other rules that ICRC would later formulate and accompany the Declaration. Various experts condemned the whole principle of giving any ANSA a special status; others believed that the legal protection offered was insufficient.

The Diplomatic Conferences for the Reaffirmation and Development of International Humanitarian Law Applicable in Armed Conflicts 1974 – 1977

The Diplomatic Conference in 1974 was set to gain final political endorsement from 126 governments of the protocol drafts which were already formulated and discussed at the Expert Conferences, when a major issue emerged concerning procedural matters, as to whether or not to invite NLMs recognised by either the OAU or the League of Arab States to the Conference. Eventually, it was decided that NLMs would be invited but they would have no voting power.

The other major issue was the status of wars of national liberation and the question of whether they ought o be regarded as international conflicts and thus come within the scope of Protocol I or if they should be treated as non- international an. be dealt with by Protocol II. Conflicting ideas regarding the application of IHL to non-international conflicts as well as the status of wars of national liberation was manifested in bitter disagreement and spitefulness at the Conference.

The scope of Protocol I was addressed in Article 1:

The present Protocol, which supplements the Geneva Conventions of 12 August 1949, for the Protection of War Victims, shall apply in the situations referred to in Article 2 common to the conventions.

These situations referred to in Article 2 are:

...all cases of declared war or of any other armed conflict which may arise between two or more of the high contracting parties, even if the state of war is not recognized by one of them.

Third World Governments proposed an addition to the above-quoted draft paragraph:

...the situations referred to in the preceding paragraph include armed conflicts in which peoples are fighting against colonial domination and alien occupation and against racist regimes in the exercise of their right of self-determination, as enshrined in the Charter of the United Nations and the Declaration of Principles of International Law concerning Friendly Relations and Co-operation among States in accordance with the Charter of the United Nations.

However, the amendment was not accepted by Western States, especially former colonial States and various objections were made to it. However, they reached an understanding that there was not a customary rule of international law granting international status to wars of national liberation. Still, the international community had already recognised the international character of wars of national liberation with the adoption of the 1970 UN Declaration of Principles of International Law concerning Friendly Relations and Co-operation among States in Accordance with the Charter of the United Nations. Hence, another amendment was submitted as an alternative to the first one and proposed adding two paragraphs to draft Article 1. The first one reaffirmed Common Article 1 and the second restated the Martens clause which called to include situations of wars of national liberation. This amendment was approved of by most of the delegates.

This clause stated:

In cases not included in this present Protocol or in other instruments of conventional law, civilians and combatants remain under the protection and the authority of the principles of international law, as they result from established custom, from the principles of humanity and the dictates of public conscience.

However, the Martens clause did not solve the dilemma of wars of national liberation because it simply reserves the application of pre-existing customary law and principles of humanity to victims of armed conflict falling *outside* the scope of the conventional apparatus.

The first session of the Conference did not offer any progress regarding Article 1. The second session of the Diplomatic Conference took place in Geneva, 1975. Even this time the national liberation movements recognised by the Organization of African Unity (OAU) and the League of Arab Nations were invited. While this session was much more productive than the first with a lot more constructive work taking place, not enough progress was made and it was decided to convene a third session of the Conference in 1976 and a fourth and final session in 1977, during which the Protocols as amended, were adopted. At the last session of the Conference in 1977, the Protocol which emerged from the Committee stage had been actually more detailed than the ICRC draft, following the template of Protocol I. Thus, national liberation movements had gained an important victory in international political and legal terms by finally gaining recognition under IHL of wars of national liberation as international conflicts.

RECENT DEVELOPMENTS AND CUSTOMARY LAW

Recent developments in practice and legal opinion signify the blurring of the distinction between international and non-international armed conflicts and the rules applicable to each. A large number of customary rules are always applicable regardless of the label of the armed conflict. So while the current situation remains, that a more comprehensive body of law regulates international conflict, the bedrock of principles and rules contained in customary international law applies regardless of the nature of the conflict. States acknowledgement that treaties and customary international law as sources of IHL are binding is laid down in the Statute of the International Court of Justice (ICJ). IHL continuous development through the process of State practice and political interactions is unstoppable.

The latest study on customary international law done by ICRC showed that a lot of customary rules corresponded with provisions in Protocol I such as the principle of distinction between civilians and combatants and between civilian objects and military objectives; the prohibition of indiscriminate attacks; the principle of proportionality in attack; the obligation to take feasible precautions in attack and against the effects of attack; the obligation to respect and protect medical and religious personnel, medical units and transports, humanitarian relief personnel and objects, and civilian journalists; the obligation to protect medical duties; the prohibition of attacks on non defended localities and demilitarized zones; the obligation to provide quarter and to safeguard an enemy *hors de combat*; the prohibition of starvation; the prohibition of attacks on objects indispensable to the survival of the civilian population; the prohibition of improper use of emblems and perfidy; the obligation to respect the fundamental guarantees of civilians and persons *hors de combat*; the obligation to account for missing persons; and the specific protections afforded to women and children.

The study even showed that there are customary rules corresponding with provisions in Protocol II such as the prohibition of attacks on civilians; the obligation to respect and protect medical and religious personnel, medical units and transports; the obligation to protect medical duties; the prohibition of starvation; the prohibition of attacks on objects indispensable to the survival of the civilian population; the obligation to respect the fundamental guarantees of civilians and persons *hors de combat*; the obligation to search for and respect and protect the wounded, sick and shipwrecked; the obligation to search for and protect the dead; the obligation to protect persons deprived of their liberty; the prohibition of forced movement of civilians; and the specific protections afforded to women and children.

Following the adoption of the Conventions, wars of national liberation increased in number and the international community recognized the need for improvement and development of the only provision applicable to internal conflicts, as it only provided minimum protection and the death and destruction caused by these conflicts called for a wider instrument. The legal quandaries that determined a legal framework for these conflicts caused at the Diplomatic Conferences of 1974-77 are very evident in the products of these conferences; Additional protocol I applicable to internal conflict of an international character and Additional Protocol II applicable to internal conflicts of non-international character. The achievement of an international legal status by wars of national liberation brings about the application of the whole *jus in bello* to such conflicts. During recent years a process of delimitation between international and non-international armed conflicts and the rules applicable to each has begun. ICJ concluded that treaties and customary international law are binding sources of IHL. However, IHL continues to develop through State practice.

NATIONAL LIBERATION MOVEMENTS

International Armed Conflicts

Traditionally international armed conflicts are defined as those in which at least two States are involved. Therefore this type of conflict is the most regulated in IHL. Indeed, it is subjected to a wide range of rules. However, in the latter half of the twentieth century armed conflicts based on the legal right to self-determination (wars of national liberation) were included in this category in contrast to the period before World War II where this distinct type of conflict was regarded as purely non-international. The reason behind the need to regulate these conflicts was that these conflicts rapidly increased in number around the decolonization period. At that time many third world States argued that wars of national liberation should be covered by the whole *jus in bello* and be treated as international armed conflicts. They even suggested that ANSAs could receive benefits, if agreed to abide by the Conventions, though very strictly and under specific conditions. This, as anticipated, was one of the most controversial issues to be dealt with at the 1949 Diplomatic Conference whose main objective was to modify the Conventions. A 4th paragraph was added to Common Article 2 and it states:

> *In all cases of armed conflict which are not of an international character, especially cases of civil war, colonial conflicts, or wars of religion, which may occur in the territory of one or more of the High Contracting Parties, the implementing of the principles of the present Convention shall be obligatory on each of the adversaries. The application of the Convention in these circumstances shall in no way depend on the legal status of the Parties to the conflict and shall have no effect on that status.*

Despite the explicit denunciation of any effect of this provision´s application to the legal status of the parties to the conflict, it faced a lot of resistance from western countries because they feared such an outcome anyway.

Definition of Wars of National Liberation

There are various forms of armed conflicts to which the term "wars of national liberation" has been employed. However four of them are recognized as such; (1) those struggles of peoples fighting a foreign invader or occupant; (2) those that have evolved within the UN and identified from the practice of States and international organizations, namely colonial and alien domination and racist regimes; (3) rebellious movements which take up arms to bring down the government and the social order it stands for; and (4) armed struggle of rebellious movements representing a component people within a plural State.

ADDITIONAL PROTOCOL I

Already the Preamble to Protocol I reaffirms the established autonomy of *jus in bello* with regard to *jus ad bellum*. State parties found it necessary to express in that same Preamble their conviction that nothing in Protocol I or in the Conventions can be interpreted as legitimizing or authorizing any act of aggression or any other use of force inconsistent with the UN Charter. They even went on expressing their belief that it is crucial to reaffirm and develop the provisions protecting the victims of armed conflicts and to supplement measures intended to reinforce their application. However, although the primary purpose of Protocol I will always be to protect civilians from the effects of hostilities, it does not mean that Protocol I does not offer a fair share of protection to members of NLMS as well.

Under the negotiation of Protocol I at the Diplomatic Conference, delegates had to find solutions for two controversial issues, namely, the status of wars of national liberation and the drafted provisions applicable to guerrilla warfare. Once acceptable solutions were found for both issues, the conference adopted Protocol I by consensus. However, still to this day the United States (US) tries to eradicate Protocol I using arguments that evidently revolve around the provisions concerning wars of national liberation and guerrilla warfare. The latest example is the arguments presented by the US claiming that the captured Taliban forces were not entitled to POW status because the Taliban regime was not recognized as the legitimate regime of Afghanistan. This of course would release the US from its obligations under the Convention concerning the protection of POWs. As anticipated, the assertion was later withdrawn, as it was shown that quite the opposite is true: the application of the Convention and Protocol I is independent of the recognition of a certain regime or even of as State. If a State entity involved in an international armed conflict has already consented to the Conventions or Protocol I, it should be considered as a party to the conflict in the meaning of the Conventions and Protocol I. The minimum requirement in this case is that it has exited de facto for a certain time as a separate independent entity, even if not recognized by a majority of States. Ironically these provisions have never been invoked by a party to an armed conflict.

It should be noted that a part of Protocol I is considered to bind all States regardless of their accession to the protocol as it is a codification of pre-existing customary rules such as the Martens Clause, that is reaffirmed in the first article of Protocol I. Protocol I has also significant influence on State's Practice which as a result transformed a lot of its provisions to become a part of customary international law. State's practice has also created a significant number of customary rules that are more detailed than the elementary provisions in Protocol II.

Article 1 (4)

The restrictive scope of Protocol I is defined in Article 1(4). This provision is a manifestation of the intentions behind the protocol, with its precise and very restricted ground for the application of IHL to internal conflicts. This provision states:

The situations referred to in the preceding paragraph include armed conflicts in which peoples are fighting against colonial domination and alien occupation and against racist regimes in the exercise of their right of self-determination, as enshrined in the Charter of the United Nations and the Declaration of Principles of International Law Concerning Friendly Relations and Co-operation among States in accordance with the Charter of the United Nations.

By this provision, the application of Protocol I applies to armed conflicts in which people are exercising their right to self-determination against a State Party to the Protocol i.e. struggles against colonial domination, alien occupation or a racist regime. It continues to recognize only three categories of wars of national liberation, the ones against a) colonial domination, b) alien occupation and c) racist regimes and only when the people oppressed by these regimes are fighting for self-determination.

However, the use of the word 'include' raises a lot of questions as it implies that the list is not comprehensive. Other categories of wars of national liberation based on the principle of self-determination could also be considered to be covered by this provision. The UN Charter and the Declaration on Friendly Relations are very clear upon the right to self-determination, granting it to all people equally and in every respect. This means that wars of national liberation or in other words struggles for self-determination cannot be limited to the cases listed in Article 1 (4). However, at the same time, and in order to limit the use of force, ICRC comments on this provision, arguing that it should be regarded as an exhaustive and complete list of the situations in which a people, in order to exercise its right of self-determination, must resort to the use of force against another people, or a racist regime.

It is not easy to say which view is more accepted or can be the one to represent an established legal position. One can only say that the scope of Article 1 (4) remains restrictive which means that a number of NLMs and the civilians involved in these unrecognized wars of national liberation are left without adequate IHL protection. This is definitely a problem, since most contemporary wars of national liberation, are struggles for self-determination against other types of regimes, e.g. authoritarian regimes. Excluding this type from the list of Article 1(4) would leave the combatants and civilians of these armed conflicts without any legal protection. Needless to say, this provision indicates that Protocol I does not apply to every ANSA which claim to be NLM fighting for self-determination. Add to it that a certain level of intensity beyond isolated acts of violence is needed for the application of this protocol.

While this has been one of the major criticisms of the Protocol by scholars, many have pointed out the importance to appreciate this restrictiveness. However, the real weakness of Article 1 (4) is that it is quite outdated. The drafters focused on three categories of conflict which rapidly declined in frequency soon after 1977. As a result, Article 1 (4) lost its practical importance. Besides any State who has a regime which could be considered to fall within the scope of Article 1 (4), would be very unlikely to accede to Protocol I. NLMs acting in such a State would therefore, find it difficult to comply with the Protocol, or to demand application of the Protocol to its armed conflict with this State´s established government. It is believed that Article 1 (4) may come to be given a less restrictive interpretation if the principle of self-determination itself undergoes an evolution and comes to be interpreted in a wider manner. In the meantime, these conflicts are not left unregulated, as customary international law applies to all kinds of conflicts anyway. These customary rules amount to the basic principles of Protocol I. At the same time that a lot of pre-existing rules were codified in Protocol I, new ones were founded and formed by this protocol too. These rules were even been observed as applicable to non-international as well as international armed conflicts.

Article 96

The uncertainties and restrictiveness with which Article 1(4) enfold protocol I, would have crippled its application to wars of national liberation if it was not for the powerful instrument that Article 96 of the same protocol provides NLMs with, as it allows them to apply and be bound by the Conventions and the Protocol.

Article 96 of Protocol I states:

1. When the Parties to the Conventions are also Parties to this Protocol, the Conventions shall apply as supplemented by this Protocol.
2. When one of the Parties to the conflict is not bound by this Protocol, the Parties to the Protocol shall remain bound by it in their mutual relations. They shall furthermore be bound by this Protocol in relation to each of the Parties which are not bound by it, if the latter accepts and applies the provisions thereof.
3. The authority representing a people engaged against a High Contracting Party in an armed conflict of the type referred to in Article 1, paragraph 4, may undertake to apply the Conventions and this protocol in relation to that conflict by means of a unilateral declaration addressed to the depositary. Such declaration shall, upon receipt by the depositary, have in relation to that conflict the following effects:
   a) The Conventions and this protocol are brought into force for the said authority as a Party to the conflict with immediate effect;

b) The said authority assumes the same rights and obligations as those which have been assumed by a High Contracting Party to the Conventions and this Protocol; and

c) The Conventions and this Protocol are equally binding upon all Parties to the conflict.

By the third paragraph, the authority representing the people struggling against the colonial, alien, or racist party to the Protocol can undertake to apply the Conventions and the Protocol by making a declaration to the depository (the Swiss Federal Council). However, certain conditions must be fulfilled first, i.e. the requirements of Article 1 (4); (a) there must be an armed conflict where a people are fighting for self-determination against colonial domination, alien occupation and racist regimes, and (b) the armed conflict must be between such a people and a Party to the Protocol. This authority must then make a declaration to the depositary which will in turn notify the other Parties to the Conventions. A similar declaration could be made under Article 7 (4) of the Weapon s Convention. A declaration under this convention can bring into force not only the Weapons Convention and its protocols, but also the Conventions, even when the State against which NLM is fighting is not a party to Protocol I.

First now, the weakness of this article reveals itself. While the regimes, against which wars of national liberation are fought, are defined in Protocol I, there is a lack of a clear definition of what might constitute an authority in Article 1 (4). Any group which engages in armed conflict against any of the three categories of regimes mentioned in Article 1 (4) could be acknowledged as NLM and thus fall within the field of application of the Protocol.

This could mean that in some wars of national liberation, there may be more than one authority claiming to represent the people struggling for self-determination. However, Article 96 may still be applicable where there is a common declaration or concordant declarations from these multiple authorities. Otherwise, it would only apply between a State Party and the authority which deposited the declaration. The rights and obligations brought into force between NLM and a State Party by such a declaration are equal to those of the State Party. Despite that, no declaration has ever been made expressly under Article 96 to date.

Does that mean that NLMs are not interested in complying with international humanitarian law? Is the law perceived as an instrument to limit their use of force, rather than providing protection to their members and the civilians whose rights they claim to represent? The IRA expressed their intention to make a declaration under this provision already at the Diplomatic Conference of 1974 – 77. Numerous unilateral declarations of this kind have been made to the ICRC. In 1980, the African National Congress (ANC) announced to the ICRC their intention to both accept and apply the Conventions and Protocol I. This Declaration made no specific reference to Article 96 or Article 1 (4). A year later, the South West Africa People´s organisation (SWAPO), followed in the footsteps of ANC and declared their intention to accept and apply IHL.

The absence of an official declaration under Article 96, which can also be a direct result of its uncertainties, prevented the application of IHL to wars of national liberation. In the absence of any declarations having been accepted, however, attention has turned to the customary status of these rules.

Members of NLMs cannot enjoy the protections offered by these treaties unless their movement formally accepts all the obligations of the Conventions and the Protocol under Article 96, in the same way as the State Parties do. NLMs could not expect to be in a position to carry out such obligations unless they are about to succeed in becoming the government of the State. This was very convenient for the States, since granting protection to members of NLMs would simply legitimize their cause, and States would do anything to avoid that. However, IHL has to apply equally to both sides if they are to be applied to the conflict at all.

COMBATANT AND POW STATUS

Already the classification of wars of national liberation as international conflicts would automatically grant the status of combatants to members of NLM who accordingly shall be treated as POW upon capture. Protocol I established new far-reaching rules regarding combatant and POW status in wars of national liberation. But the lack of official declarations under Article 96, made it impossible for members of NLMs to claim this POW status.

Furthermore, Article 1 of the regulations annexed to the 1907 Hague Convention IV, contains established conditions which must be met for a combatant to be recognized as a lawful combatant and thus afforded a special status under IHL. However, this article is intended to deal only with entities that could become subject to IHL. At that time, that meant only States.

Article 1 of these Regulations states:

The laws, rights, and duties of wars apply not only to armies, but also to militia and volunteer corps fulfilling the following conditions:

1. To be commanded by a person responsible for his subordinates;
2. To have a fixed distinctive emblem recognizable at a distance;
3. To carry arms openly; and
4. To conduct their operation in accordance with the laws and customs of war.

In countries where militia or volunteer corps constitute the army, or form part of it, they are included under the denomination "army." These conditions are restated in the first, the second and the third Geneva Conventions where an indication is expressed as to the application of these criteria to members of NLMs. Article 4A(2) of the third (POW) Geneva Convention of 1949 extended the class of lawful combatants. The article states:

Members of other militias and members of other volunteer corps, including those of organized resistance movements, belonging to a party to the conflict and operating within or outside their own territory, even if this territory is occupied, provided that such militias or volunteer corps, including such organized resistance movements, fulfil the following conditions ....

A proper analysis of these age-old conditions goes beyond the scope of this paper; however, a few indications of their complexity may be pointed out. First of all, it should be noted that already in 1949, these conditions were considered unrealistic because of the nature of these movements and the difficulties they face to fulfil these conditions, especially the "distinction" condition. This particular condition was discussed on several occasions before the first Diplomatic Conference in 1974. Under these discussions suggestions were being made that the open carrying of arms during military operations could be adequate to distinguish members of NLMS from civilians. However, when the issue of distinction was coupled with the possibility of internationalising wars of national liberation at the Diplomatic Conference in 1974, various delegations opposed claiming that such a concession to members of NLMs would lead to the eradicating of the obligation that IHL is to be respected in military operations carried out by members of NLMs, while still granting the latter the status of legitimate combatants and of POW in case of capture.

Conducting the hostilities in accordance with IHL uncovered great concerns as it also carried the possibility of internationalizing wars of national liberation. IHL compliance implicates the probability of receiving a belligerent status. Such recognition would mean that these movements are lawfully conducting hostile actions, hence legitimizing their cause and bringing wars of national liberation into the international sphere.

There is even controversy around the meaning of the first requirement. Does this responsibility mean operational subordination, disciplinary subordination or something in between? Although traditional law seems to assume disciplinary subordination at least to the State upon which these members depend, the question cannot be considered answered.

Of course these conditions should be viewed disjunctively. While the failure to carry arms openly would not suggest that the members of NLMs concerned are conducting their military operations unlawfully, the failure to have a distinctive sign would. Still the unanimously adopted Article 43 of Protocol I that defines armed forces is lacking the "distinction" requirement.

This article states:

1. The armed forces of a Party to a conflict consist of all organized armed forces, groups and units which are under a command responsible to that Party for the conduct of its subordinates, even if that Party is represented by a government or an authority not recognized by an adverse Party. Such armed forces shall be subject to an internal disciplinary system which, inter alia, shall enforce compliance with the rules of international law applicable in armed conflict.
2. Members of the armed forces of a Party to a conflict (other than medical personnel and chaplains covered by Article 33 of the Third Convention) are combatants, that is to say, they have the right to participate directly in hostilities.
3. Whenever a Party to a conflict incorporates a paramilitary or armed law of enforcement agency into its armed forces it shall so notify the other Parties to the conflict.

The significance with this article is that it rejects the traditional distinction between combatant and non-combatant members of armed forces and introduces a new radical definition of armed forces, which allows members of NLMs within the meaning of Article 1(4) to be recognized and included when defining armed forces.

Nonetheless the unrealistic conditions of Article 1 of the Hague Regulation were still a problem for these movements. Article 44 of Protocol I came to modify these conditions in order to make them achievable. This Article states:

1. Any combatant, as defined in Article 43, who falls into the power of an adverse Party shall be a prisoner of war.

2. While all combatants are obliged to comply with the rules of international law applicable in armed conflict, violations of these rules shall not deprive a combatant of his right to be a combatant or, if he falls into the power of an adverse Party, of his right to be a prisoner of war, except as provided in paragraphs 3 and 4.
3. In order to promote the protection of the civilian population from the effects of hostilities, combatants are obliged to distinguish themselves from the civilian population while they are engaged in an attack or in a military operation preparatory to an attack. Recognizing, however, that there are situations in armed conflicts where, owing to the nature of the hostilities an armed combatant cannot so distinguish himself, he shall retain his status as a combatant, provided that, in such situations, he carries his arms openly:
   a) During each military engagement, and
   b) During such time as he is visible to the adversary while he is engaged in a military deployment preceding the launching of an attack in which he is to participate. Acts which comply with the requirements of this paragraph shall not be considered as perfidious within the meaning of Article 37, paragraph 1 (c).
4. A combatant who falls into the power if an adverse Party while failing to meet the requirements set forth in the second sentence of paragraph 3 shall forfeit his right to be a prisoner of war, but he shall, nevertheless, be given protections equivalent in all respects to those accorded to prisoners of war by the Third Convention and by this Protocol. This protection includes protections equivalent to those accorded to prisoners of war by the Third Convention in the case where such a person is tried and punished for any offences he has committed.
5. Any combatant who falls into the power of an adverse Party while not engaged in an attack or in a military operation

preparatory to an attack shall not forfeit his rights to be a combatant and a prisoner of war by virtue of his prior activities.

6. This Article is without prejudice to the right of any person to be a prisoner of war pursuant to Article 4 of the Third Convention.
7. This Article is not intended to change the generally accepted practice of States with respect to the wearing of the uniform by combatants assigned to the regular, uniformed armed units of a Party to the conflict.
8. In addition to the categories of persons mentioned in Article 13 of the First and Second Conventions, all members if the armed forces of a Party to the conflict, as defined in Article 43 of this Protocol, shall be entitled to protection under those Conventions if they are wounded or sick or, in the case of the Second Convention, shipwrecked at sea or in other waters.

According to this article a member of NLM does not lose his status as a combatant if, in narrowly defined situations, he does not distinguish himself from the civilians. However, in the lack any specified manner in which combatants have to distinguish themselves, how can one judge if the member has distinguished himself or not. There is no reference to a fixed or distinctive sign. The article only specifies in its third paragraph that the obligation to distinguish combatants from the civilian surroundings applies during "an attack or a military operation preparatory to an attack". At the same time an exception to the "distinction" condition is presented for the first time. This exception, however, would certainly cause new problems, such as determining the nature and the existence of the hostilities that can bring this exception into application. Still, the general understanding of this provision is that members o NLM must carry arms openly throughout the time when they are visible to the enemy and while relocating to a place from which an attack is to be initiated. This unmistakably corresponds with the text and drastically limits the effects of the exceptional rule. To be clear, combatant or POW status does not grant immunity from criminal prosecution for acts contrary to IHL.

CONCLUSION

NLMs involved in wars of national liberation – an international armed conflict - can become a party to the Conventions and Protocol I. However, in order for NLMs to qualify as such they needed to fulfill the strict conditions set up by Protocol I. If these conditions are met, the specific NLM assumes the same rights and obligations in an armed conflict as those of a State. This presumed privilege made States worry that Article 1 (4) and Article 96 (3) of this protocol would lead to the modification of *jus ad bellum.* For that reason they restricted the scope of Article 1 (4) so that it only applies to three categories of struggles for self-determination. To be fair, self-determination struggles against other regimes than the one listed in Article 1 (4) might not have been anticipated then. And because Article 96 (3) is dependent on the fulfilment of the requirements set out in Article 1 (4), it was made unpractical.

Already with the qualification of wars of national liberation as non-international conflict, the granting of combatant status to members of NLMS is ruled out. However, the POW status offered in Article 44 is almost impossible to achieve. The modification of the antique conditions in Article 1 of the regulations annexed to the Hague Convention, requiring a considerable element of (a) control, (b) identification, (c) openness, and (d) compliance with IHL from NLMs, is insufficient. Apart from the difficulty to meet these conditions, uncertainties still exist as to the legal consequences of any failure and as to which of these conditions are applicable to the whole group, which to the individual in the group, and which to both the group and the individual.

5

NON-INTERNATIONAL ARMED CONFLICTS

ANSAs are often involved in internal conflicts restricted to the territory of a single State and involve at least one ANSA. These conflicts are defined as non-international armed conflicts by IHL as a contrast to wars of national liberation which have been internationalized with the adoption of Protocol I. The key to the identification of these armed conflicts is ANSA´s concentrated use of violence under a relatively long period of time. This intensity is an established requirement which constitutes a threshold or a cut-off that hostilities such as internal disturbances, tensions, riots or other isolated and sporadic acts of violence do not cross and thereby are left beyond the reach of international law. This requirement has become a problem for the application of IHL since armed conflicts have always taken diverse appearances. Therefore, the scrutiny of each armed conflict is very essential in order to decide if IHL should apply. The question that imposes itself here is: at what point on the scale of intensity are we justified in designating an armed conflict as non-international? Unfortunately the transition from a common disturbance to an internal conflict of a non-international dignity is not like the freezing point of water.

There is also the problem of the emergence of new groups of armed conflicts. Globalization has not only internationalized the effects of internal armed conflicts, but also facilitated the transformation of internal armed conflicts into transnational conflicts.

Adding to that the intervention of a third State in an otherwise internal armed conflict, to either stop or support one or both parties. IHL avoids dealing with this type of intervention although it is not a new phenomenon. This, nevertheless, does not mean that these rather complex situations are left unregulated. Such intervention might internationalize the conflict and in that case the entire IHL would be applicable, otherwise customary international law is always applicable.

RELEVANT PROVISIONS APPLICABLE TO NON-INTERNATIONAL ARMED CONFLICTS

Due to the frequency of these internal armed conflicts, the international community was forced to realise that some form of regulation of non-international conflicts was needed. The effort to extend IHL to non-international armed conflicts ultimately resulted in the bold and ambiguous Common Article 3. IHL applicable in non-international armed conflict is the result of a compromise between the concept of sovereignty and humanitarian concerns. Internal conflicts involve a high intensity of violence and cannot remain beyond the reach of international law providing protection to both civilians and combatants. Non-international armed conflicts are covered by Common Article 3, Protocol II (156 State Parties to date), several other treaties, as well as by customary law. Customary law acts both as a complement and a confirmation of the basic standards set by both Protocol II and Common Article 3. As already noted, many provisions applicable in international armed conflicts have also become applicable in non-international armed conflicts as customary international law. Under the following analysis you should have in mind that the part of IHL governing non-international armed conflict is the result of a compromise between the concept of sovereignty and humanitarian concerns.

COMMON ARTICLE 3

When Common article 3 was first adopted, it was considered a major step in the right direction in the development of the IHL.

Indeed, it is the result of the first attempt ever to impose some basic humanitarian legal restraints upon both parties to an internal conflict carried out within the territory of a State Party to the Conventions. As is well known, States do not welcome any interference in their domestic security matters. So to agree upon imposing limitations in dealing with internal violence directed against? is still considered a great achievement. This "mini convention" is viewed as a part of *jus cogens.*

The article states that:

In the case of armed conflict not of an international character occurring in the territory of one of the High Contracting Parties, each party to the conflict shall be bound to apply, as a minimum, the following provisions:

1. Persons taking no active part in the hostilities, including members of armed forces who have laid down their arms and those placed *hors de combat* by sickness, wounds, detention, or any other cause, shall in all circumstances be treated humanely, without any adverse distinction founded on race, colour, religion or faith, sex, birth or wealth, or any other similar criteria.

To this end the following acts are and shall remain prohibited at any time and in any place whatsoever with respect to the above-mentioned persons:

a) violence to life and person, in particular murder of all kinds, mutilation, cruel treatment and torture;

b) taking of hostages;

c) outrages upon personal dignity, in particular, humiliating and degrading treatment;

d) the passing of sentences and the carrying out of executions without previous judgment pronounced by a regularly constituted court affording all the judicial guarantees which are recognized as indispensable by civilized peoples.

2. The wounded and sick shall be collected and cared for. An impartial humanitarian body, such as the International Committee of the Red Cross, may offer its services to the Parties to the conflict. The Parties to the conflict should further endeavour to bring into force, by means of special agreements, all or part of the other provisions of the present Convention.

The application of the preceding provisions shall not affect the legal status of the Parties to the conflict.

Despite the undisputed significance of Common Article 3, as an improvement of the traditional international law approach to internal conflicts, it barely employs the most basic principles preserved in the Conventions onto non-international conflicts. It is true that the parties to the armed conflict are encouraged to apply all the provisions of the Conventions, but it fails to provide the full application of the entire body of IHL on its own. When governments have been reluctant to recognize the lower threshold in Common Article 3, namely that there is an internal conflict taking place within their territory, it seems rather unlikely that they would consider applying any additional provisions from the Conventions. To be clear, the application of Common Article 3 starts automatically when the objective criteria listed in this article are met.

Nevertheless, the government´s refusal to acknowledge this rule may contaminate the attitude of the armed group involved in the conflict, especially that they neither participated in the process that produced this rule, nor were allowed to become a party to the treaty. The reciprocity between the government and the ANSA remains important, though it is not a direct requirement for its application. Of course they may be other reasons why an armed group might refuse to comply with the law. Armed groups that do not have an aspiration to achieve international recognition and legitimacy, lack the intention to comply with international norms. They are merely interested in controlling economical/natural resources or running criminal activities. On the other hand, a government´s reluctance to admit that an internal conflict existed within its territory had totally different reasons. It was grounded in its concern that such recognition would give legitimacy to the armed group´s cause and at the same time reveal the weak points of the State. It should be pointed out in this context that Common article 3 does not confer by any means recognition to the ANSA involved in the conflict, nor does it change their status in international law. It certainly does not provide any legitimization to their cause.

By this provision, it is no longer required that the members of ANSA exercise control over any amount of territory or that they have the characteristic of a government. The threshold for the application of Common Article 3 is lower than that for recognised belligerency; such recognition would bring the whole corpus of IHL, not just the minimum rules of common Article 3, into application. As already mentioned, there are a lot of violent activities left outside the scope of this provision. Under this provision´s rather low threshold lies a range of conflicts, from passing sporadic challenges to State authority to insurgency, which could, conceivably, come within the scope of Common Article 3.

The greatest weakness in Common Article 3 is the absence of a clear definition of what is to be considered a non-international conflict. This ambiguity of its threshold makes it uncertain if and when violent actions in a State can be regarded as a non-international armed conflict and thereby trigger its application. Common Article 3 also lacks of the expression of the necessity or even better the formation of a competent authority who can decide if a certain conflict constitutes an ' Article 3 conflict'. As if all these deficiencies are not enough, Common Article 3 fails to take into account the special type of warfare involved in most internal conflicts, i.e. guerrilla warfare. Yet the article fails to take it into account. The Diplomatic Conference of 1949 failed to define the scope of the conflict which is covered by Common Article 3. A lot of difficulties and disputes had to be resolved by the committee of the non-international conflict at the Diplomatic Conference when the drafting of the provision of non-international conflicts came up for discussion. Judging from the conclusion of the article, they obviously had a hard time reaching a consensus. So the limitations and defects of this article's final composition must be regarded with this in mind. Indeed, Common article 3 has been the object of more attention and dispute than any other provision in the Conventions. In the end its conclusion can be regarded as an achievement despite the defects it holds.

ADDITIONAL PROTOCOL II

Protocol II, like Common Article 3, was considered innovative as it was the first separate treaty to establish standards for the protection of persons involved in internal armed conflicts. It provided basic rules on methods of warfare applicable by both States and ANSAs involved in non-international armed conflicts. Protocol II was meant to define and supplement Common Article 3. But the strong resistance it received from developing States that, although they supported a distinctive treatment for ANSAs fighting against colonial and racist regimes, strived to secure their fragile existence by decreasing the regulations in non-international armed conflicts that occurs within their territory and threaten their authority, led to the failure of this intention. The States severely limited Protocol II and introduced a high threshold for its applicability, since the status of ANSAs combating colonial and racist regimes was established, and they had no interest in adopting a comprehensive framework in Protocol II. It should be stressed at this point that a compliance with the provisions of Protocol II does not imply recognition of any particular status for armed opposition groups.

Protocol II turned out to be limited to ensuring the application of the basic rules of IHL to internal conflicts. Thereby, it does not limit the rights of the States or the means available to them to maintain or restore law and order. It cannot even be used to justify humanitarian intervention. A government faced with an insurrection can in no circumstances use the argument that the insurgents have illegally taken up arms to justify refusing to apply Protocol II, since the instrument was adopted precisely to govern situations of that nature. With respect to the obligations it creates, Protocol II therefore rules out any subordination of *jus in bello* to jus ad bellum. Nevertheless, Protocol II has had a significant influence on State Practice and the following formation of customary law applicable in non-international armed conflicts. As a result, many of its provisions are now considered to be part of customary international law. States practice has also created a significant number of customary rules that are more detailed than the elementary provisions in Protocol II. Customary law has a very important complementary role as it fixes the deficiencies and fills the gaps in both Protocol II and Common Article 3.

Both Article 3 and Protocol II can apply simultaneously to a conflict, providing for the minimum amount of protection. However, protocol II provides a much greater substantive protection, introducing new fundamental rules concerning the protection of civilians against the effects of hostilities, as well as the protection of medical personnel and transports.

Article 1

Article 1 of Protocol II comprises the foundation of the protocol as it lays down the scope of its application. In order to remedy the shortage of Common Article 3, mentioned earlier, and to improve the protection of victims of non-international conflicts it was necessary to develop rules and define objective criteria to determine the applicability of Protocol II. The uncertainty regarding definitions often led to the rejection of the applicability of Common Article 3. At the same time a strict and rigid definition would have also led to the same result. Article 1 is the result of many extensive and protracted negotiations. The outcome of the entire protocol hinged on this single provision.

The article states:

1) This Protocol, which develops and supplements Article 3 common to the Geneva Conventions of 12 August 1949 without modifying its existing conditions of application, shall apply to all armed conflicts which are not covered by Article 1 of the Protocol Additional to the Geneva Conventions of 12 August 1949, and relating to the Protection

of Victims of International Armed Conflicts (Protocol I) and which take place in the territory of a High Contracting Party between its armed forces and dissident armed forces or other organized armed groups which, under responsible command, exercise such control over a part of its territory as to enable them to carry out sustained and concerted military operations and to implement this Protocol.

2) This Protocol shall not apply to situations of internal disturbances and tensions, such as riots, isolated and sporadic acts of violence and other acts of a similar nature, as not being armed conflicts.

While Common Article 3 does not provide a definition of "non-international armed conflict", Article 1 of Protocol II, clarifies that the Protocol applies to armed conflicts which take place (1) in the territory of a State Party to the protocol, (2) between its armed forces and ANSAs which (a) are organized under a responsible command, (b) exercise control over part of its territory, (c) are able to carry out continuous and intensive military operations and to implement the Protocol.

The condition of having a responsible authority and an organization does not imply that a hierarchical system of guerilla organization similar to that of regular armed forces is required. It simply points out the obligation of having an organization that exercise control over a certain amount of territory and capable of planning and carrying out continuous and concerted military operations. In addition to that, it should have a *de facto* authority imposing discipline on its members and capable of implementing this protocol. The amount of territory which should be occupied is not stated and in fact is not relevant: the occupation of the territory only has to be such as to allow sustained and concerted military operations and to apply the protocol. Therefore, internal conflicts resulting in a temporary occupation of a small territory without total control over another national territory do not fall under Protocol II. On the other hand being under command and in control of a large amount of the territory is a crucial requirement to be able to implement the protocol, for instance to set up of hospitals and prison camps. So this rather high threshold is fairly realistic since the conditions provided in this article correspond with actual circumstances in which the parties may reasonably be expected to apply the rules developed in Protocol II. In practical terms, if the ANSA is organized in accordance with the requirements of the Protocol, the extent of territory it can claim to control will be that which escapes the control of the government´s armed forces. However, there must be some degree of stability in the control of even a modest area of land for it to be capable of effectively applying the rules of the Protocol. This condition of territory control in the mother State is rarely achieved as most ANSAs have their base outside of the mother State. Obviously, these criteria restrict the scope of application of the Protocol to conflicts of a high intensity only. Therefore, only very few non-international conflicts are covered by Protocol II, unlike Common Article 3.

Once this threshold is passed, the Protocol applies to the conflict in question. The application of Protocol II is automatic, i.e. no declaration has to be made by the parties to the conflict as long as the requirements of Article 1 are met. Therefore, the question of the applicability of Protocol II can be answered differently in each case, according to the prevailing circumstances. Despite the efforts made to clarify the problem of the threshold of Protocol II, much ambiguity still surrounds its application. Protocol II does not clearly state how much territory must be under the control of the non-government party to the conflict. Even the implementation of this Protocol by the ANSA remains unclear. A lot is left up to the discretion of the State, which is not a very satisfactory position. If States are allowed to characterise a situation and in accordance with that dictates of their individual disposition, then the broader base of humanitarian concerns may be sacrificed in the process.

The second paragraph of Article 1 reveals the exclusion of situations of internal disturbances and tensions, such as riots, isolated and sporadic acts of violence and other acts of a similar nature, from the scope of Protocol II. As already mentioned, these forms of hostilities are not considered as armed conflicts, not even in the framework of Common Article 3. A State may use armed force to maintain order caused by or even causing internal tensions or when force is used as a preventative measure to maintain respect for law and order without getting to be considered internal disturbances. However, situations of this kind are covered by regional and universal human rights according to the article.

Nevertheless, practice has laid down certain criteria to draw up the boundaries of non- international armed conflicts from internal disturbances. Firstly, the hostilities have to be carried out by force of arms and reveal such intensity that the government is compelled to utilize its armed forces against ANSA. Secondly, the hostilities are meant to be carried out by the entire ANSA, and not by a single group within. Additionally, the ANSA has to exhibit a minimum amount of organization. Its armed forces should be under a responsible command and thereby be capable of meeting humanitarian requirements. The conflict must demonstrate certain similarities to an armed conflict without fulfilling all conditions necessary for the recognition of belligerency.

While in conflicts that come within the scope of Common Article 3, the ANSA and the State party involved are also encouraged to apply all the other provisions of the Conventions relating to international armed conflicts, thus offering a much broader base of protection to those involved in wars of national liberation, including a limit on the means and methods of warfare and on the conduct of hostilities. Protocol II only applies to situations of conflicts between ANSA and the established government and not between two or more ANSAs, resulting in a scope of application that is much narrower than that of Common Article 3.

COMBATANT AND POW STATUS

The status of combatants in internal conflicts differs dramatically from the status of combatants in international conflicts. However, the restrictive combatant status offered in Common Article 3 can be accorded to both recognized and unrecognized ANSAs. But

Article 4 of the POW Convention, which automatically applies in international conflicts, does not apply to a non-international conflict unless the parties to such conflict choose to apply it, either by an expressed agreement or by concession. For instance, US Military command applied this article to the captured enemy in Vietnam.

The combatant status offered in Common Article 3 and Protocol II fail in providing any protection from prosecution to captured combatants. This is rather peculiar considering that both instruments establish a separation, if only to a limited extent, between *jus ad bellum* and *jus in bello.*

The constraints on States provided by Common article 3 or Protocol II, such as the obligation to treat members of ANSAs in a humane manner, have been proven difficult to achieve. Indeed these instruments fail to achieve any constraints on the penalties these combatants are forced to endure for participating in the hostilities. This failure is extremely alarming bearing in mind the absence of specific rules and definitions with respect to the principles of distinction and proportionality that makes the distinction between combatants and civilians very minimal in Protocol II.

Article 44 (3, 4, and 5) of Protocol II states:

3. In order to protect the civilian population from hostilities, civilians are not to be harmed if they are not taking part in attacks or war activities or preparing attacks. Because in certain armed situations it is not possible to differentiate between the combatants and the civilians, people are to be granted combatants status if they: a) are openly carrying a weapon during a military manoeuvre; b) are openly carrying a weapon in view of the enemy while on a military march prior to an attack which they are supposed to take part in.
4. A combatant who falls into enemy hands and who is not covered by the provisions of Section 3/2 is to be considered a Prisoner of War; he is entitled to all rights guaranteed by the Third Convention and this Protocol.

5. A combatant who falls into enemy hands, not while taking part in an attack or preparing for an attack, is not considered a combatant or a Prisoner of War because of his prior activity.

To be regarded as combatants, members of ANSAs have to fulfill certain conditions. They have to be carrying arms openly either during the attack or in the preparation preceding the attack that they are participating in. If the combatants are caught participating in a military operation or preparing such but not abiding by the distinction rules they are still granted a POW status. Even civilians participating in these conflicts are granted both combatant and POW status under the same conditions. However unlike Protocol I, Protocol II does not grant either combatant or POW status on members of any armed group, for their mere membership. In addition to that domestic law still remains in force in situations where Protocol II is applicable. Obviously the protection offered by Protocol I regarding combatants and POW, is to be much preferred. However, Article 6, concerning penal prosecutions, lays down the judicial guarantees provided for in Common Article 3; independence of the courts, rights of defence, individual responsibility, non-retroactivity of penalties, presumption of innocence, information on judicial remedies. The fifth paragraph of this article contains a provision that even urge the established government to grant amnesty to the participants. There are also various resolutions granting POW status to members of ANSAs when captured, especially those fighting for a certain political objective, such as freedom. Most recently the US Supreme Court has declared the applicability of Common Article 3 with regard to trying individuals captured in Afghanistan during the conflict there between US and Al Qaeda. The Supreme Court declared that Common Article 3 applies even to that conflict. In the meanwhile, since neither common Article 3 nor Protocol II contains any provision on criminal responsibility for any violations of IHL in an internal armed conflict, the International Criminal Tribunal for the former Yugoslavia (ICTY) concluded in an important decision that horrific crimes committed in a non-international armed conflict are to be considered as international crimes. As a result, rules concerning international armed conflicts apply when trying a person prosecuted for a crime committed in a non-international armed conflict.

Both Common Article 3 and Protocol II apply simultaneously and automatically to internal conflicts when certain threshold criteria are reached. However, the ambiguity surrounding the application and scope of Common Article 3, caused by its lack of definition of what constitutes an internal conflict, made it difficult to distinguish between a non-international armed conflict and internal disturbances or other sporadic acts of violence. This has expectedly helped States escape their international obligation in applying these instruments by denying that such a conflict is taking place in their territory. Protocol II, however, describes its scope in considerable detail, excluding low-intensity conflicts. Article 1 makes the application of Protocol II dependent on the exercise of *de facto* control of part of the national territory and on the ability of on material circumstances linked to the nature of the hostilities, i.e. the ability to carry out organized and sustained acts of violence and to implement the Protocol. It applies to all armed conflicts in which these conditions are met, regardless of who triggered the conflict and why. Protocol II rules out any subordination of *jus in bello* to *jus ad bellum*. Protocol II, reaffirms the separation between *jus ad bellum* and *jus in bello* established by Common Article only as far as the obligations it creates are concerned and only to a limited extent as it fails to provide any protection from arbitrary persecution to the participants in these conflicts. It is fair to say that the protection offered by both Protocol II and Common Article 3, to captured members of unrecognized NSAs is very modest and in many cases non-existence.

CONCLUSION

Final Remarks

We stand at the dawn of the 21st century with so much violence and blood in our past, present and inescapably in our future too. To our consternation IHL has been proven repeatedly ineffective especially when dealing with the changed nature of global violence. The increase in armed conflicts generated by ANSAs presents both theoretical and practical challenges to international law. The impact of the violent activities of ANSAs on world politics is growing to such an extent that the traditionally exclusive role of States in international law must be reassessed. The first authoritative recognition of the existence and relevance of ANSAs from an international legal perspective came from ICJ. Even today when the existence of ANSAs is frequently acknowledged in international law books and journals, the State-centred conception of international law still prevails.

It is rather obvious that ANSAs are not a new phenomenon; however our perception of them is much different today. Does this mean that the instruments provided by IHL are unsuited to the realities of today's conflicts? It should be remembered that IHL has always aimed at balancing between legitimate concern for the security of the State and its population on the one hand and the preservation of human life, health and dignity on the other.

This chapter sought to examine the rules that affirm the applicability of IHL on ANSAs and the armed conflicts in which they are involved. At the same time, it offers some explanation as to why these rules are not applied in such situations. Some light has even been shed over the international development that led to the current wording and form of these provisions to give a bigger picture when evaluating these instruments.

Traditional law allowed the applicability of the whole body of *jus in bello* only when a state of belligerency was recognized by the involved State or a third State. While such recognition of belligerency rarely occurred, the application of IHL was more of a political expediency with the involved State requiring the principle of reciprocity. Typically, this recognition came at a late stage of the conflict with much destruction and death already having taken place.

State sovereignty played a central role during the drafting period of the conventions, resulting in States refusal to adopt a comprehensive framework for internal armed conflicts since they regarded these conflicts as falling within their domestic jurisdiction and the members of ANSAs as criminals not deserving the protection of IHL. Ultimately this produced the ambiguous Common Article 3 that raised a lot of criticism. While some opine that the uncertainty surrounding the definition of an internal armed conflict as well as the confusion regarding its threshold and automatic applicability made it unpractical. Others argue that its scope covers all cases of armed conflicts not of an international character, especially in the absence of a clear definition for a non-international armed conflict. In any case, Common Article 3 still remains very significant as it is the first move towards legal intrusion of IHL into the conventional sphere of internal affairs of sovereign States.

By 1977 and as wars of national liberation became more frequent, Protocol I came to confer international status on these conflicts. If NLMS were viewed as a 'Power' under Common Article 2 (3), the possibility then existed that they could apply and agree to be bound by these Conventions under article 96, and the whole body of IHL would apply to the conflict in which they were involved. There are divergent opinions regarding the scope of the application of Protocol I as laid down in Article 1 (4), especially regarding inclusion and exclusion of some self-determination struggles, thus its scope has been seen to be very restrictive. However, our belief in the universality of human rights (HR) forces us to realize the inevitability of the transformation of a people's right to self-determination to even include people who are subject to apartheid, persecution, discrimination and other violations of HR by another group whether it is a minority or majority which prevents the affected group from the realisation of HR and fundamental freedoms. If it is of any comfort conflicts that do not fall within the scope of this article are rescued by Protocol II, and Common Article 3.

The other product of 1977 was Protocol II, which sought to extend the scope of Common Article 3 and present a definition of non-international armed conflicts making States definition or recognition of these situations irrelevant. Protocol II supplements and develops Common Article 3, but it does not substitute its provisions. In other words, Common Article 3 and Protocol II exist autonomously. Thus they can be applied simultaneously to a non-international armed conflict. However Protocol II provides more substantive protection for civilians. But, like Common Article 3, it does not offer any protection to the members of the ANSA. These would still be regarded as criminals and persecuted under domestic laws.

This paper shows that the applicability of IHL to ANSAs and the conflicts in which they are involved has been made unpractical by either the restrictiveness of the provisions or political reluctance. In theory State´s denial of the existence of an armed conflict within its borders, or their being a party to the conventions or the protocols is irrelevant. In practice, however, States prefer to classify internal conflicts of both international and non-international conflicts as internal disturbances or indeed manifestations of terrorism, and deal with them under municipal law, in order to preserve their State sovereignty and image. If they, against all expectations, concede to apply IHL, then it is just an act of "selective humanitarianism".

IHL´s restrictive applicability to armed conflicts, international and non-international, hinders its application to internal tensions or disturbances or other isolated acts of violence. At the same time, these supposedly unregulated hostilities are the ones causing most harm and the possibility of applying similar protection to these cases is very important to discuss. It has, therefore, been argued that the qualification of the conflict as international or non-international is declining in relevancy, since a considerable amount of customary rules applies regardless of that. However, customary rules cannot weaken the applicable treaty obligations of the Signatory Party. Customary international humanitarian law only fills in certain gaps in protection provided to victims of armed conflict by treaty law. These gaps result either from the lack of ratification of relevant treaties or from the lack of detailed rules on non-international armed conflicts in treaty law. The advantage of customary law is that it is not necessary for a State to formally accept a rule in order to be bound by it. Bearing in mind that IHL strives to ease the suffering caused by armed conflicts, we have to admit that it is rather absurd that we still categorize armed conflicts as an international or a non-international conflict. This triggers different instruments offering different measures of protection to members of ANSA and civilians; when the scourges of the armed conflicts are virtually the same and sometimes even worse in non-international conflicts. If an armed conflict is considered to be an international conflict, the whole *jus in bello* would apply. But, if the same conflict is considered to be of a non-international character, then it is simply the basic rules of Common Article 3 or/and Protocol II which will be applicable, significantly limiting the protection offered to those involved in such conflict. On top of that States frequently tried to deny any applicability of IHL to the activities of ANSAs in their territory or in other territories for that matter, warring of granting legitimacy to ANSAs and their cause. The application of IHL does not confer any legal status on a group or their particular use of force. More important, the applicability of IHL cannot be judged upon the legality of the cause and conduct of hostilities. The rules of IHL apply equally to all parties to an armed conflict irrespective of which is the aggressor or the self-defender or which is a State or an armed group.

Many conflicts today are internal conflicts clashed between ANSAs without an obvious State involvement. These conflicts claim thousands of lives and affect millions of people every year. But because they are less politically sensitive than conflicts in which a State is a party to the conflict they do not get much attention in IHL or the international community. So if the nature of the conflict makes such a difference, maybe blurring the distinction between different categories would make the protection offered by IHL available to civilians and combatants against the barbarism that occurs in these conflicts.

In the end it should be stressed that there is no need to change the existing or to come up with new laws, because that will only lead to more confusion and additional inefficient laws. However let´s face it, States today are no longer capable of controlling ANSAs.

Globalisation facilitated the expansion of ANSA´s activities and thereby helped create a space removed from the effective control of any State. This has allowed them to act with virtual impunity; escape their internationally recognized humanitarian obligations and the consequences of their actions. If ANSAs are to be held accountable for violations of humanitarian norms, they have to be addressed directly, even those designated as terrorists by the international community. Although there have been calls for measures to address "all parties" in armed conflicts, States remain reluctant to place ANSAs on their political agenda. International organizations engaging ANSAs are left to work in an often ad hoc manner without any international political support. The most important questions facing the world today are: Is the State still a central actor of international law? Is she the only one ruling and regulating on the national and international level? And of course whether the UN with its member States ignoring ANSAs can cope with the new era? Is it so that the UN ´s influence and good reputation is in decline?

The law ought to be made more effective and inclusive. Tomorrow´s mission should not be to determine what the rules are, or how to apply them to a specific situation, or even whether the existing rules are adequate or not, but rather how to secure or compel compliance with the law at all. It may be that we have now passed from the phase of law-making to a period where the focus is not on new substantive law but on how to make existing law effective.

6

Political Correctness

INTRODUCTION

As Russell Kirk wrote, one of conservatism's most important insights is that all ideologies are wrong. Ideology takes an intellectual system, a product of one or more philosophers, and says, "This system must be true." Inevitably, reality ends up contradicting the system, usually on a growing number of points. But the ideology, by its nature, cannot adjust to reality; to do so would be to abandon the system.

Therefore, reality must be suppressed. If the ideology has power, it uses its power to undertake this suppression. It forbids writing or speaking certain facts. Its goal is to prevent not only expression of thoughts that contradict what "must be true," but thinking such thoughts. In the end, the result is inevitably the concentration camp, the gulag and the grave.

While some Americans have believed in ideologies, America itself never had an official, state ideology – up until now. But what happens today to Americans who suggest that there are differences among ethnic groups, or that the traditional social roles of men and women reflect their different natures, or that homosexuality is morally wrong? If they are public figures, they must grovel in the dirt in endless, canting apologies. If they are university students, they face star chamber courts and possible expulsion. If they are employees of private corporations, they may face loss of their jobs. What was their crime? Contradicting America's new state ideology of "Political Correctness." But what exactly is "Political Correctness?" Marxists have used the term for at least 80 years, as a broad synonym for "the General Line of the Party." It could be said that Political Correctness is the General Line of the Establishment in America today; certainly, no one who dares contradict it can be a member of that Establishment. But that still does not tell us what it really is.

This short book, which Free Congress has decided to make available free over its website, seeks to answer that question. It does so in the only way any ideology can be understood, by looking at its historical origins, its method of analysis and several key components, including its place in higher education and its ties with the Feminist movement. Finally, it offers an annotated bibliography for those who wish to pursue the subject in greater depth.

Perhaps the most important question facing Americans today is, "Do we really want America to be an ideological state?" Because conservatives know where all ideologies lead, our answer, resoundingly, is "NO!" But if we expect to prevail and restore our country to full freedom of thought and expression, we need to know our enemy. We need to understand what Political Correctness really is. As you will soon see, if we can expose the true origins and nature of Political Correctness, we will have taken a giant step to its overthrow.

WHAT IS "POLITICAL CORRECTNESS"?

Most Americans look back on the 1950s as a good time. Our homes were safe, to the point where many people did not bother to lock their doors. Public schools were generally excellent, and their problems were things like talking in class and running in the halls. Most men treated women like ladies, and most ladies devoted their time and effort to making good homes, rearing their children well and helping their communities through volunteer work. Children grew up in two–parent households, and the mother was there to meet the child when he came home from school. Entertainment was something the whole family could enjoy.

What Happened?

If a man from America of the 1950s were suddenly introduced into America in the 2000s, he would hardly recognize it as the same country. He would be in immediate danger of getting mugged, carjacked or worse, because he would not have learned to live in constant fear.

He would not know that he shouldn't go into certain parts of the city, that his car must not only be locked but equipped with an alarm, that he dare not go to sleep at night without locking the windows and bolting the doors – and setting the electronic security system.

If he brought his family with him, he and his wife would probably cheerfully pack their children off to the nearest public school. When the children came home in the afternoon and told them they had to go through a metal detector to get in the building, had been given some funny white powder by another kid and learned that homosexuality is normal and good, the parents would be uncomprehending.

In the office, the man might light up a cigarette, drop a reference to the "little lady," and say he was happy to see the firm employing some Negroes in important positions. Any of those acts would earn a swift reprimand, and together they might get him fired.

When she went into the city to shop, the wife would put on a nice suit, hat, and possibly gloves. She would not understand why people stared, and mocked. And when the whole family sat down after dinner and turned on the television, they would not understand how pornography from some sleazy, blank-fronted "Adults Only" kiosk had gotten on their set.

Were they able, our 1950s family would head back to the 1950s as fast as they could, with a gripping horror story to tell. Their story would be of a nation that had decayed and degenerated at a fantastic pace, moving in less than a half a century from the greatest country on earth to a Third World nation, overrun by crime, noise, drugs and dirt. The fall of Rome was graceful by comparison.

Why did it Happen?

Over the last forty years, America has been conquered by the same force that earlier took over Russia, China, Germany and Italy. That force is ideology. Here, as elsewhere, ideology has inflicted enormous damage on the traditional culture it came to dominate, fracturing it everywhere and sweeping much of it away. In its place came fear, and ruin. Russia will take a generation or more to recover from Communism, if it ever can.

The ideology that has taken over America goes most commonly by the name of "Political Correctness." Some people see it as a joke. It is not. It is deadly serious. It seeks to alter virtually all the rules, formal and informal, that govern relations among people and institutions. It wants to change behavior, thought, even the words we use. To a significant extent, it already has. Whoever or whatever controls language also controls thought. Who dares to speak of "ladies" now?

Just what is "Political Correctness?" "Political Correctness" is in fact cultural Marxism – Marxism translated from economic into cultural terms. The effort to translate Marxism from economics into culture did not begin with the student rebellion of the 1960s. It goes back at least to the 1920s and the writings of the Italian Communist Antonio Gramsci. In 1923, in Germany, a group of Marxists founded an institute devoted to making the translation, the Institute of Social Research (later known as the Frankfurt School). One of its founders, George Lukacs, stated its purpose as answering the question, "Who shall save us from Western Civilization?" The Frankfurt School gained profound influence in American universities after many of its leading lights fled to the United States in the 1930s to escape National Socialism in Germany.

The Frankfurt School blended Marx with Freud, and later influences (some Fascist as well as Marxist) added linguistics to create "Critical Theory" and "deconstruction." These in turn greatly influenced education theory, and through institutions of higher education gave birth to what we now call "Political Correctness."

The lineage is clear, and it is traceable right back to Karl Marx. The parallels between cultural Marxism and classical, economic Marxism are evident. Cultural Marxism, or Political Correctness, shares with classical Marxism the vision of a "classless society" i.e., a society not merely of equal opportunity, but equal condition. Since that vision contradicts human nature – because people are different, they end up unequal, regardless of the starting point – society will not accord with it unless forced. So, under both variants of Marxism, it is forced. This is the first major parallel between classical and cultural Marxism: *both are totalitarian ideologies.* The totalitarian nature of Political Correctness can be seen on campuses where "PC" has taken over the college: freedom of speech, of the press, and even of thought are all eliminated. The second major parallel is that both cultural Marxism and classical, economic Marxism have *single-factor explanations of history.* Classical Marxism argues that all of history was determined by ownership of the means of production. Cultural Marxism says that history is wholly explained by which groups – defined by sex, race and sexual normality or abnormality – have power over which other groups.

The third parallel is that both varieties of Marxism *declare certain groups virtuous and others evil a priori*, that is, without regard for the actual behavior of individuals. Classical Marxism defines workers and peasants as virtuous and the bourgeoisie (the middle class) and other owners of capital as evil. Political Correctness defines blacks, Hispanics, Feminist women, homosexuals and some additional minority groups as virtuous and white men as evil. (Political Correctness does not recognize the existence of non-Feminist women and defines blacks who reject Political Correctness as whites).

The fourth parallel is in means: *expropriation.* Economic Marxists, where they obtained power, expropriated the property of the bourgeoisie and handed it to the state, as the "representative" of the workers and the peasants. Cultural Marxists, when they gain power (including through our own government), lay penalties on white men and others who disagree with them and give privileges to the groups they favor. Affirmative action is an example.

Finally, both varieties of Marxists employ a method of analysis *designed to show the correctness of their ideology in every situation.* For classical Marxists, the analysis is economic. For cultural Marxists, the analysis is linguistic: deconstruction. Deconstruction "proves" that any "text," past or present, illustrates the oppression of blacks, women, homosexuals, etc. by reading that meaning into words of the text (regardless of their actual meaning). Both methods are, of course, phony analyses that twist the evidence to fit preordained conclusions, but they lend a "scientific" air to the ideology. These parallels are neither remarkable nor coincidental. They exist because Political Correctness is directly derived from classical Marxism, and is in fact merely a variant of Marxism. Through most of the history of Marxism, cultural Marxists were "read out" of the movement by classical, economic Marxists. Today, with economic Marxism dead, cultural Marxism has filled its shoes. The medium has changed, but the message is the same: a society of radical egalitarianism enforced by the power of the state.

Political Correctness now looms over American society like a colossus. It has taken over both political parties – recent Republican conventions were choreographed according to its dictates, while cultural conservatives were shown the door – and is enforced by many laws and government regulations. It almost totally controls the most powerful element in our culture, the entertainment industry. It dominates both public and higher education: many a college campus is a small, ivy-covered North Korea. It has even captured the clergy in many Christian churches. Anyone in the Establishment who departs from its dictates swiftly ceases to be a member of the Establishment. The remainder of this short book will explore the subject of Political Correctness further: its history, its method of analysis (deconstruction), and the means by which it has attained its influence, especially through education.

But one more question must be addressed at the outset, the most vital question: how can Americans combat Political Correctness and retake their society from the cultural Marxists? To that end, it is not sufficient to criticize Political Correctness. It tolerates a certain amount of criticism, even gentle mocking. It does so through no genuine tolerance for other points of view, but in order to disarm its opponents, to let itself seem less menacing than it is. The cultural Marxists do not yet have total power, and they are too wise to appear totalitarian until their victory is assured.

Rather, those who would defeat cultural Marxism must defy it. They must use words it forbids, and refuse to use the words it mandates; remember, sex is better than gender. They must shout from the housetops the realities it seeks to suppress, such as the facts that violent crime is disproportionately committed by blacks and that most cases of AIDS are voluntary, i.e., acquired from immoral sexual acts. They must refuse to turn their children over to public schools.

Above all, those who would defy Political Correctness must behave according to the old rules of our culture, not the new rules the cultural Marxists lay down. Ladies should be wives and homemakers, not cops or soldiers, and men should still hold doors open for ladies. Children should not be born out of wedlock. Open homosexuals should be shunned. Jurors should not accept race as an excuse for murder. Defiance spreads. When other Americans see one person defy Political Correctness and survive – and you still can, for now – they are emboldened. They are tempted to defy it, too, and some will. The ripples from a single act of defiance, of one instance of walking up to the clay idol and breaking off its nose, can range far. There is nothing the Politically Correct fear more than open defiance, and for good reason; it is their chief vulnerability. That should lead cultural conservatives to defy cultural Marxism at every turn.

While the hour is late, the battle is not decided. Very few Americans realize that Political Correctness is in fact Marxism in a different set of clothes. As that realization spreads, defiance will spread with it. At present, Political Correctness prospers by disguising itself. Through defiance, and through education on our own part (which should be part of every act of defiance), we can strip away its camouflage and reveal the Marxism beneath the window-dressing of "sensitivity," "tolerance" and "multiculturalism." Who dares, wins.

THE HISTORICAL ROOTS

America is today dominated by an alien system of beliefs, attitudes and values that we have come to know as "Political Correctness." Political Correctness seeks to impose a uniformity of thought and behavior on all Americans and is therefore totalitarian in nature. Its roots lie in a version of Marxism which seeks a radical inversion of the traditional culture in order to create a social revolution.

Social revolution has a long history, conceivably going as far back as Plato's *Republic*. But it was the French Revolution of 1789 that inspired Karl Marx to develop his theories in the nineteenth century. In the twentieth century, the success of the Bolshevik Revolution of 1917 in Russia set off a wave of optimistic expectation among the Marxist forces in Europe and America that the new proletarian world of equality was finally coming into being. Russia, as the first communist nation in the world, would lead the revolutionary forces to victory.

The Marxist revolutionary forces in Europe leaped at this opportunity. Following the end of World War I, there was a Communist "Spartacist uprising in Berlin, Germany lead by Rosa Luxemburg; the creation of a "Soviet" in Bavaria led by Kurt Eisner; and a Hungarian communist republic established by Bela Kun in 1919. At the time, there was great concern that all of Europe might fall under the banner of Bolshevism. This sense of impeding doom was given vivid life by Trotsky's Red Army invasion of Poland in 1919. However, the Red Army was defeated by Polish forces at the battle of the Vistula in 1920. The Spartacist, Bavarian Soviet and Bela Kun governments all failed to gain widespread support from the workers and after a brief time they were all overthrown. These events created a quandary for the Marxist revolutionaries in Europe. Under Marxist economic theory, the oppressed workers were supposed to be the beneficiaries of a social revolution that would place them on top of the power structure. When these revolutionary opportunities presented themselves, however, the workers did not respond. The Marxist revolutionaries did not blame their theory for these failures. They blamed the workers.

One group of Marxist intellectuals resolved their quandary by an analysis that focused on society's cultural "superstructure" rather than on the economic substructures as Marx did. The Italian Marxist Antonio Gramsci and Hungarian Marxist Georg Lukacs contributed the most to this new cultural Marxism.

Antonio Gramsci worked for the Communist International during 1923-24 in Moscow and Vienna. He was later imprisoned in one of Mussolini's jails where he wrote his famous "Prison Notebooks." Among Marxists, Gramsci is noted for his theory of cultural hegemony as the means to class dominance. In his view, a new "Communist man" had to be created before any political revolution was possible. This led to a focus on the efforts of intellectuals in the fields of education and culture. Gramsci envisioned a long march through the society's institutions, including the government, the judiciary, the military, the schools and the media. He also concluded that so long as the workers had a Christian soul, they would not respond to revolutionary appeals.

Georg Lukacs was the son a wealthy Hungarian banker. Lukacs began his political life as an agent of the Communist International. His book *History and Class Consciousness* gained him recognition as the leading Marxist theorist since Karl Marx. Lukacs believed that for a new Marxist culture to emerge, the existing culture must be destroyed. He said, "I saw the revolutionary destruction of society as the one and only solution to the cultural contradictions of the epoch," and, "Such a worldwide overturning of values cannot take place without the annihilation of the old values and the creation of new ones by the revolutionaries."

When he became Deputy Commissar for Culture in the Bolshevik Bela Kun regime in Hungary in 1919, Lukacs launched what became known as "Cultural Terrorism." As part of this terrorism he instituted a radical sex education program in Hungarian schools. Hungarian children were instructed in free love, sexual intercourse, the archaic nature of middle-class family codes, the out-datedness of monogamy, and the irrelevance of religion, which deprives man of all pleasures. Women, too, were called to rebel against the sexual mores of the time. Lukacs's campaign of "Cultural Terrorism" was a precursor to what Political Correctness would later bring to American schools. In 1923, Lukacs and other Marxist intellectuals associated with the Communist Party of Germany founded the Institute of Social Research at Frankfurt University in Frankfurt, Germany. The Institute, which became known as the Frankfurt School, was modeled after the Marx-Engels Institute in Moscow. In 1933, when Nazis came to power in Germany, the members of the Frankfurt School fled. Most came to the United States.

The members of the Frankfurt School conducted numerous studies on the beliefs, attitudes and values they believed lay behind the rise of National Socialism in Germany. The Frankfurt School's studies combined Marxist analysis with Freudian psychoanalysis to form the basis of what became known as "Critical Theory." Critical Theory was essentially destructive criticism of the main elements of Western culture, including Christianity, capitalism, authority, the family, patriarchy, hierarchy, morality, tradition, sexual restraint, loyalty, patriotism, nationalism, heredity, ethnocentrism, convention and conservatism. These criticisms were reflected in such works of the Frankfurt School as Erich Fromm's *Escape from Freedom* and *The Dogma of Christ*, Wilhelm's Reich's *The Mass Psychology of Fascism* and Theodor Adorno's *The Authoritarian Personality*. *The Authoritarian Personality*, published in 1950, substantially influenced American psychologists and social scientists. The book was premised on one basic idea, that the presence in a society of Christianity, capitalism and the patriarchal-authoritarian family created a character prone to racial prejudice and German fascism. *The Authoritarian Personality* became a handbook for a national campaign against any kind of prejudice or discrimination on the theory that if these evils were not eradicated, another Holocaust might occur on the American continent. This campaign, in turn, provided a basis for Political Correctness.

Critical Theory incorporated sub-theories which themselves were intended to chip away at specific elements of the existing culture, including "matriarchal theory," "androgyny theory," "personality theory," "authority theory," "family theory," "sexuality theory," "racial theory," "legal theory" and "literary theory." Put into practice, these theories were to be used to overthrow the prevailing social order and usher in social revolution based on cultural Marxism.

To achieve this, the Critical Theorists of the Frankfurt School recognized that traditional beliefs and the existing social structure would have to be destroyed and then replaced. The patriarchal social structure would be replaced with matriarchy; the belief that men and women are different and properly have different roles would be replaced with androgyny; and the belief that heterosexuality is normal would be replaced with the belief that homosexuality is "normal."

As a grand scheme intended to deny the intrinsic worth of white, heterosexual males, the Critical Theorists of the Frankfurt School opened the door to the racial and sexual antagonisms of the Trotskyites. Leon Trotsky believed that oppressed blacks could be the vanguard of a communist revolution in North America. He denounced white workers who were prejudiced against blacks and instructed them to unite with the blacks in revolution. Trotsky's ideas were adopted by many of the student leaders of the 1960s counterculture movement, who attempted to elevate the black revolutionaries to positions of leadership in their movement.

The student revolutionaries were also strongly influenced by the ideas of Herbert Marcuse, another member of the Frankfurt School. Marcuse preached the "Great Refusal," a rejection of all basic Western concepts, sexual liberation and the merits of feminist and black revolutions. His primary thesis was that university students, ghetto blacks, the alienated, the asocial, and the Third World could take the place of the proletariat in the Communist revolution. In his book, *An Essay on Liberation*, Marcuse proclaimed his goals of a radical transvaluation of values; the relaxation of taboos, cultural subversion; Critical Theory; and a linguistic rebellion that would amount to a methodical reversal of meaning. As for racial conflict, Marcuse wrote that white men are guilty and that blacks are the most natural force of rebellion.

Marcuse may be the most important member of the Frankfurt School in terms of the origins of Political Correctness, because he was the critical link to the counterculture of the 1960s. His objective was clear: "One can rightfully speak of a cultural revolution, since the protest is directed toward the whole cultural establishment, including morality of existing society..." His means was liberating the powerful, primeval force of sex from its civilized restraints, a message preached in his book, *Eros and Civilization*, published in 1955. Marcuse became one of the main gurus of the 1960s adolescent sexual rebellion; he himself coined the expression, "make love, not war." With that role, the chain of Marxist influence via the Frankfurt School was completed: from Lukacs's service as Deputy Commissar for Culture in the Bolshevik Hungarian government in 1919 to American students burning the flag and taking over college administration buildings in the 1960s. Today, many of these same colleges are bastions of Political Correctness, and the former student radicals have become the faculties.

One of the most important contributors to Political Correctness was Betty Friedan. Through her book *The Feminine Mystique,* Friedan became the mother of the modern feminist movement in America. Friedan was not a member of the Frankfurt School, but she was strongly influenced by it. Her work offers a useful case study of the Marxist roots of Political Correctness.

Friedan devoted almost a full chapter of *The Feminine Mystique* to Abraham Maslow's theory of self-actualization. Maslow was a social psychologist who in his early years did research on female dominance and sexuality. Maslow was a friend of Herbert Marcuse at Bandeis University and had met Erich Fromm in 1936. He was strongly impressed by Fromm's Frankfurt School ideology. He wrote an article, "The Authoritarian Character Structure," published in 1944, that reflected the personality theory of Critical Theory. Maslow was also impressed with the work of Wilhelm Reich, who was another Frankfurt School originator of personality theory.

The significance of the historical roots of Political Correctness cannot be fully appreciated unless Betty Friedan's revolution in sex roles is viewed for what it really was – a manifestation of the social revolutionary process begun by Karl Marx. Friedan's reliance on Abraham Maslow's reflection of Frankfurt School ideology is simply one indicator. Other indicators include the correspondence of Friedan's revolution in sex roles with Georg Lukacs' annihilation of old values and the creation of new ones, and with Herbert Marcuse's transvaluation of values. But the idea of transforming a patriarchy into a matriarchy – which is what a sex-role inversion is designed to do – can be connected directed to Friedrich Engels book *The Origin of the Family, Private Property, and the Sate.* First published in 1884, this book popularized the now-accepted feminist belief that deep-rooted discrimination against the oppressed female sex was a function of patriarchy. The belief that matriarchy was the solution to patriarchy flows from Marx's comments in *The German Ideology*, published in 1845. In this work Marx advanced the idea that wives and children were the first property of the patriarchal male. The Frankfurt School's matriarchal theory (and its near-relation, androgyny theory) both originated from these sources.

When addressing the general public, advocates of Political Correctness – or cultural Marxism, to give it its true name – present their beliefs attractively. It's all just a matter of being "sensitive" to other people, they say. They use words such as "tolerance" and "diversity," asking, "Why can't we all just get along?"

The reality is different. Political Correctness is not at all about "being nice," unless one thinks gulags are nice places. Political Correctness is Marxism, with all that implies: loss of freedom of expression, thought control, inversion of the traditional social order and, ultimately, a totalitarian state. If anything, the cultural Marxism created by the Frankfurt School is more horrifying than the old, economic Marxism that ruined Russia. At least the economic Marxists did not exalt sexual perversion and attempt to create a matriarchy, as the Frankfurt School and its descendants have done.

This short essay has sought to show one critical linkage, that between classical Marxism and the ingredients of the "cultural revolution" that broke out in America in the 1960s. The appendices to this paper offer a "wiring diagram" which may make the trail easier to follow, along with a more detailed look at some of the main actors. Of course, the action does not stop in the '60s; the workings of Frankfurt School are yet very much with us, especially in the field of education. That topic, and other present-day effects of Frankfurt School thinking, will be the subjects of future chapters in this book.

Profiles

Georg Lukacs

- He began his political life as a Kremlin agent of the Communist International.
- His *History and Class-Consciousness* gained him recognition as the leading Marxist theorist since Karl Marx.
- In 1919 he became the Deputy Commissar for Culture in the Bolshevik Bela Kun Regime in Hungary. He instigated what become known as the "Cultural Terrorism."
- The Cultural Terrorism was a precursor of what was to happen in American schools.
- He launched an "explosive" sex education program. Special lectures were organized in Hungarian schools and literature was printed and distributed to instruct children about free love, the nature of sexual intercourse, the archaic nature of the bourgeois family codes, the outdatedness of monogamy and the irrelevance of religion, which deprives man of all pleasure. Children urged thus to reject and deride paternal authority and the authority of the Church, and to ignore precepts of morality, were easily and spontaneously turned

into delinquents with whom only the police could cope. This call to rebellion addressed to Hungarian children was matched by a call to rebellion addressed to Hungarian women.

- In rejecting the idea that Bolshevism spelled the destruction of civilization and culture, Lukacs stated: "Such a worldwide overturning of values cannot take place without the annihilation of the old values and the creation of new ones by the revolutionaries."
- Lukacs' state of mind was expressed in his own words:
    - o "All the social forces I had hated since my youth, and which I aimed in spirit to annihilate, now came together to unleash the First Global War."
    - o "I saw the revolutionary destruction of society as the one and only solution to the cultural contradictions of the epoch."
    - o "The question is, Who will free us from the yoke of Western Civilization?"
    - o "Any political movement capable of bringing Bolshevism to the West would have to be 'Demonic'."
    - o "The abandonment of the soul's uniqueness solves the problem of 'unleashing' the diabolic forces lurking in all the violence which are needed to create a revolution."
- Lukacs' state of mind was typical of those who represented the forces of Revolutionary Marxism.
- At a secret meeting in Germany in 1923, Lukacs proposed the concept of inducing "Cultural Pessimism" in order to increase the state of hopelessness and alienation in the people of the West as a necessary prerequisite for revolution.
- This meeting led to the founding of the Institute for Social Research at Frankfurt University in Germany in 1923 – an organization of Marxist and Communistoriented psychologists, sociologists and other intellectuals that came to be known as the Frankfurt School, which devoted itself to implementing Georg Lukacs's program.

Antonio Gramsci

- He was an Italian Marxist on an intellectual par with Georg Lukacs who arrived by analysis at the same conclusions as Lukacs and the Frankfurt School regarding the critical importance of intellectuals in fomenting revolution in the West.
- He had traveled to the Soviet Union after the Bolshevik Revolution of 1917 and made some accurate observations that caused him to conclude that a Bolshevikstyle uprising could not be brought about by Western workers due to the nature of their Christian souls.
- Antonio Gramsci became the leader of the Italian Communist Party, which earned him a place in one of Mussolini's jails in the 1930s, where he wrote *Prison Notebooks* and other documents.
- These works became available in English to Americans.
- His advice to the intellectuals was to begin a long march through the educational and cultural institutions of the nation in order to create a new Soviet man before there could be a successful political revolution.
- This reflected his observations in the Soviet Union that its leaders could not create such a new Soviet man after the Bolshevik Revolution.
- This blueprint for mind and character change made Gramsci a hero of Revolutionary Marxism in American education and paved the way for creation of the New American Child in the schools by the education cartel.
- The essential nature of Antonio Gramsci's revolutionary strategy is reflected in Charles A. Reich's *The Greening of America*: "There is a revolution coming. It will not be like revolutions in the past. It will originate with the individual and the culture, and it will change the political structure as its final act. It will not require violence to succeed, and it cannot be successfully resisted by violence. This is revolution of the New Generation."

Wilhelm Reich

- In his 1933 book entitled *The Mass Psychology of Fascism*, he explained that the Frankfurt School departed from the Marxist sociology that set "Bourgeois" against "Proletariat." Instead, the battle would be between "reactionary" and "revolutionary" characters.
- He also wrote a book entitled *The Sexual Revolution*, which was a precursor of what was to come in the 1960s.
- His "sex-economic" sociology was an effort to harmonize Freud's psychology with Marx's economic theory.
- Reich's theory was expressed in his words: "The authoritarian family is the authoritarian state in miniature. Man's authoritarian character structure is basically produced by the embedding of sexual inhibitions and fear in the living substance of sexual impulses. Familial imperialism is ideologically reproduced in national imperialism…the authoritarian family…is a factor where reactionary ideology and reactionary structures are produced."
- Wilhelm Reich's theory, when coupled with Georg Lukacs' sex education in Hungary, can be seen as the source for the American education cartel's insistence on sex education from kindergarten onwards and its complete negation of the paternal family, external authority, and the traditional character structure.
- Reich's theory encompassed other assertions that seem to have permeated American education:
    - The organized religious mysticism of Christianity was an element of the authoritarian family that led to Fascism.
    - The patriarchal power in and outside of man was to be dethroned.
    - Revolutionary sexual politics would mean the complete collapse of authoritarian ideology.
    - Birth control was revolutionary ideology.

  - o Man was fundamentally a sexual animal.
- Reich's *The Mass Psychology of Fascism* was in its ninth printing as of 1991, and is available in most college bookstores.

Erich Fromm

- Like Wilhelm Reich, Fromm was a social psychologist of the Frankfurt School who came to America in the 1930s.
- His book *Escape from Freedom*, published in 1941, is an ideological companion to Wilhelm Reich's *The Mass Psychology of Fascism*.
- Fromm asserted that early capitalism created a social order that bred a sadomasochistic and authoritarian character of which Martin Luther and Adolph Hitler were prime examples.
- He asserted that the same capitalistic social order resulted in Calvin's Theory of Predestination, which reflected the principle of the basic inequality of men that was revived in Nazi ideology.
- He asserted the authoritarian character experiences only domination or submission and "differences, whether sex or race, to him are necessarily of superiority or inferiority."
- He asserted that "Positive Freedom" implies the principle that there is no higher power than the unique individual self; that man is the center and purpose of life; that the growth and realization of man's individuality is an end that can never be subordinated to purposes which are supposed to have a greater dignity.
- Fromm made the real meaning of this "Positive Freedom" clear in another of his many books – *The Dogma of Christ...* wherein he describes a revolutionary character such as himself as: the man who has emancipated himself from the ties of blood and soil, from his mother and father, and from special loyalties to state, race, party or religion.
- Fromm makes his revolutionary intent very clear in *The Dogma of Christ...* "We might define revolution in a

psychological sense, saying that a revolution is a political movement led by people with revolutionary characters, and attracting people with revolutionary characters."

Herbert Marcuse

- Like Wilhelm Reich and Erich Fromm, Herbert Marcuse was an intellectual of the Frankfurt School who came to America in the 1930s.
- He has often been described as a Marxist philosopher, but he was in fact a fullblooded social revolutionary who contemplated the disintegration of American society just as Karl Marx and Georg Lukacs contemplated the disintegration of German society: "One can rightfully speak of a cultural revolution, since the protest is directed toward the whole cultural establishment, including the morality of existing society...there is one thing we can say with complete assurance: the traditional idea of revolution and the traditional strategy of revolution has ended. These ideas are old-fashioned...What we must undertake is a type of diffuse and dispersed disintegration of the system."
- Marcuse published *Eros and Civilization* in 1955, which became the founding document of the 1960s counterculture and brought the Frankfurt School into the colleges and universities of America.
- He asserted that the only way to escape the one-dimensionality of modern industrial society was to liberate the erotic side of man, the sensuous instinct, in rebellion against "technological rationality."
- This erotic liberation was to take the form of the "Great Refusal," a total rejection of the capitalist monster and its entire works, including technological reason and ritual-authoritarian language.
- He provided the obtuse intellectual justifications for adolescent sexual rebellion, and the slogan "Make Love, Not War."

- His theory included the belief that the Women's Liberation Movement was to be the most important component of the opposition, and potentially the most radical.
- His revolutionary efforts would blossom into a full-scale war by revolutionary Marxism against the European white male in the schools and colleges.

Theodor Adorno

- He was another Marxist revolutionary and member of the Frankfurt School who came to America in the 1930s.
- Along with others, Adorno authored *The Authoritarian Personality*, which was published in 1950.
- Adorno's book was inspired by the same kind of theoretical assertions revealed in the works of Wilhelm Reich, Erich Fromm and Herbert Marcuse based on analytical studies of German society that were begun in 1923.
- The basic theme was the same. There was such a thing as an authoritarian character that was the opposite of the desired revolutionary character. This authoritarian character was a product of capitalism, Christianity, conservatism, the patriarchal family and sexual repression. In Germany, this combination induced prejudice, anti-Semitism and fascism according to Frankfurt School theory.
- It so happened that most Americans were products of capitalism, Christianity, conservatism, the patriarchal family and sexual repression in their youth. So Theodor Adorno and other members of the Frankfurt School had a golden opportunity to execute Georg Lukacs's and Antonio Gramsci's program for creating social revolution in America instead of Germany.
- They would posit the existence of authoritarian personalities among Americans with tendencies toward prejudice, and then exploit this to force the "scientifically planned re-education" of Americans with the excuse that it was being done in order to eradicate prejudice.

- This scientifically-planned re-education would become the master plan for the transformation of America's system of fundamental values into their opposite revolutionary values in American education so that school children would become replicas of the Frankfurt School revolutionary characters and thus create the New American Child.
- This can be confirmed by noting that *The Authoritarian Personality* is the key source of the affective domain of Benjamin Bloom's *Taxonomy of Educational Objectives* of 1964, which guided the education cartel thereafter.

CORRECTNESS IN HIGHER EDUCATION

On a growing number of university campuses the freedom to articulate and discuss ideas – a principle that has been the cornerstone of higher education since the time of Socrates – is eroding at an alarming rate. Consider just one increasing trend: hundreds (sometimes thousands) of copies of conservative student newspapers have been either stolen or publicly burned by student radicals. In many cases these acts have taken place with the tacit support of faculty and administrators. The perpetrators are rarely disciplined.

While it would be easy to dismiss such demonstrations of intolerance as student pranks, these incidents are the surface manifestations of a more pervasive and insidious trend – a trend that has as its goal the destruction of the liberal arts tradition that has helped create and sustain Western civilization.

Though some pundits have claimed that the prevalence of the ideological intolerance known as Political Correctness has been exaggerated, the opposite is closer to the truth. Political Correctness has become so deeply ingrained in American higher education that many campuses are now dominated by an atmosphere of uncertainty and apprehension. An increasing number of dedicated students and faculty members now live in fear that their intellectual pursuit of truth will offend the Grand Inquisitors of Political Correctness. The techniques of Political Correctness are now well known: attacks on the curriculum in the name of "multiculturalism," the imposition of restrictive and vaguelyworded "speech codes" and mandatory "sensitivity training" courses for freshman that are little more than systematic efforts at ideological indoctrination. But the influence of Political Correctness has spread in other disturbing ways. Consider a few recent incidents from the university battlefield.

- At Amherst College in Massachusetts, a homosexual student group covered the university's sidewalks with graffiti, including the slogan "Queer by Divine Right," which was scrawled in front of the campus chapel on Good Friday. When the *Amherst Spectator*, a conservative student newspaper, criticized these chalkings as promoting "hatred and division," student protestors publicly burned copies of the paper.
- When the *Cornell Review*, another conservative student newspaper, published a parody of the course descriptions from Cornell's heavily-politicized Africana Department, campus militants blocked traffic at the center of the campus for several hours and burned stolen copies of the *Review* in a metal trash can. The militants went on to demand that the university provide "racial sensitivity" classes for incoming freshman, a campus speech code and more money for segregated minority programs such as a blacks-only dormitory.
- Students who participate in ROTC programs have told friends and family that they are afraid to show up for class wearing their uniforms because their grades have been arbitrarily marked down by faculty members who are hostile to the military.
- In the wake of a rash of sexual harassment charges that have been filed by extreme feminists against their alleged enemies, some professors have begun to take out insurance policies to protect themselves from the crushing financial burden of malicious and frivolous lawsuits.
- A faculty questionnaire at the University of Massachusetts asks professors what "contribution to multi-culturalism" they have made. The questionnaire is then used in making

decisions about tenure and promotion. It is worth remembering that for every dramatic and well-publicized example of Political Correctness, there are innumerable instances where its influence is more subtle, but just as real.

The Origins of Political Correctness in Higher Education

While the ideology of Political Correctness is hardly restricted to our campuses, there is no doubt it originated there. The intellectual roots of this phenomenon stretch back over centuries. Ultimately, the origins of PC can be traced to the rise of modern ideology and its quest for power. In contrast to the classical and Judeo-Christian traditions, which stressed man's need to understand the moral order and conform himself to it, modern ideologies have sought to dominate and control the world. In the twentieth century these ideologies finally gained political power in Communist states. But in the West, ideology has not been able to make such a direct assault on our traditions of ordered liberty. Rather, radical intellectuals have sought to undermine the foundations of knowledge itself, concentrating their efforts on the transformation of the university. The turning point in the academy came in the 1960s, when militant students launched a guerilla attack on the traditions of Western culture and the liberal arts. Seeing that they could not gain lasting power through demonstrations alone, many of these militants opted to remain "in the system," going on to become professors themselves. This generation of "tenured radicals" (to use Roger Kimball's phrase) has now become the establishment in the vast majority of our institutions of higher learning. As university presidents, deans, and department chairmen, they have set about hiring other ideologues in their own image and have instigated the repressive policies we know as Political Correctness. These politicized academics will be extremely difficult to dislodge from their current positions of power.

Ideology vs. Liberal Education

The stakes in this war of ideas are high, for they include the very concept of freedom itself. Americans have always understood the intimate and vital connection between liberal education and political liberty. That is why Political Correctness is nothing less than a death blow aimed at the heart of our republic. In his seminal book, *The Idea of a University*, Cardinal John Henry Newman defined the "liberal arts" as a pursuit of knowledge for its own sake. By way of contrast, he defined the "servile arts" as those modes of study that serve only specific, immediate ends. The liberal arts are liberating, Newman argued, because they enable men to discover the underlying principles that guide us toward wisdom and virtue. Were he alive today, Newman would view Political Correctness as "servile" because its purpose is to advance a political agenda to a position of national power. Militant professors in increasing numbers are shamelessly turning their podiums into pulpits, abandoning the search for objective truth and setting about the task of indoctrinating their students.

The Devastated Curriculum

The proponents of Political Correctness have concentrated their efforts on the core of a liberal education, the curriculum. Their efforts will radically alter what new generations of Americans will learn. In this battle the handmaiden of Political Correctness has been the "multicultural" movement. A number of critics have rightly pointed out that multiculturalism is more than an argument for courses that concentrate on groups that at one time were disadvantaged or oppressed. Rather, multiculturalism involves the systematic restructuring of the curriculum so as to hinder students from learning about the Western tradition. Since the ulterior motive behind Political Correctness is an attempt to restructure American society along egalitarian lines, it is imperative for its proponents to instill in the minds of students a thoroughgoing cultural relativism.

Perhaps the most disturbing aspect of the Politically Correct assault on the curriculum is that it has occurred at many of America's elite universities. Take, for example, the case of Stanford University, an institution that has long played a leadership role in American higher education. Stanford eliminated its long-standing Western civilization requirement in 1988 and replaced it with a multicultural program known as "Cultures, Ideas, and Values." Under this new program freshmen at Stanford can just as easily study Marxist revolutionaries in Central America as they can Plato, Shakespeare or Newton.

Stanford has also led the movement away from serious study of history. Students at Stanford, like students at all but one of the other top 50 universities in the United States, are not required to take a single course in history. Instead, they are offered a choice of courses under the heading of "American Cultures." According to one recent graduate of Stanford, it is impossible to fulfill the "American Cultures" requirement by studying Protestantism, Irish Americans, or the American West, while courses that do fulfill the requirement include "Film and Literature: US-Mexico Border Representations" and "Contemporary Ethnic Drama." Stanford students must also take courses in "World Cultures" and "Gender Studies" that include "Chicana Expressive Culture" and "Misogyny and Feminism in the Renaissance."

Because elite institutions such as Stanford set an example for the rest of American higher education, other universities eagerly adopt these devastating assaults on the curriculum. This "trickle-down" effect will have a long-lasting impact on the way future generations of Americans will be educated.

Intolerance and the Assault on Freedom

The two pillars that have traditionally sustained the liberal arts are academic freedom and freedom of speech. Without the freedom to pursue the truth and to write and speak freely, authentic scholarship is impossible. But both of these fundamental freedoms have been routinely abrogated by the establishment of speech codes, "sensitivity" classes, and a general atmosphere of fear and intimidation on campus.

For example, younger professors who have not received tenure must not only be careful of what they say, but of what they publish. Ideological university administrators in the 1990s have created an environment dominated by suspicion that is far more intense than anything spawned by anti-Communist Senator Joseph McCarthy in the 1950s. The most tragic victims of this age of Political Correctness are the students. The traditional goal of a liberal arts education – acculturation, whereby students absorb the inherited wisdom of the past – has been set aside. Increasingly, a university education today seems to involve rote learning of political opinions. When all is said and done, Political Correctness substitutes smug feelings of righteousness for the traditional habits of critical thinking. One distinguished scholar recently lamented that "higher education is increasingly about acquiring attitudes and opinions that one puts on like a uniform." Because the academy is a relatively isolated world, it can allow politicized administrators to turn the campus into a laboratory for experiments in social transformation. When critics of Political Correctness have compared the atmosphere on campus to that of a totalitarian state, liberal pundits have been quick to denounce them as hysterical. Few of these pundits have any first-hand experience of daily life on campus.

The Movement for Academic Reform

Despite the institutional power of the campus radicals, forces are at work seeking to spur authentic academic reform. The academic reform movement relies on the principles of accountability, communication and a commitment to authentic scholarship. One force of academic reform is a growing demand among parents for greater accountability from colleges and universities. At a time when studies show that students are paying more and learning less than ever before, parents in increasing numbers are becoming discriminating consumers.

Another force is independent student newspapers whose journalists publicize the antics of Political Correctness on campus. In the past, campus radicals thrived in the enclosed world of the university, but their actions are no longer going undetected. The advent of conservative student newspapers on dozens of campuses has forced campus militants into the open where they are most vulnerable to the scrutiny of an exasperated public. Two years ago, those who fund the Collegiate Network asked the Intercollegiate

Studies Institute to take over the administration of their program to support and enhance responsible student journalism. The Collegiate Network contributes seed money, practical help and intellectual guidance to the 60 conservative student newspapers which provide alternative forums of discussion at many of the nations most elite (and closedminded) universities.

These alternatives papers have identified abuses at all levels of academic life and engaged in investigative journalism that has been remarkably fair and accurate. Perhaps the most well-known "scoop" came from Yale University's alternative paper, *Light & Truth*, a publication supported by the Collegiate Network. The editors of *Light & Truth* discovered that the $20 million gift of alumnus Lee Bass was not being used for its intended purpose of supporting an integrated course in Western civilization. Their report broke open the scandal, which ended when Yale returned Mr. Bass's money. The subsequent furor cost Yale a great deal more than Mr. Bass's $20 million – both in monetary terms and in the loss of confidence of many Yale donors that the current administration can be trusted.

Not all the scandals uncovered by alternative campus papers are of this magnitude, but there are innumerable abuses that can be exposed by investigative student journalism. The law school at the University of North Carolina, Chapel Hill, banned representatives of the U.S. military from setting up recruiting tables there, despite receiving federal tax dollars from the Defense Department. An article about this outrageous assault on freedom that ran in both the student-run *Carolina Review* and in the national student newspaper published by ISI, *CAMPUS*, raised a hue and cry on and off campus. North Carolina legislators took immediate action and passed a bill prohibiting taxpayer-supported schools from discriminating against the military when prospective employers come to the university.

At the University of Wisconsin, Madison, the *UWM Times*, a conservative student newspaper, revealed that a university administrator had been soliciting signatures for local Democrat candidates for public office, in direct violation of a state law forbidding university employees from engaging in political campaigning. The university chancellor, despite having issued a directive against such campaigning, refused to reprimand the administrator in question – perhaps because the chancellor himself violated both the state law and his own directive by signing one of the petitions while at work. The story was picked up by the *Milwaukee Journal-Sentinel* and the abuse was brought to an end. Now that alternative newspapers and organizations dedicated to academic reform are spreading the word, the larger communities that surround our institutions of higher education are getting more involved in serious academic reform. For example, the National Association of Scholars is encouraging university trustees to take a more active and vocal role in opposing the excesses of Political Correctness. Efforts of this type must be expanded and intensified.

In the long run, the most direct method of defeating the inquisitors of Political Correctness is simply to stand up to them. Individual acts of defiance often entail serious risks: students can face star-chamber proceedings that are humiliating and demoralizing while faculty can lose their bids to receive tenure. But every act of resistance causes a ripple, encouraging others to stand up to ideological intimidation. With the support of a significant number of parents, donors and alumni, these Davids may yet slay the Goliaths who tower over them.

The Fire of True-Learning

Perhaps the strongest force for true academic reform is that which seeks to defeat the ideological depredations of Political Correctness by winning the war of ideas. The best students have a questioning intelligence that cannot be satisfied with political slogans. When such students have access to serious scholarship they respond with enthusiasm. Even today acculturation still takes place under the mentorship of outstanding scholars at various institutions around the country. Moreover, some colleges and universities continue to swim against the ideological tides of our time. The Intercollegiate Studies Institute (ISI), in conjunction with the Templeton Foundation, has identified the best professors, departments, colleges and textbooks in American higher education today. This program, the Templeton Honor Rolls for Education in a Free Society, celebrates excellence and serves as a guide for parents and students contemplating the daunting choice of which college or university to attend. By singling out the best in higher education, the Templeton Honor Rolls also encourage donors to reward universities that preserve the traditions of the free society.

Prospective college students, their parents and donors can also benefit from a comprehensive guide to 100 of the top institutions of higher learning in America published by the ISI. The guide contains substantial, essay-length treatments of all 100 institutions, including 80 elite schools that were selected on the basis of competitive admissions standards and 20 schools that ISI particularly recommends for their commitment to a liberal arts education. The ISI college guide warns students about the ideological dangers on the campuses and steers them in the direction of the best professors and departments. As best-selling author William J. Bennett wrote of this project, "All too often, Americans treat colleges and universities with a deference that prevents them from asking hard questions and demanding real results. But if there is ever to be genuine, long-lasting education reform, parents and students will have to become shrewder and better-informed consumers of education. The ISI guide is a powerful tool in this effort."

One of Edmund Burke's most famous sayings is that "the only thing necessary for the triumph of evil is for good men to do nothing." For generations, Americans have treated higher education with respect and awe – a token of their faith in the liberating power of the liberal arts. But in the face of Political Correctness, it is time for the American public to temper its respect with a critical sensibility and to undertake a more direct effort to call academia to account. It is time for good men and women to demand that American higher education live up to its best traditions and eschew the tyranny of Political Correctness.

DECONSTRUCTION AND LITERATURE

Literature is, if not the most important cultural indicator, at least a significant benchmark of a society's level of civilization. Our nature and environment combine to form each individual mind, which in turn expresses itself in words. Literature, as the words society collectively holds up as exemplary, is then a starting point of sorts – a window into the culture.

Today's literary field is therefore worth examining for the insights it provides into our current cultural milieu. The contemporary American literary field is awash in "isms:" Marxism, Freudianism, feminism, and so on. Most of these are the academic cousins of what is called in the common culture "Political Correctness." Literary theorists take their particular brand of criticism and apply it to literature in an effort to find self-affirmation in a "discovered" meaning of the text. For a feminist critic, for example, no longer does Andrew Marvel's "Upon Appleton House" have the beauty of the grounds as its theme; it speaks instead of the evils of a patriarchal line of inheritance. These "cultural critics," so named because they critique literature based on the point of view of a particular culture, arose in the 1960s, but their schools of criticism only truly began to pick up steam with the arrival of the school of deconstruction in the 1970s. The works of the father of deconstruction, Jacques Derrida, began to be translated from the French by American professor Gayatri Spivak in the mid-1970s, a time when the U.S. literary scene was ripe for its influence. The economic Marxists were alive and well on American campuses, and the cultural critics were still being fed by the radicalism of the times. Feminists, "queer theorists" and "literature-by-people of color" critics had gained a foothold in the earlier decade, but they had in their meager arsenals only a vague feeling of repression. What they lacked was philosophical backing– the courage prompted by having their own *logos*. The arrival of deconstruction from France provided that philosophy.

At that time, that generation of academics was doing what all academics do, telling the previous generation that it had it all wrong.

In this case the rebellion was against the New Critics – so-called even now, decades after their prime. The New Critics specialized in finding the meaning of texts without regard to background information such as authorial intent, a process that had "the text is everything" as its guiding principle.

The new generation of critics set out to turn that principle on its head. Instead of "the text is everything," the new generation claimed that "everything is text" and turned to analyzing anything and everything in relation to the literary work. If a poet wrote a poem that included a female character, the critics would look into the poet's relationship with his mother, his wife, his sister and so on in an effort to offer up an interpretation of the work. This could have (and often did have) the positive effect of using biographic information to gain new understanding of the work; however, these new interpretations were not attempts to discern the true meaning of the work (as the New Critics had done) or even to discover the author's intended meaning (as traditional readings attempted). This new generation of critics instead became prime practitioners of what is known in literary circles as "cultural criticism." They strained to view literature from the "woman's point of view" or the "gay point of view" or the "radical minority point of view." Their attempts were not to find meaning – they were influenced too greatly by relativists for that – but to find sexism, racism or "homophobia" in the works of male, European or heterosexual authors.

Derridean deconstruction became a tool for these cultural critics. Simply stated, deconstruction is a school of thought that posits that words have no meaning. Instead, words have "traces" of meaning. The meaning of a word is continually disappearing, leaving us with only the memory, or trace, of what that meaning once was. (Similar to Heidegger's term being, Derrida often uses the crossed-out word trace in an effort to indicate a meaning that is simultaneously present and disappearing.) A metaphor may be helpful to understand the underlying philosophy of deconstructionism. If I say the word "pen," then you think of the object there in the desk drawer. But if I throw the pen at someone, then the word "pen" begins to lose the benign meaning of a writing apparatus with ink; to use deconstructionist terms, the original understanding of the word "pen" undergoes erasure to leave only a trace. Instead the word "pen" becomes associated with a weapon, a projectile, a means of expressing (perhaps) anger. If the pen strikes someone, then the word "pen" to that person means something painful, a personal injury, impetus for striking back and so on. These meanings constantly grow and change because the human mind is always interpreting and reinterpreting. Because of this, deconstruction argues, it never fully settles on *the* stable meaning for the word "pen." Based on this linguistic argument, deconstructionists conclude that since any meanings in words are so quickly diffused, we can never really communicate at all. Words no longer have meaning.

The postmodern catch word "differance," along with terms like "erasure" and "trace," entered American scholarship through Derrrida's writings. By combining the concepts of (and the French words for) "deferment" and "difference," Derrida came up with this name for the endless deferment of meaning that takes place. Derrida claims that differance is the reason that words cannot have meanings; the mind continually understands things in different ways so that the original meaning loses its importance as the *proper* meaning - it becomes a mere trace.

Ultimately this is insufficient for today's cultural critics – they need words to mean things so that they can point to artistic works and bemoan how they illustrate or exemplify the repression of minority cultures. But other than its general philosophy, deconstruction offered something more important. It offered the techniques to "show" how all language deconstructs itself.

The deconstructionists specialized in "deconstructing" literary works – although they steadfastly insist that the works deconstruct themselves and the critic only illustrates how this happens. These techniques of deconstruction usually involve isolating the surface meaning of the literary work – the "traditionalist" meaning – and attempting to show how the work itself violates that traditional meaning. For example, they will take a love poem and pick apart the language until they find something that they can interpret as unloving. Elizabeth Barrett Browning's sonnet "How Do I Love Thee? Let Me Count The Ways," ends with the words "I shall but love thee better in death." The clever deconstructionists might combine these with Browning's earlier words, "when feeling out of bounds for the edge of beauty and ideal grace," to conclude that Mrs. Browning is actually reaching for her husband's death. "Why is she looking for the *edge* of beauty?" the deconstructionist asks. "She clearly does not want to remain in or before beauty; instead, she is seeking some way around it." The deconstructionist attributes this apparent disparity to the problem with language, "differance," and quickly concludes that the poem – like all other language – has no meaning.

Once they realized the power of this school of thought, the cultural critics embraced it readily, for here they discovered a method of attack on the traditional interpretations of literary works. They used deconstruction to remove traditional meaning and replaced it with *new* meaning. That meaning was the Political Correctness that infests our society today. For example, after the traditional meaning of "How Do I Love Thee?" has been destabilized in the process described above, a feminist critic might come along and - in the absence of a stable traditional interpretation – declare that the poem is "really" concerned with how women in nineteenth-century England were conditioned to see themselves as secondary to men.

Since "everything is text" in the postmodern mantra, the cultural critics did not hesitate to apply their methods to music, movies, television and anything they encountered. They found that they could remove the meaning from all cultural phenomena and substitute the values of whichever group they preferred. For example, homosexual analysts could remove the truth from the Bible and instead interpret it as full of homophobic hate – God's truth was torn down, and a human political agenda was inserted.

This example is not particularly outrageous, as Derrida's stated goal in deconstructionism was to remove the idea of what he called the "transcendental signified." Standard models of linguistics operate with respect to a signifier-signified pair. The signifier is the word, and the signified is that which the word represents. When differance enters the picture, the thing signified is deferred continually until it can be deferred no longer – that is, until it reaches into the realm of metaphysics. The final meaning reached by any word is God, as He is the ultimate meaning of traditional Western thought.2 The "transcendental signified" of which Derrida is trying to rid himself and the Western world is in fact God. Derrida labels belief in God a product of deficient Western thinking, and in true Nietzchean fashion he claims that God is a construct of language rather than the other way around.

Naturally, Derrida quickly became the darling of the American university establishment. He lectured at universities along the Eastern seaboard, and grew to love that area of America. Soon America returned that affection by granting him a position in the English department of Yale University. Yale then began to draw to other deconstructionists and postmodernists; J. Hillis Miller, Geoffrey Hartman and others. Another European, Paul DeMan, also came to America and began teaching deconstruction. DeMan's history provides yet another reason why deconstructionists sought so avidly to remove meaning from language. In pre-World War II Belgium, DeMan had worked for an explicitly pro-Nazi newspaper. DeMan's detractors note that removing the meaning from language was an excellent way to dismiss his pro-Nazi writings.

Through deconstruction the cultural critics adopted a tool that turned literature, philosophy and culture into nonsense. For instance, in his own writing, in order to remain true to his own philosophy, Derrida eschews all forms of the verb "to be." In deconstructionist terms the verb "to be" implies meaning; thus, it cannot exist. Derrida therefore goes back and crosses out all "to be" verbs, making his writing all but incomprehensible. In beginning to attack the signifier-signified construction, Derrida writes "the sign is that ill-named thing, the only one, that escapes the instituting question of philosophy: 'What is…?'" At the same time Derrida is attempting to communicate his ideas about traditional linguistic models, he is forced by his own philosophy to scratch out the very words that allow him to communicate. If Derrida were to follow the logic of his own theories he would find that the very concept of communicating his ideas by written or spoken word should be impossible. If deconstructionist theories were even remotely accurate, all verbal communication – and by extension all other forms of communication – would be impossible. As New Critic Dr. M. H. Abrams of Cornell University states, "I hope that Derrida remembers that words do mean things next time someone warns him of an oncoming bus."

Not only does the embrace of deconstruction harm logical philosophy, it also renders the creation of literature virtually impossible. If words mean nothing, then they are nothing more than sounds. True, Lewis Carroll did create a well-known poem using nonsensical but pleasant-sounding words, but how many poems like "jabberwocky" can be created before we reach the saturation point? (Some would argue that we have already reached that point.)

As university literature departments "progress," the divide widens between those who produce literature and those who analyze and teach it. While Samuel Taylor Coleridge, T.S. Eliot and an entire cadre of great authors were well-educated men, it seems that a literary education in an American university actually *hinders* one's ability to write well. As professors of literature embrace the philosophy of deconstruction they lose the ability to write beautifully because meaning is necessary for beautiful writing. As a result, a distinction has emerged within English departments between M.F.A. (Master of Fine Arts) and Ph.D. programs – to the extent that they now have distinct faculties. America's greatest hope for good literature today lies not in the universities, but in the "amateurs" writing after their nine to five work days or while the kids are at school. The intelligentsia has forgotten its literature in its haste to promote its politics. Already there is a backlash against deconstructionism. Just as the current thriving generation of critics looked upon New Criticism as passé, so the students of today are beginning to look upon deconstruction as obsolete. Derrida still lectured up to his recent death (he spoke in Washington, D.C. as recently as 1995), but, like their forebears, today's literature students are beginning to rise up and tell their predecessors that they had it all wrong. A primary factor in this backlash is the difficulty that lies in communicating deconstructionist ideas (note that what is offered here is merely an outline, not the actual methods of deconstructing a literary work). As a result of this difficulty, today's MTV generation has stumbled upon a positive side effect of their fifteen-second attention spans: They lack the patience to wade through Derrida's nearly unintelligible syntax and decipher his terminology.

Unfortunately, that has not stopped the cultural critics from indoctrinating this new generation in feminist interpretation, Marxist philosophy and so-called "queer theory." Requirements for reading Shakespeare, Milton, Chaucer, and other dead white males are disappearing to be replaced by options to take studies in "the Roles of Women in the Renaissance" (an excuse to lament the sexism of the past) or "The Bible as Literature" (a course designed to denigrate the Bible as cleverly crafted fiction instead of God's truth).

Deconstruction has succeeded in destabilizing the traditional meanings of texts. What happens next remains to be seen, but there are indications that its influence is waning. Already we see Shakespearean plays revived in the cinema; "Much Ado About Nothing," "Hamlet," and "Romeo and Juliet" – all recently adapted for the screen – have long since been abandoned by the American academy in favor of lesser works. Jane Austen's novels, once highly touted by the intelligentsia as undiscovered works of a female author, are now derided in our universities as being too conservative because of their themes of love and marriage. The popular culture has, in a moment of taste, seen the worth of these and revived them as cinema adaptations.

But the real death knell for deconstruction will sound when the next generation of literary critics realizes that the very nature of what it does – read, think, analyze – is antithetical to deconstruction's philosophical goals. The reliable savior of the intelligentsia is the common man and his common sense. Common sense dictates that words do mean things, and as deconstruction posits otherwise it will be relegated to the margins of society. Sadly, its effects will linger on – it has given a sense of validity to cultural criticism and established a marketplace for its ideas. The deconstructionists are already abandoning their enclave at Yale as their school of thought is eclipsed by trendier, simpler and narrower ideologues. These are the feminists, Marxists and queer theorists – none of whom are leaving their tenured offices peacefully. Instead, they have begun to recruit and train new graduate students to take their places. Applications for graduate and teaching degrees are at an all time high as these campus establishment "radicals" encourage the next generation to help them enshrine their ideology permanently in the American university system.

RADICAL FEMINISM AND POLITICAL CORRECTNESS

Perhaps no aspect of Political Correctness is more prominent in American life today than feminist ideology. Is feminism, like the rest of Political Correctness, based on the cultural Marxism imported from Germany in the 1930s? While feminism's history in America certainly extends longer than sixty years, its flowering in recent decades has been interwoven with the unfolding social revolution carried forward by cultural Marxists.

Where do we see radical feminism ascendant? It is on television, where nearly every major offering has a female "power figure" and the plots and characters emphasize inferiority of the male and superiority of the female. It is in the military, where expanding opportunity for women, even in combat positions, has been accompanied by double standards and then lowered standards, as well as by a decline in enlistment of young men, while "warriors" in the services are leaving in droves. It is in government-mandated employment preferences and practices that benefit women and use "sexual harassment" charges to keep men in line. It is in colleges where women's gender studies proliferate and "affirmative action" is applied in admissions and employment. It is in other employment, public and private, where in addition to affirmative action, "sensitivity training" is given unprecedented time and attention. It is in public schools, where "self awareness" and "self-esteem" are increasingly promoted while academic learning declines. And sadly, we see that "a woman's right to choose" leads many fellow Americans, including many with stewardship of public law and culture, to believe it is "the right thing to do" to allow the most helpless to be put to death.

While it is the theme of this essay that the radical feminist movement is embraced by present day Political Correctness ideology, derived from cultural Marxism, feminism as such does have earlier roots. Feminism was conceived and birthed in America in the 1830s, in the generation experiencing the first stage of the industrial revolution. Women, who for centuries had shared the challenges of surviving in an agrarian life, were becoming part of a middle-class gentry with more time and energy to spend writing newspaper articles and novels for their "sisters." The initial stages of the feminization of American culture had started.

These feminists, radical in their time, became a staple of the idealistic Transcendentalists, who included Ralph Waldo Emerson, Henry David Thoreau and many radical Unitarian ministers of the day. They were also abolitionists, bent on destroying slavery and Southern culture as well. Spurred by the rhetoric of Harriet Beecher Stowe (author of *Uncle Tom's Cabin*), Julia Ward Howe (author of the words to "The Battle Hymn of the Republic"), and Margaret Fuller (the first radical feminist newspaper columnist), the men and women of this idealist Transcendentalist generation propelled our nation toward Civil War.

Who were these Transcendentalist idealists, and why should we be reminded of them today? They were the precursors of today's idealistic Boomer generation. While we cannot draw a continuous link between the Transcendentalists and today's Boomers, their characteristics are very similar. We may glimpse where the elite Boomers are leading us by reviewing the history of the Transcendentalists and their causes.

The Transcendentalists supported abolition of slavery, women's rights, temperance, pacifism (but not in the anti-slavery cause), and other causes which we now observe in New Age popular culture. They developed into spiritualism (talking with the dead), Eastern mysticism and phrenology (discerning personality by the shape of one's skull). They would be right at home in today's New Age milieu. Luther George Williams points out, referring to women's groups and civil rights groups that: Freed slaves secured the vote only after the 13th, 14th and 15th Amendments (ratified in 1870), but women fared worse. They did not receive the vote until the passage of the 19th Amendment in 1920. However, the substantial political victories that these groups achieved (during the Civil War period) guaranteed that they would remain allies. Today, their political organizations dominate every aspect of society, politics and education in America – including the military.2 Indeed, the present-day radical feminist assault on VMI and the Citadel has a political parallel to the Transcendentalist activism of the Civil War period. This current assault is in part a continuation of a century-old effort to destroy Southern culture. In contrast to today's radical feminists, social feminists of the 1890s and early 20th century were of a less totalitarian character. They stood for women's suffrage but also advocated the strengthening of the family.

Today, the feminization of American culture, moving rapidly since the 1960s continues to intensify. Radical Feminists demand that women be allowed to "choose" entry to the infantry, artillery, special forces and combat engineering positions in the Army and Marine Corps. These demands follow the Feminization of combat aviation in the U.S. Navy, Air Force and Army since 1993.

The feminization of American politics was advanced in the 1996 presidential election, when parties produced "feminized" conventions featuring soft, emotional, Oprah Winfrey-type orations and sentimental film clips of the presidential candidates. Both candidates were portrayed as soft, gentle, emotion-driven creatures sufficiently in touch with their feelings that all women across America would feel "comfortable" in their care.3 With 60 million female votes at stake, both parties pandered to America's "feminine" side.

There is no doubt in the media that the "man of today" is expected to be a touchyfeely subspecies who bows to the radical feminist agenda. He is a staple of Hollywood, the television network sitcoms and movies, and the political pundits of talk shows.5 The feminization is becoming so noticeable that newspapers and magazines are picking up on it. For example, the *Washington Times* and *National Review* magazines combined to tell us that "behind the breezy celebration of 'guy stuff' in today's men's magazine lurks a crisis of confidence. What does it mean to be masculine in the 90s?" It is revealed that today's men's magazines (*Esquire, GQ, Men's Health, Men's Fitness, Men's Journal, Details, Maxim, Men's Perspective)*"are all geared to a new feminized man...."6 Some examples? The old masculine attitude toward personal appearance is disappearing. If memory serves, our fathers' acts of personal upkeep were mostly limited to shaving and putting on a tie. According to Lowry:

It's hard to imagine them interested in articles on 'A Flat Belly for the Beach' (Verge), or the three new men's fragrances for the fall season (GQ), or even 'The New Fall Suit' (Esquire). But somewhere along the line men became less concerned with being strong and silent, and more worried about making themselves pretty.

Indeed the feminization of American culture is nearly completed. And the last bastion of male domination, the U.S. military, is under assault. If this "feminization" trend were driven only by radical feminists seeking to pull down a perceived male-dominated hierarchy, there would be more hope that the cycles of history would move America toward a stable accommodation between men and women. But the drive is deeper, and it will not be satisfied by any accommodation. The radical feminists have embraced and been embraced by the wider and deeper movement of cultural Marxism. For dedicated Marxists, the strategy is to attack at every point where an apparent disparity leaves a potential constituency of "oppressed" persons – in this case women, who are the largest of all constituencies. Cultural Marxists, men and women, are making the most of it, and the theory developed by the Frankfurt School provides the ideology.

The Frankfurt School theorized that the authoritarian personality is a product of the patriarchal family. This idea is in turn directly connected to Engels's *The Origins of the Family, Private Property and the State,* which promotes matriarchy. Furthermore, it was Karl Marx who wrote in *The Communist Manifesto* about the radical notion of a "community of women." He also, in 1845, wrote disparagingly in his *The German Ideology* of the idea that the family was the basic unit of society.

The concept of the "authoritarian personality" is not just to be interpreted primarily as a model for the conduct of warfare against prejudice as such. It is a handbook for psychological warfare against the American male, to render him unwilling to defend traditional beliefs and values. In other words, the aim was to emasculate him. Undoubtedly the Institute for Social Research at Frankfurt University meant this, as it used the term "psychological techniques for changing personality." The "authoritarian personality," studied in the 1940s and 1950s by American followers of the Frankfurt School, prepared the way for such psychological warfare against the male gender role. The aim was promoted by Herbert Marcuse and others under the guise of "women's liberation" and under the New Left movement in the 1960s. Evidence that psychological techniques for changing personality are intended to focus in particular on the emasculation of the American male has also been provided by Abraham Maslow, founder of "third force humanist psychology" and promoter of psychotherapeutic techniques in public school classrooms. 8 He wrote that "the next step in personal evolution is a transcendence of both masculinity and femininity to general humanness."

Cultural Marxist stalwarts apparently know exactly what they want to do and how they plan to do it. They have actually already succeeded in accomplishing much of their agenda.

How did this situation come about in American universities? Gertrude Himmelfarb has observed that it slipped past traditional academics almost unobserved until it was too late. It occurred so "quietly" that when they "looked up", postmodernism was upon them with a vengeance. "They were surrounded by such a tidal wave of faddish multicultural subjects such as radical feminism, deconstructed relativism as history and other courses" which undermine the perpetuation of Western civilization.10 Indeed, this tidal wave slipped by just as Antonio Gramsci and the Frankfurt School had envisioned – a quiet revolution that could not be resisted by force. The Frankfurt School had devised the concept of designating the opponents of the Marxist cultural revolution as "authoritarian characters." According to available accounts:

There was a meeting of American scholars at a conference on religious and racial prejudice in 1944. Over the next five years, a Frankfurt School team under the direction of Max Horkheimer conducted in-depth social and psychological profiles of Americans under a project entitled "Studies of Prejudice." One of the results was a book entitled "The Authoritarian Personality" by Theodor Adorno, et al, that summarized one of the largest public opinion surveys ever undertaken in the United States. It was published in 1950, and conformed to the original Critical Theory in every respect. As a document which testified to the belief system of the Frankfurt School revolutionaries it was essentially anti-God, anti- Christian, anti-family, anti-nationalist, anti-patriot, anti conservative, antihereditarian, anti-ethnocentric, anti-masculine, anti-tradition, and anti-morality. All of these are elements in critical theory.

"Cultural Marxism," as preached by the Frankfurt School alumni in the U.S., is being implemented by the elite Boomers. This has laid the foundation for and spurred the widely popular and destructive concepts of "affirmative action," "multiculturalism" and "diversity." One can't escape these terms today. They have grown from the study of anti-Semitism and discrimination by the Institute for Social Research during the 1940s and the systematic infusion of the language of "discrimination," "civil rights," 'women's rights," and other "minority rights" into American culture. According to Raehn:

Critical Theory as applied mass psychology has led to the deconstruction of gender in the American culture. Following Critical Theory, the distinction between masculinity and femininity will disappear. The traditional roles of the mothers and fathers are to be dissolved so that patriarchy will be ended. Children are not to be raised according to their biological genders and gender roles according to their biological differences. This reflects the Frankfurt School rationale for the disintegration of the traditional family.

Thus, one of the basic tenets of Critical Theory was the necessity to break down the traditional family. The Frankfurt School scholars preached: Even a partial breakdown of parental authority in the family might tend to increase the readiness of a coming generation to accept social change.

The transformation of American culture envisioned by the cultural Marxists goes further than pursuing gender equality. Embodied in their agenda is "matriarchal theory," under which they purpose to transform American culture to be female-dominated. This is a direct throwback to Wilhelm Reich, a Frankfurt School member who considered matriarchal theory in psychoanalytic terms. In 1993, he wrote in "The Mass Psychology of Fascism" that matriarchy was the only genuine family type of "natural society."

Erich Fromm, another charter member of the Institute, was one of the most active advocates of matriarchal theory. Fromm was especially taken with the idea that all love and altruistic feelings were ultimately derived from the maternal love necessitated by the extended period of human pregnancy and postnatal care: Love thus was not dependent on sexuality, as Freud had supposed. In fact, sex was more often tied to hatred and destruction. Masculinity and femininity were not reflections of "essential" sexual differences, as the romantics had thought. They were derived instead from differences in life functions, which were in part socially determined.

This dogma was a precedent for today's radical feminist pronouncements appearing in newspapers and in TV programs, including TV newscasts. For its promoters, male and female roles result from cultural indoctrination – an indoctrination carried out by the male patriarchy to the detriment of women. Indeed, cultural Marxism has, in the 1990s, melded with radical feminism in the elite

Boomer generation, that throwback to the dangerous Transcendentalists of the early 19th century. A cauldron of discontent is forming in our nation, a discontent which has the potential to dismantle American civilization.

Destructive criticism of primary elements of American culture inspired the 1960s counter-culture revolution. Idealistic Boomers coming of age strove to transform the prevailing culture into its opposites, in the spirit of social revolution. Now the elite Boomers are in positions of power, and they are working to destroy the nation's historic institutions. They aim to destroy as well the heritage we call "Western Civilization." Richard Bernstein has written in his book on multiculturalism, "the Marxist revolutionary process for the past several decades in America has centered on race and sex warfare rather than class warfare" as in earlier times. This reflects a scheme more total than economics to restructure American society. As the social revolutionaries readily proclaim, their purpose is to destroy the hegemony of white males. To accomplish this, all barriers to the introduction of more women and minorities throughout the "power structure" are to be brought down by all means available. Laws and lawsuits, intimidation, and demonizing of white males as racists and sexists are pursued through the mass media and the universities. The psycho–dynamic of the revolutionary process aim for psychic disempowerment – decapitation – of those who oppose. Steve Forbes has emphasized:

> This country's founders recognized three primal values in the Declaration of Independence, and they ranked them properly: Life, liberty, and the pursuit of happiness.

Forbes observes that if the order of these fundamental human rights is switched – with happiness before liberty or liberty before life – we come to moral chaos and social anarchy.

This very condition is what Judge Robert Bork describes as "modern liberalism." He defines its characteristics as "'radical egalitarianism' (equality of outcomes rather than of opportunities) and 'radical individualism' (the drastic reduction of limit to personal gratification)." Judge Bork also identifies radical feminism as "the most destructive and fanatical" element of this modern liberalism. He further describes radical feminism as "totalitarian in spirit."

Most Americans do not realize that they, through their institutions, are being led by social revolutionaries who think in terms of the continuing destruction of the existing social order in order to create a new one. The revolutionaries are New Age Elite Boomers.18 They now control the public institutions in the United States. Their "quiet" revolution, beginning with the counter-culture revolution of their youth, is nearing completion. A key, or even a dominant element because purportedly it represents that largest political and social constituency among their potential followers, is feminism. The Marxist movement in its "quiet" cultural latter-day phase is seemingly sweeping all before it. With its sway over the media, fully in the grip of feminism, it is hard to discern the stirrings of a counter-culture. Are the elite Boomers, the New Totalitarians, the most dangerous generation in America's history? William Strauss and Neil Howe suggest so, in their book *Generations: The History of America's Future – 1584 – 2069.* 19 James Kurth writes:

> The United States itself has become a great power that opposes much of what was once thought of as Western Civilization, especially its cultural achievements and its social arrangements. The major American elites – those in power in politics, business, the media, and academia – now use American power, especially the "soft power" of information, communications, and popular entertainment, to displace Western Civilization not only in America but also in Europe.

Will American men, of every race, and more traditionalist women of every age and circumstances – who may well be a silent majority of their sex – rise to challenge Political Correctness? Or will American men continue in voluntary submission toward a future of peonage under a new American matriarchy? Would that be a precursor to a condition of anarchy, and an end to America's experiment with democracy? It may well be that the fate of American civilization depends on American men steadfastly resisting Politically Correct feminism. Even more, they must resourcefully oppose the wider grip of Political Correctness, the cultural Marxism for which radical feminism is only one avenue of attack.

READINGS ON THE FRANKFURT SCHOOL

This is the sixth and final chapter in the Free Congress Foundation's book on Political Correctness, or – to call it by its real name – cultural Marxism. It is a short bibliographical essay intended not as an exhaustive resource for scholars but as a guide for interested citizens who want to learn more about the ideology that is taking over America.

As readers of the earlier chapters in this book already know, to understand Political Correctness and the threat it poses it is necessary to understand its history, particularly the history of the institution most responsible for creating it, the Frankfurt School. The Frankfurt School, or the Institute for Social Research as it was formally known, was established at Frankfurt University in Germany in 1923. This fact alone is important, because it tells us that Political Correctness is not merely a leftover of the American student rebellion of the 1960s.

Another fact from that long-ago year, 1923, is equally significant: the intended name for the Frankfurt School was the Institute for Marxism. The Institute's father and funder, Felix Weil, wrote in 1971 that he "wanted the Institute to become known, and perhaps famous, due to its contributions to Marxism as a scientific discipline..."1 Beginning a tradition Political Correctness still carries on, Weil and others decided that they could operate more effectively if they concealed their Marxism; hence, on reflection, they chose the neutral-sounding name, the Institute for Social Research (Insitut für Sozialforschung). But "Weil's heartfelt wish was still to create a foundation similar to the Marx-Engels Institute in Moscow – equipped with a staff of professors and students, with libraries and archives – and one day to present it to a German Soviet Republic." In 1933, this disguised "Institute for Marxism" left Germany and reestablished itself in New York City, where in time it shifted its focus to injecting its ideology into American society. The most readable English-language history of the Frankfurt School is Martin Jay's book, The Dialectical Imagination: A History of the Frankfurt School and the Institute for Social Research, 1932 - 1950 (University of California Press, Berkeley, CA, 1973 – new edition in 1996). This book is in print in paperback and can be ordered through any bookstore. The reader should be aware that Jay's book is, in the words of another work on the Frankfurt School, a "semiofficial' history3, which is to say that it is largely uncritical. Like virtually all other English-language authors on the Institute, Jay is on the political left. Nonetheless, the book provides a solid factual introduction to the Frankfurt School, and the reader should have little trouble discerning in it the roots and origins of today's Political Correctness.

In his first chapter, "The Creation of the Institut für Sozialforschung and Its First Frankfurt Years," Jay lays bare the Institute's Marxist origins and nature, and equally its efforts to conceal both: "The original idea of calling it the Institut für Marxismus (Institute for Marxism) was abandoned as too provocative, and a more Aesopian alternative was sought (not for the last time in the Frankfurt School's history)." Of the Institute's first director, Carl Grünberg, Jay writes, "Grünberg concluded his opening address by clearly stating his personal allegiance to Marxism as a scientific methodology. Just as liberalism, state socialism, and the historical school had institutional homes elsewhere, so Marxism would be the ruling principle at the Institut."5 Jay's first chapter also introduces the Institute's critical shift that laid the basis for today's Political Correctness, a.k.a. cultural Marxism: "if it can be said that in early years of its history the Institut concerned itself primarily with an analysis of bourgeois society's socio-economic substructure, in the years after 1930 its prime interest lay in its cultural superstructure." The second chapter, "The Genius of Critical Theory," gets at the heart of the "Critical Studies" departments that now serve as the fonts of Political Correctness on American college campuses. All of these are branches and descendants of the Critical Theory first developed in the 1930s by the Frankfurt School. The term "Critical Theory" is itself something of a play on words. One is tempted to ask, "OK, what is the theory?" The answer is, "The theory is to criticize." Jay writes, "Critical Theory, as its name implies, was expressed through a series of critiques of other thinkers and philosophical traditions...Only by confronting it in its own terms, as a gadly of other systems, can it be fully understood." The goal of Critical Theory was not truth, but praxis, or revolutionary action: bringing the current society and culture down through unremitting, destructive criticism. According to Jay, "The true object of Marxism, Horkheimer argued (Max Horkheimer succeeded Carl Grünberg as director of the Institute in July, 1930), was not the uncovering of immutable truths, but the fostering of social change."

The central question facing the Institute in the early 1930s was how to apply Marxism to the culture. The title of Jay's third chapter gives the answer: "The Integration of Psychoanalysis." Here, Jay's book falls down to some extent, in that it does not offer a clear understanding of how the Institute integrated Marx and Freud. The answer appears to be that Freud's later critiques were made conditional on a capitalist, bourgeois order: a revolutionary, post-capitalist society could "liberate" man from his Freudian repression.

Here again one sees key aspects of Political Correctness emerging, including a demand for sexual "liberation" and the attack on "patriarchal" Western culture. If the precise nature of the blending of Marx and Freud is left open by Jay, his next chapter makes the blend's application clear: "The Institute's First Studies of Authority." The Institute left Germany for New York in 1933 because the Nazis came to power in Germany. Not surprisingly, one of the Institute's first tasks in New York was to oppose Nazism. It did so largely by concocting a psychological "test" for an "authoritarian personality." Supposedly, people with this authoritarian personality were likely to support Nazism. Both the concept and the methodology were doubtful at best. But the Institute's work laid down an important tool for the left, namely a notion that anyone on the right was psychologically unbalanced. And it marked a key turning for the Institute in the birth of Political Correctness in America, in that the empirical research the studies demanded was done on Americans.

Ultimately, the result was Institute member Theodor Adorno's vastly influential book, The Authoritarian Personality, published in 1950.

Jay's fifth chapter, "The Institute's Analysis of Nazism," continues the theme of the "authoritarian personality." But his sixth, "Aesthetic Theory and the Critique of Mass Culture," provides an answer to the question of why most "serious" modern art and music is so awful. It is intended to be. Theodor Adorno was the Institute's lead figure on high culture – he began life as a music critic and promoter of Schönberg – and his view was that in the face of the "repressiveness" of bourgeois society, art could only be "true" if it were alienating, reflecting the alienated society around it. Jay quotes Adorno: "A successful work…is not one which resolves objective contradictions in a spurious harmony, but one which expresses the idea of harmony negatively by embodying the contradictions, pure and uncompromised, in its innermost structure."

Adorno despised the new mass culture – film, radio, and jazz – in what seems to be a case of missed opportunity: today, the entertainment industry is the single most powerful promoter of Political Correctness. Another key Frankfurt School figure, Walter Benjamin, did see the potential: "he paradoxically held out hope for the progressive potential of politicized, collectivized art."10 At some point, someone – the question of who lies beyond the boundaries of Jay's book – put Benjamin's perception together with the Frankfurt School's general view, which Jay summarizes as "the Institut came to feel that the culture industry enslaved men in far more subtle and effective ways than the crude methods of domination practiced in earlier eras."11 In the remainder of the book, Jay traces the (sort of) empirical work of the Institute in the 1940s, which was beset by the same problems as their earlier survey "research," and follows the Institute in its return to Frankfurt, Germany after World War II. But by this point, the reader will already have the picture. He will have seen how Marxism was translated from economic into cultural terms; discerned the themes of sexual liberation, feminism, "victims" and so on that make up today's Political Correctness; and found in Critical Theory the origins of the endless wailing about "racism, sexism and homophobia" that "PC" pours forth. One key piece of history is missing: "an analysis of Marcuse's influential transmission of the Frankfurt School's work to a new American audience in the 1960s,"12 as Jay puts it in his epilogue. Also, Jay curiously passes over with only the most minimal discussion the effective move of the Institute, in the persons of Horkheimer and Adorno, to Los Angeles during the war. Did the connections they built there play any role in injecting the Frankfurt School's philosophy into American film and, after the war, television? Jay does not touch upon the subject.

But for the reader new to the Frankfurt School as the source of today's Political Correctness, Jay's The Dialectical Imagination offers a solid base. The book concludes with an extensive (though not annotated) bibliography of works by and about the Frankfurt School.

As to other accessible works about the Frankfurt School, the definitive modern work in German has recently been translated into English: The Frankfurt School: Its History, Theories and Political Significance by Rolf Wiggershaus, (translated by Michael Robertson, The MIT Press, Cambridge, MA, first paperback edition 1995). This covers much of the same ground as Martin Jay's book, although it also follows the Institute from its post-war return to Germany up to Adorno's death in 1969. Wiggershaus is more detailed than Jay, and, although he too is on the left politically, he is more critical than Jay. In the book's Afterword, Wiggershaus offers a brief look (and a hostile one) at some German conservative critiques of the Frankfurt School. A picture emerges that will seem familiar to Americans entrapped in the coils of Political Correctness:

Since the publication in 1970 of his book The Poverty of Critical Theory, Rohrmoser has promulgated, in constantly varying forms, the view that Marcuse, Adorno, and Horkheimer were the terrorists' intellectual foster-parents, who were using cultural revolution to destroy the traditions of the Christian West. Academics such as Ernst Topitsch and Kurt Sontheimer, who saw themselves as educators and liberal democrats, followed in Rohrmoser's footsteps. In 1972 Topitsch, a critical rationalist who was Professor of Philosophy in Graz, had stated that behind the slogans of "rational discussion" and "dialogue free of domination" there was being established at the universities "a distinct terrorism of political convictions such as never existed before, even under Nazi tyranny."

Additional works on the Frankfurt School include:

- The Frankfurt School by T.B. Bottomore (Tavistock, London, 1984). Another history written by a sympathizer; you are better off with Jay or Wiggershaus.
- "The New Dark Age: The Frankfurt School and 'Political Correctness'" by Michael Minnicino, in Fidelio, Vol. 1, No. 1, Winter 1992 (KMW Publishing, Washington, DC) One of the few looks at the Frankfurt School by someone not a sympathizer, this long journal article explains the role of the Institute for Social Research in creating the ideology we now know as "Political Correctness." Unfortunately, its value is reduced by some digressions that lack credibility.
- Angela Davis: An Autobiography by Angela Davis (Random House, New York 1974) Angela Davis, a leading American black radical and Communist Party member, was described by Frankfurt School member Herbert Marcuse as "my best student." She also studied in Frankfurt under Adorno. This book shows the link between the Institute for Social Research and the New Left of the 1960s through the eyes of a key participant.
- The Young Lukacs and the Origins of Western Marxism by Andrew Arato (Seabury Press, New York, 1979). The author is, as usual, a sympathizer, but this work shows the key role Lukacs played in the thinking of the Frankfurt School and, later, the New Left.
- The Origin of Negative Dialectics: Theodor W. Adorno, Walter Benjamin and the Frankfurt Institute by Susan Buck-Morss (Free Press, New York, 1977). An important book

on the relationship of the Frankfurt School and Critical Theory to the New Left.

- Introduction to Critical Theory: Horkheimer to Habermas by David Held (University of California Press, Berkeley, 1980). Yet another history by a fan of the Frankfurt School, but valuable for its discussion of the impact of Nietzsche on key Frankfurt School figures.

Beyond these secondary works lies the vast literature produced by members of the Frankfurt School itself. Some key works were written in English, and many of those written in German are available in translation. As is usually the case with Marxist works, the prose style and vocabulary are often so convoluted as to make them almost unreadable. Further, the refusal of the Frankfurt School to make its own future vision plain led many of its members to write in aphorisms, which adds yet another layer of impenetrableness.

One work, however, is of such importance that it must be recommended despite its difficulty: Eros and Civilization by Herbert Marcuse (Beacon Press, Boston, first paperback edition in 1974 and still in print). Subtitled A Philosophical Inquiry into Freud, this book holds center stage for two reasons. First, it completes the task of integrating Marx and Freud. While the Marxism is *sotto voce*, the whole framework of the book is in fact Marxist, and it is through the framework that Freud is considered. Second, Eros and Civilization and its author were the key means of transmission by which the intellectual work of the Frankfurt School was injected into the student rebellion of the 1960s. This book became the bible of the young radicals who took over America's college campuses from 1965 onward, and who are still there as faculty members. In brief, Eros and Civilization urges total rebellion against traditional Western culture – the "Great Refusal" – and promises a Candyland utopia of free sex and no work to those who join the revolution. About two-thirds of the way through the book, Marcuse offers this summary of its arguments:

Our definition of the specific historical character of the established reality principle led to a reexamination of what Freud considered to be universal validity. We questioned this validity in view of the historical possibility of the abolition of the repressive controls imposed by civilization. The very achievements of this civilization seemed to make the performance principle obsolete, to make the repressive utilization of the instincts archaic. But the idea of a non-repressive civilization on the basis of the achievements of the performance principle encountered the argument that instinctual liberation (and consequently total liberation) would explode civilization itself, since the latter is sustained only through renunciation and work (labor) – in other words, through the repressive utilization of instinctual energy. Freed from these constraints, man would exist without work and without order; he would fall back into nature, which would destroy culture. To meet this argument, we recalled certain archetypes of imagination which, in contrast to the culture-heroes of repressive productivity, symbolized creative receptivity. These archetypes envisioned the fulfillment of man and nature, not through domination and exploitation, but through release of inherent libidinal forces. We then set ourselves the task of "verifying" these symbols – that is to say, demonstrating their truth value as symbols of a reality beyond the performance principle. We thought that the representative content of the Orphic and Narcissistic images was the erotic reconciliation (union) of man and nature in the aesthetic attitude, where order is beauty and work is play.14 Marcuse continues after this summary to lay out the erotic content of the "reality beyond the performance principle," i.e., a new civilization where work and productivity were unimportant. "The basic experience in this (aesthetic) dimension is sensuous rather than conceptual,"15 that is, feelings are more important than logic: "The discipline of aesthetics installs the *order of sensuousness* as against the *order of reason*."

"In German, *sensuousness* and *sensuality* are still rendered by one and the same term: *Sinnlichkeit.* It connotes instinctual (especially sexual) gratification…17 No longer used as a full-time instrument of labor, the body would be resexualized… (which) would first manifest itself in a reactivation of all erotogenic zones and, consequently, in a resurgence of pre-genital polymorphous sexuality and in a decline of genital supremacy. The body in its entirety would become an object of cathexis, a thing to be enjoyed – an instrument of pleasure. This change in the value and scope of libidinal relations would lead to a disintegration of the institutions in which the private interpersonal relations have been organized, particularly the monogamic and patriarchal family."

This in a book which Marcuse dedicated to Sophie Marcuse, his wife of fifty years! It is easy to see how this message – "If it feels good, do it" – published in 1955 resonated with the student rebels of the 1960s. Marcuse understood what most of the rest of his Frankfurt School colleagues did not: the way to destroy Western civilization – the objective set forth by George Lukacs in 1919 – was not through abstruse theory, but through sex, drugs, and rock 'n' roll. Marcuse wrote other works for the new generation that spawned the New Left – One Dimensional Man (1964), Critique of Pure Tolerance (1965), An Essay on Liberation (1969), Counterrevolution and Revolt (1972). But Eros and Civilization was and remains the key work, the one that put the match to the tinder. Other central works by members of the Frankfurt School include:

- The Authoritarian Personality by Theodor Adorno (Harper, New York, 1950). This book is the basis for everything that followed that portrayed conservatism as a psychological defect. It had enormous impact, not least on education theory.
- Dialectic of Enlightenment by Theodor Adorno and Max Horkheimer (trans. by John Cumming, Verso, London, 1979). A complex philosophical work written during World War II largely in response to Nazism (and extensively devoted to discussions of anti-Semitism), this work seeks to find a kernel of "liberating" reason in the ruins of the Enlightenment.
- Minima Moralia: Reflections from a Damaged Life by Theodor Adorno (trans. E.F.N. Jophcott, New Left Books,

London, 1974). A book of aphorisms, almost entirely incomprehensible, but the effective conclusion of Adorno's work.

- Escape from Freedom by Erich Fromm (Farrar & Rinehart, New York, 1941, still in print in paperback) Fromm was the Institute's "happy face," and this book was often required reading at colleges in the 1960s. The thesis is that man's nature causes him to throw his freedom away and embrace fascism unless he "masters society and subordinates the economic machine to the purposes of human happiness," i.e., adopts socialism. At this point Fromm was in the process of breaking away from the Institute and his subsequent works cannot be considered as part of the Frankfurt School corpus.
- Eclipse of Reason (Oxford University Press, New York, 1947). Essentially a sequel to Dialectic of Enlightenment, the book is heavily the work of Adorno and other Frankfurt School personages, although only Horkheimer name appeared on it. Its contents are based on a series of lectures Horkheimer gave at Columbia University in 1944. The prose style is surprisingly readable, but the contents are odd; there is throughout a strong nostalgia, which was normally anathema to the Frankfurt School. The key chapter, "The Revolt of Nature," reflects a strange Retro anarchism: "The victory of civilization is too complete to be true. Therefore, adjustment in our times involves an element of resentment and suppressed fury."
- Critical Theory: Selected Essays by Max Horkheimer (trans. Matthew O'Connell, Seabury Press, New York, 1972). The essay, "Traditional and Critical Theory" is especially important.
- The Essential Frankfurt School Reader, ed. By Andrew Arato and Eike Gebhardt (Continuum, New York, 1982, in print in paperback) Not an introduction to the Frankfurt School, but rather a reprinting of Frankfurt School essays

not available elsewhere, this book is more useful to the specialist than the novice. Nonetheless, both the editors' lengthy introductions and some of the essays are useful (once again, the editors are solidly on the Left politically, and their style is as heavy as that of the Frankfurt School's members). This small bibliography will be enough to get an interested reader started; the full literature on and by the Frankfurt School is immense, as the bibliographies in Jay's and Wiggershaus's books attest. What has been missing from it, at least in English, is a readable book, written for the layman, that explains the Frankfurt School and its works in terms of the creation of Political Correctness. This short volume is at least a start in filling that gap.

7

Politics in South Korea and United States

S.-North Korea relations developed primarily during the Korean War, but in recent years have been largely defined by the United States' suspicions regarding North Korea's nuclear programs, and North Korea's perception of an imminent US attack.

BACKGROUND

Although hostility between the two countries remains largely a product of Cold War politics, there were earlier conflicts and animosity between the US and Korea. In the mid-19th century Korea closed its borders to Western trade, much as North Korea has today. In the General Sherman Incident, Korean forces attacked a US gunboat sent to negotiate a trade treaty and killed its crew, after it defied instructions from Korean officials. A US retribution attack, the Sinmiyangyo, followed.

Korea and the US ultimately established trade relations in 1882. Relations soured again when the US negotiated peace in the Russo-Japanese War. Japan persuaded the US to accept Korea as part of Japan's sphere of influence, and the US did not protest when Japan annexed Korea five years later. Korean nationalists petitioned the US to support their cause at the Versailles Treaty conference under Woodrow Wilson's principle of national self-determination, without success.

The US divided Korea after World War II along the 38th parallel, intending it as a temporary measure. However, the breakdown of relations between the US and USSR prevented a reunification. The North Korean government came to see the US as an imperalist successor to Japan, a view it still holds today. The United States maintains economic sanctions against the DPRK under the Trading with the Enemy Act.

DENUCLEARIZATION OF THE KOREAN PENINSULA

North Korea joined the nuclear Non-Proliferation Treaty (NPT) as a non-nuclear weapons state in 1985, and North and South Korean talks begun in 1990 resulted in a 1992 Denuclearization Statement. However, lack of progress in developing and implementing an agreement with the International Atomic Energy Agency (IAEA) for the inspection of the North's nuclear facilities led to North Korea's March 1993 announcement of its withdrawal from the NPT. A UN Security Council resolution in May 1993 urged North Korea to cooperate with the IAEA and to implement the 1992 North-South Denuclearization Statement. It also urged all member states to encourage North Korea to respond positively to this resolution and to facilitate a solution of the nuclear issue.

U.S.-North Korea talks beginning in June 1993 led to the U.S.-North Korea Agreed Framework in October 1994:

- North Korea agreed to freeze its existing plutonium enrichment program, to be monitored by the IAEA;
- Both sides agreed to cooperate to replace North Korea's graphite-moderated reactors with light water reactor (LWR) power plants, to be financed and supplied by an international consortium (later identified as the Korean Peninsula Energy Development Organization or KEDO);
- The United States and North Korea agreed to work together to store safely the spent fuel from the five-megawatt reactor and dispose of it in a safe manner that does not involve reprocessing in North Korea;

- The two sides agreed to move toward full normalization of political and economic relations;
- Both sides agreed to work together for peace and security on a nuclear-free Korean Peninsula; and
- Both sides agreed to work together to strengthen the international nuclear non-proliferation regime.

In accordance with the terms of the Agreed Framework, North Korea decided to freeze its nuclear program and cooperate with United States and IAEA verification efforts, and in January 1995 the U.S. eased economic sanctions against North Korea. North Korea agreed to accept the decisions of KEDO, the financier and supplier of the LWRs, with respect to provision of the reactors. KEDO subsequently identified Sinpo as the LWR project site and held a groundbreaking ceremony in August 1997. In December 1999, KEDO and the (South) Korea Electric Power Corporation (KEPCO) signed the Turnkey Contract (TKC), permitting fullscale construction of the LWRs. In January 1995, as called for in the Agreed Framework, the United States and North Korea negotiated a method to store safely the spent fuel from the five-megawatt reactor. According to this method, U.S. and North Korean operators would work together to can the spent fuel and store the canisters in the spent fuel pond. Actual canning began in 1995. In April 2000, canning of all accessible spent fuel rods and rod fragments was declared complete.

In 1998, the United States identified an underground site in Kumchang-ni, which it suspected of being nuclear-related. In March 1999, North Korea agreed to grant the U.S. "satisfactory access" to the site. In October 2000, during Special Envoy Jo Myong Rok's visit to Washington, and after two visits to the site by teams of U.S. experts, the U.S. announced in a Joint Communiqué with North Korea that U.S. concerns about the site had been resolved.

As called for in Dr. William Perry's official review of U.S. policy toward North Korea, the United States and North Korea launched new negotiations in May 2000 called the Agreed Framework Implementation Talks.

NORTH KOREA POLICY UNDER GEORGE W. BUSH

Following the inauguration of President George W. Bush in January 2001, the new Administration began a review of North Korea policy. At the conclusion of that review, the Administration announced on June 6, 2001, that it had decided to pursue continued dialogue with North Korea on the full range of issues of concern to the Administration, including North Korea's conventional force posture, missile development and export programs, human rights practices, and humanitarian issues. In 2002, the Administration also became aware that North Korea was developing a uranium enrichment program for nuclear weapons purposes. U.S.-D.P.R.K. tensions mounted, when Bush categorized North Korea as part of the "Axis of Evil" in his 2002 State of the Union address.

When U.S.-D.P.R.K. direct dialogue resumed in October 2002, this uranium- enrichment program was high on the U.S. agenda. North Korean officials acknowledged to a U.S. delegation, headed by Assistant Secretary of State for East Asian and Pacific Affairs James A. Kelly, the existence of the uranium enrichment program. Such a program violated North Korea's obligations under the NPT and its commitments in the 1992 North-South Denuclearization Declaration and the 1994 Agreed Framework. The U.S. side stated that North Korea would have to terminate the program before any further progress could be made in U.S.-D.P.R.K. relations. The U.S. side also made clear that if this program were verifiably eliminated, the U.S. would be prepared to work with North Korea on the development of a fundamentally new relationship. In November 2002, the members of KEDO agreed to suspend heavy fuel oil shipments to North Korea pending a resolution of the nuclear dispute.

In December 2002, Spanish troops boarded and detained a shipment of Scud missiles from North Korea destined for Yemen, at the United States' request. After two days, the United States released the ship to continue its shipment to Yemen. This further strained the relationship between the US and North Korea, with North Korea characterizing the boarding an "act of piracy".

In late 2002 and early 2003, North Korea terminated the freeze on its existing plutonium-based nuclear facilities, expelled IAEA inspectors and removed seals and monitoring equipment, quit the NPT, and resumed reprocessing of spent nuclear fuel to extract plutonium for weapons purposes. North Korea subsequently announced that it was taking these steps to provide itself with a deterrent force in the face of U.S. threats and the U.S.' "hostile policy". Beginning in mid-2003, the North repeatedly claimed to have completed reprocessing of the spent fuel rods previously frozen at Yongbyon and later publicly said that the resulting fissile material would be used to bolster its "nuclear deterrent force". There is no independent confirmation of North Korea's claims.

President Bush has stated that the United States has no plans at this time to invade North Korea now or in the forseeable future. He also stated that the United States intends to make every effort to achieve a peaceful end to North Korea's nuclear program in cooperation with North Korea's neighbors, who have also expressed concern over the threat to regional stability and security they believe it poses. The Bush Administration's stated goal is the complete, verifiable, and irreversible elimination of North Korea's nuclear weapons program. North Korea's neighbors have joined the United States in supporting a nuclear weapons-free Korean Peninsula.

In the last months of 2005, relations between the countries have been further strained by US allegations of North Korean counterfeiting of American dollars. The US alleges that North Korea produces $15 million worth of 'supernotes' every year, and has induced banks in Macau and elsewhere to end business with North Korea.

SIX-PARTY TALKS : SIX-PARTY TALKS

In early 2003 multilateral talks were proposed to be held among the six most relevant parties aimed at reaching a settlement through diplomatic means. North Korea initially opposed such a process, maintaining that the nuclear dispute was purely a bilateral matter between themselves and the United States. However, under pressure from its neighbors and with the active involvement of the People's Republic of China, North Korea agreed to preliminary three-party talks with China and the United States in Beijing in April 2003.

After this meeting, North Korea then agreed to six-party talks, between the United States, North Korea, South Korea, China, Japan and Russia. The first round of talks was held in August 2003, with subsequent rounds being held at regular intervals. However, since the last round (5th round, 1st phase) was held in November 2005, North Korea has refused to return to the talks. This was in retaliation for the US freezing offshore North Korean bank accounts in Macau.

In early 2005, US government told its East Asia allies that Pyongyang had exported nuclear material to Libya. This backfired when the Asia allies discovered that US government had concealed involvement of Pakistan; a key U.S. ally was the weapon's middle man. In March 2005, Condoleezza Rice had to travel to East Asia in an effort to repair the damage.

2006 Nuclear Test

U.S. intelligence agencies have been unable to confirm that a test has occurred, but are presently looking into the situation. Tony Snow, President George W. Bush's White House Press Secretary, said that the United States would now go to the United Nations to determine "what our next steps should be in response to this very serious step."President Bush stated in a televised speech Monday morning, that such a claim of a test is a "provocative act" and U.S condemns such acts. President Bush stated that the United States is "committed to diplomacy" but will "continue to protect America and America's interests."

Press Say About This.

WASHINGTON North Korea said Monday that it had set off its first nuclear test, becoming the eighth country in history, and arguably the most unstable and most dangerous, to proclaim that it has joined the club of nuclear weapons states. The test came just two days after the country was warned by the United Nations Security Council that the action could lead to severe consequences.

American officials cautioned that they had not yet received any confirmation that the test had occurred. The United States Geological Survey said it had detected a tremor of 4.2 magnitude on the Korean Peninsula.

China called the test a "flagrant and brazen" violation of international opinion and said it "firmly opposes" North Korea's conduct.

Senior Bush administration officials said that they had little reason to doubt the announcement, and warned that the test would usher in a new era of confrontation with the isolated and unpredictable country run by President Kim Jong-il.

Early Monday morning, even before the test was confirmed, Bush administration officials were holding conference calls to discuss ways to further cut off a country that is already subject to sanctions, and hard-liners said the moment had arrived for neighboring countries, especially China and Russia, to cut off the trade and oil supplies that have been Kim's lifeline.

In South Korea, the country that fought a bloody war with the North for three years and has lived with an uneasy truce and failed efforts at reconciliation for more than half a century, officials said they believed that an explosion occurred around 10:36 p.m. New York time - 11:36 a.m. Monday in Korea.

They identified the source of the explosion as North Hamgyong Province, roughly the area where American spy satellites have been focused for several years on a variety of suspected underground test sites.

That was less than an hour after North Korean officials had called their counterparts in China and warned them that a test was just minutes away. The Chinese, who have been North Korea's main ally for 60 years but have grown increasingly frustrated by the its defiance of Beijing, sent an emergency alert to Washington through the United States Embassy in Beijing. Within minutes, President Bush was notified, shortly after 10 p.m., by his national security adviser, Stephen Hadley, that a test was imminent.

North Korea's decision to conduct the test demonstrated what the world has suspected for years: the country has joined India, Pakistan and Israel as one of the world's "undeclared" nuclear powers. India and Pakistan conducted tests in 1998; Israel has never acknowledged conducting a test or possessing a weapon. But by actually setting off a weapon, if that is proven, the North has chosen to end years of carefully crafted and diplomatically useful ambiguity about its abilities.

The North's decision to set off a nuclear device could profoundly change the politics of Asia.

The test occurred only a week after Japan installed a new, more nationalistic prime minister, Shinzo Abe, and just as the country was renewing a debate about whether its ban on possessing nuclear weapons - deeply felt in a country that saw two of its cities incinerated in 1945 - still makes strategic sense.

And it shook the peninsula just as Abe was arriving in South Korea for the first time as prime minister, in an effort to repair a badly strained relationship, having just visited with Chinese leaders in Beijing. It places his untested administration in the midst of one of the region's biggest security crises in years, and one whose outcome will be watched closely in Iran and other states suspected of attempting to follow the path that North Korea has taken.

Now, Tokyo and Washington are expected to put even more pressure on the South Korean government to terminate its "sunshine policy" of trade, tourism and openings to the North - a policy that has been the source of enormous tension between Seoul and Washington since Bush took office.

The explosion was the product of nearly four decades of work by North Korea, one of the world's poorest and most isolated countries. The nation of 23 million people appears constantly fearful that its far richer, more powerful neighbors - and particularly the United States - will try to unseat its leadership. The country's founder, Kim Il-sung, who died in 1994, emerged from the Korean War determined to equal the power of the United States, and acutely aware that Gen. Douglas MacArthur had requested nuclear weapons to use against his country.

But it took decades to put together the technology, and only in the past few years has the North appeared to have made a political decision to speed forward. "I think they just had their military plan to demonstrate that no one could mess with them, and they weren't going to be deterred, not even by the Chinese," a senior American official who deals with the North said late Sunday evening. "In the end, there was just no stopping them."

But the explosion was also the product of more than two decades of diplomatic failure, spread over at least three presidencies. American spy satellites saw the North building a good-size nuclear reactor in the early 1980's, and by the early 1990's the C.I.A. estimated that the country could have one or two nuclear weapons. But a series of diplomatic efforts to "freeze" the nuclear program - including a 1994 accord signed with the Clinton administration - ultimately broke down, amid distrust and recriminations on both sides.

Three years ago, just as President Bush was sending American troops toward Iraq, the North threw out the few remaining weapons inspectors living at their nuclear complex in Yongbyon, and moved 8,000 nuclear fuel rods they had kept under lock and key. Those rods contained enough plutonium, experts said, to produce five or six nuclear weapons, though it is unclear how many the North now stockpiles.

For years, some diplomats assumed that the North was using that ambiguity to trade away its nuclear capability, for recognition, security guarantees, aid and trade with the West. But in the end, the country's reclusive leader, Kim Jong-il, who inherited the mantle of leadership from his father, still called the "Great Leader," appears to have concluded that the surest way of getting what he seeks is to demonstrate that he has the capability to strike back if attacked.

Assessing the nature of that ability is difficult. If the test occurred as the North claimed, it is unclear whether it was an actual bomb or a more primitive device. Some experts cautioned that it could try to fake an explosion, setting off conventional explosives; the only way to know for sure will be if American "sniffer" planes, patrolling the North Korean coast, pick up evidence of nuclear byproducts in the air.

Even then, it is not clear that the North could fabricate that bomb into a weapon that could fit atop its missiles, one of the country's few significant exports.

But the big fear about North Korea, American officials have long said, has less to do with its ability to lash out than it does with its proclivity to proliferate. The country has sold its missiles and other weapons to Iran, Syria and Pakistan; at various moments in the six-party talks that have gone on for the past few years, North Korean representatives have threatened to sell nuclear weapons. But in a statement issued last week, announcing that it intends to set off a test, the country said it would not sell its nuclear products.

The fear of proliferation prompted President Bush to declare in 2003 that the United States would never "tolerate" a nuclear-armed North Korea. He has never defined what he means by "tolerate," and on Sunday night Tony Snow, Bush's press secretary, said that, assuming the report of the test is accurate, the United States would now go to the United Nations to determine "what our next steps should be in response to this very serious step."

Nuclear testing is often considered a necessary step to proving a weapon's reliability as well as the most forceful way for a nation to declare its status as a nuclear power.

"Once they do that, it's serious," said Harold M. Agnew, a former director of the Los Alamos weapons laboratory, which designed most of the nation's nuclear arms. "Otherwise, the North Koreans are just jerking us around."

Networks of seismometers that detect faint trembles in the earth and track distant rumbles are the best way to spot an underground nuclear test.

The big challenge is to distinguish the signatures of earthquakes from those of nuclear blasts. Typically, the shock waves from nuclear explosions begin with a sharp spike as earth and rock are compressed violently. The signal then tends to become fuzzier as surface rumblings and shudders and after shocks create seismologic mayhem.

With earthquakes, it is usually the opposite. A gentle jostling suddenly becomes much bigger and more violent.

Most of the world's seismic networks that look for nuclear blasts are designed to detect explosions as small as one kiloton, or equal to 1,000 tons of high explosives. On instruments for detecting earthquakes, such a blast would measure a magnitude of about 4, like a small tremor.

Philip E. Coyle III, a former head of weapons testing at the Pentagon and former director of nuclear testing for the Lawrence Livermore National Laboratory, a weapons-design center in California, said the North Koreans could learn much from a nuclear test even if it was small by world standards or less than an unqualified success.

"It would not be totally surprising if it was a fizzle and they said it was a success because they learned something," he said. "We did that sometimes. We had a missile defense test not so long ago that failed, but the Pentagon said it was a success because they learned something, which I agree with. Failures can teach you a lot."

William J. Broad contributed reporting from New York, and Thom Shanker from Washington.

WASHINGTON North Korea said Monday that it had set off its first nuclear test, becoming the eighth country in history, and arguably the most unstable and most dangerous, to proclaim that it has joined the club of nuclear weapons states.

The test came just two days after the country was warned by the United Nations Security Council that the action could lead to severe consequences.

American officials cautioned that they had not yet received any confirmation that the test had occurred. The United States Geological Survey said it had detected a tremor of 4.2 magnitude on the Korean Peninsula.

China called the test a "flagrant and brazen" violation of international opinion and said it "firmly opposes" North Korea's conduct.

Senior Bush administration officials said that they had little reason to doubt the announcement, and warned that the test would usher in a new era of confrontation with the isolated and unpredictable country run by President Kim Jong-il.

Early Monday morning, even before the test was confirmed, Bush administration officials were holding conference calls to discuss ways to further cut off a country that is already subject to sanctions, and hard-liners said the moment had arrived for neighboring countries, especially China and Russia, to cut off the trade and oil supplies that have been Kim's lifeline.

In South Korea, the country that fought a bloody war with the North for three years and has lived with an uneasy truce and failed efforts at reconciliation for more than half a century, officials said they believed that an explosion occurred around 10:36 p.m. New York time - 11:36 a.m. Monday in Korea.

They identified the source of the explosion as North Hamgyong Province, roughly the area where American spy satellites have been focused for several years on a variety of suspected underground test sites.

That was less than an hour after North Korean officials had called their counterparts in China and warned them that a test was just minutes away. The Chinese, who have been North Korea's main ally for 60 years but have grown increasingly frustrated by the its defiance of Beijing, sent an emergency alert to Washington through the United States Embassy in Beijing. Within minutes, President Bush was notified, shortly after 10 p.m., by his national security adviser, Stephen Hadley, that a test was imminent.

North Korea's decision to conduct the test demonstrated what the world has suspected for years: the country has joined India, Pakistan and Israel as one of the world's "undeclared" nuclear powers. India and Pakistan conducted tests in 1998; Israel has never acknowledged conducting a test or possessing a weapon. But by actually setting off a weapon, if that is proven, the North has chosen to end years of carefully crafted and diplomatically useful ambiguity about its abilities.

The North's decision to set off a nuclear device could profoundly change the politics of Asia.

The test occurred only a week after Japan installed a new, more nationalistic prime minister, Shinzo Abe, and just as the country was renewing a debate about whether its ban on possessing nuclear weapons - deeply felt in a country that saw two of its cities incinerated in 1945 - still makes strategic sense.

And it shook the peninsula just as Abe was arriving in South Korea for the first time as prime minister, in an effort to repair a badly strained relationship, having just visited with Chinese leaders in Beijing. It places his untested administration in the midst of one of the region's biggest security crises in years, and one whose outcome will be watched closely in Iran and other states suspected of attempting to follow the path that North Korea has taken.

Now, Tokyo and Washington are expected to put even more pressure on the South Korean government to terminate its "sunshine policy" of trade, tourism and openings to the North - a policy that has been the source of enormous tension between Seoul and Washington since Bush took office.

The explosion was the product of nearly four decades of work by North Korea, one of the world's poorest and mcst isolated countries. The nation of 23 million people appears constantly fearful that its far richer, more powerful neighbors - and particularly the United States - will try to unseat its leadership. The country's founder, Kim Il-sung, who died in 1994, emerged from the Korean War determined to equal the power of the United States, and acutely aware that Gen. Douglas MacArthur had requested nuclear weapons to use against his country.

But it took decades to put together the technology, and only in the past few years has the North appeared to have made a political decision to speed forward. "I think they just had their military plan to demonstrate that no one could mess with them, and they weren't going to be deterred, not even by the Chinese," a senior American official who deals with the North said late Sunday evening. "In the end, there was just no stopping them."

But the explosion was also the product of more than two decades of diplomatic failure, spread over at least three presidencies. American spy satellites saw the North building a good-size nuclear reactor in the early 1980's, and by the early 1990's the C.I.A. estimated that the country could have one or two nuclear weapons. But a series of diplomatic efforts to "freeze" the nuclear program - including a 1994 accord signed with the Clinton administration - ultimately broke down, amid distrust and recriminations on both sides.

Three years ago, just as President Bush was sending American troops toward Iraq, the North threw out the few remaining weapons inspectors living at their nuclear complex in Yongbyon, and moved 8,000 nuclear fuel rods they had kept under lock and key. Those rods contained enough plutonium, experts said, to produce five or six nuclear weapons, though it is unclear how many the North now stockpiles.

For years, some diplomats assumed that the North was using that ambiguity to trade away its nuclear capability, for recognition, security guarantees, aid and trade with the West. But in the end, the country's reclusive leader, Kim Jong-il, who inherited the mantle of leadership from his father, still called the "Great Leader," appears to have concluded that the surest way of getting what he seeks is to demonstrate that he has the capability to strike back if attacked.

Assessing the nature of that ability is difficult. If the test occurred as the North claimed, it is unclear whether it was an actual bomb or a more primitive device. Some experts cautioned that it could try to fake an explosion, setting off conventional explosives; the only way to know for sure will be if American "sniffer" planes, patrolling the North Korean coast, pick up evidence of nuclear byproducts in the air.

Even then, it is not clear that the North could fabricate that bomb into a weapon that could fit atop its missiles, one of the country's few significant exports.

But the big fear about North Korea, American officials have long said, has less to do with its ability to lash out than it does with its proclivity to proliferate. The country has sold its missiles and other weapons to Iran, Syria and Pakistan; at various moments in the six-party talks that have gone on for the past few years, North Korean representatives have threatened to sell nuclear weapons. But in a statement issued last week, announcing that it intends to set off a test, the country said it would not sell its nuclear products.

The fear of proliferation prompted President Bush to declare in 2003 that the United States would never "tolerate" a nuclear-armed North Korea. He has never defined what he means by "tolerate," and on Sunday night Tony Snow, Bush's press secretary, said that, assuming the report of the test is accurate, the United States would now go to the United Nations to determine "what our next steps should be in response to this very serious step."

Nuclear testing is often considered a necessary step to proving a weapon's reliability as well as the most forceful way for a nation to declare its status as a nuclear power.

"Once they do that, it's serious," said Harold M. Agnew, a former director of the Los Alamos weapons laboratory, which designed most of the nation's nuclear arms. "Otherwise, the North Koreans are just jerking us around."

Networks of seismometers that detect faint trembles in the earth and track distant rumbles are the best way to spot an underground nuclear test.

The big challenge is to distinguish the signatures of earthquakes from those of nuclear blasts. Typically, the shock waves from nuclear explosions begin with a sharp spike as earth and rock are compressed violently. The signal then tends to become fuzzier as surface rumblings and shudders and after shocks create seismologic mayhem.

With earthquakes, it is usually the opposite. A gentle jostling suddenly becomes much bigger and more violent.

Most of the world's seismic networks that look for nuclear blasts are designed to detect explosions as small as one kiloton, or equal to 1,000 tons of high explosives. On instruments for detecting earthquakes, such a blast would measure a magnitude of about 4, like a small tremor.

Philip E. Coyle III, a former head of weapons testing at the Pentagon and former director of nuclear testing for the Lawrence Livermore National Laboratory, a weapons-design center in California, said the North Koreans could learn much from a nuclear test even if it was small by world standards or less than an unqualified success.

"It would not be totally surprising if it was a fizzle and they said it was a success because they learned something," he said. "We did that sometimes. We had a missile defense test not so long ago that failed, but the Pentagon said it was a success because they learned something, which I agree with. Failures can teach you a lot."

William J. Broad contributed reporting from New York, and Thom Shanker from Washington.

WASHINGTON North Korea said Monday that it had set off its first nuclear test, becoming the eighth country in history, and arguably the most unstable and most dangerous, to proclaim that it has joined the club of nuclear weapons states.

The test came just two days after the country was warned by the United Nations Security Council that the action could lead to severe consequences.

American officials cautioned that they had not yet received any confirmation that the test had occurred. The United States Geological Survey said it had detected a tremor of 4.2 magnitude on the Korean Peninsula.

China called the test a "flagrant and brazen" violation of international opinion and said it "firmly opposes" North Korea's conduct.

Senior Bush administration officials said that they had little reason to doubt the announcement, and warned that the test would usher in a new era of confrontation with the isolated and unpredictable country run by President Kim Jong-il.

Early Monday morning, even before the test was confirmed, Bush administration officials were holding conference calls to discuss ways to further cut off a country that is already subject to sanctions, and hard-liners said the moment had arrived for neighboring countries, especially China and Russia, to cut off the trade and oil supplies that have been Kim's lifeline.

In South Korea, the country that fought a bloody war with the North for three years and has lived with an uneasy truce and failed efforts at reconciliation for more than half a century, officials said they believed that an explosion occurred around 10:36 p.m. New York time - 11:36 a.m. Monday in Korea.

They identified the source of the explosion as North Hamgyong Province, roughly the area where American spy satellites have been focused for several years on a variety of suspected underground test sites.

That was less than an hour after North Korean officials had called their counterparts in China and warned them that a test was just minutes away. The Chinese, who have been North Korea's main ally for 60 years but have grown increasingly frustrated by the its defiance of Beijing, sent an emergency alert to Washington through the United States Embassy in Beijing. Within minutes, President Bush was notified, shortly after 10 p.m., by his national security adviser, Stephen Hadley, that a test was imminent.

North Korea's decision to conduct the test demonstrated what the world has suspected for years: the country has joined India, Pakistan and Israel as one of the world's "undeclared" nuclear powers. India and Pakistan conducted tests in 1998; Israel has never acknowledged conducting a test or possessing a weapon. But by actually setting off a weapon, if that is proven, the North has chosen to end years of carefully crafted and diplomatically useful ambiguity about its abilities. The North's decision to set off a nuclear device could profoundly change the politics of Asia.

The test occurred only a week after Japan installed a new, more nationalistic prime minister, Shinzo Abe, and just as the country was renewing a debate about whether its ban on possessing nuclear weapons - deeply felt in a country that saw two of its cities incinerated in 1945 - still makes strategic sense.

And it shook the peninsula just as Abe was arriving in South Korea for the first time as prime minister, in an effort to repair a badly strained relationship, having just visited with Chinese leaders in Beijing. It places his untested administration in the midst of one of the region's biggest security crises in years, and one whose outcome will be watched closely in Iran and other states suspected of attempting to follow the path that North Korea has taken.

Now, Tokyo and Washington are expected to put even more pressure on the South Korean government to terminate its "sunshine policy" of trade, tourism and openings to the North - a policy that has been the source of enormous tension between Seoul and Washington since Bush took office.

The explosion was the product of nearly four decades of work by North Korea, one of the world's poorest and most isolated countries. The nation of 23 million people appears constantly fearful that its far richer, more powerful neighbors - and particularly the United States - will try to unseat its leadership. The country's founder, Kim Il-sung, who died in 1994, emerged from the Korean War determined to equal the power of the United States, and acutely aware that Gen. Douglas MacArthur had requested nuclear weapons to use against his country.

But it took decades to put together the technology, and only in the past few years has the North appeared to have made a political decision to speed forward. "I think they just had their military plan to demonstrate that no one could mess with them, and they weren't going to be deterred, not even by the Chinese," a senior American official who deals with the North said late Sunday evening. "In the end, there was just no stopping them." But the explosion was also the product of more than two decades of diplomatic failure, spread over at least three presidencies. American spy satellites saw the North building a good-size nuclear reactor in the early 1980's, and by the early 1990's the C.I.A. estimated that the country could have one or two nuclear weapons. But a series of diplomatic efforts to "freeze" the nuclear program - including a 1994 accord signed with the Clinton administration - ultimately broke down, amid distrust and recriminations on both sides. Three years ago, just as President Bush was sending American troops toward Iraq, the North threw out the few remaining weapons inspectors living at their nuclear complex in Yongbyon, and moved 8,000 nuclear fuel rods they had kept under lock and key. Those rods contained enough plutonium, experts said, to produce five or six nuclear weapons, though it is unclear how many the North now stockpiles.

For years, some diplomats assumed that the North was using that ambiguity to trade away its nuclear capability, for recognition, security guarantees, aid and trade with the West. But in the end, the country's reclusive leader, Kim Jong-il, who inherited the mantle of leadership from his father, still called the "Great Leader," appears to have concluded that the surest way of getting what he seeks is to demonstrate that he has the capability to strike back if attacked.

Assessing the nature of that ability is difficult. If the test occurred as the North claimed, it is unclear whether it was an actual bomb or a more primitive device. Some experts cautioned that it could try to fake an explosion, setting off conventional explosives; the only way to know for sure will be if American "sniffer" planes, patrolling the North Korean coast, pick up evidence of nuclear byproducts in the air. Even then, it is not clear that the North could fabricate that bomb into a weapon that could fit atop its missiles, one of the country's few significant exports. But the big fear about North Korea, American officials have long said, has less to do with its ability to lash out than it does with its proclivity to proliferate. The country has sold its missiles and other weapons to Iran, Syria and Pakistan; at various moments in the six-party talks that have gone on for the past few years, North Korean representatives have threatened to sell nuclear weapons. But in a statement issued last week, announcing that it intends to set off a test, the country said it would not sell its nuclear products.

The fear of proliferation prompted President Bush to declare in 2003 that the United States would never "tolerate" a nuclear-armed North Korea. He has never defined what he means by "tolerate," and on Sunday night Tony Snow, Bush's press secretary, said that, assuming the report of the test is accurate, the United States would now go to the United Nations to determine "what our next steps should be in response to this very serious step."

Nuclear testing is often considered a necessary step to proving a weapon's reliability as well as the most forceful way for a nation to declare its status as a nuclear power. "Once they do that, it's serious," said Harold M. Agnew, a former director of the Los Alamos weapons laboratory, which designed most of the nation's nuclear arms. "Otherwise, the North Koreans are just jerking us around."

Networks of seismometers that detect faint trembles in the earth and track distant rumbles are the best way to spot an underground nuclear test. The big challenge is to distinguish the signatures of earthquakes from those of nuclear blasts. Typically, the shock waves from nuclear explosions begin with a sharp spike as earth and rock are compressed violently. The signal then tends to become fuzzier as surface rumblings and shudders and after shocks create seismologic mayhem. With earthquakes, it is usually the opposite. A gentle jostling suddenly becomes much bigger and more violent. Most of the world's seismic networks that look for nuclear blasts are designed to detect explosions as small as one kiloton, or equal to 1,000 tons of high explosives. On instruments for detecting earthquakes, such a blast would measure a magnitude of about 4, like a small tremor.

Philip E. Coyle III, a former head of weapons testing at the Pentagon and former director of nuclear testing for the Lawrence

Livermore National Laboratory, a weapons-design center in California, said the North Koreans could learn much from a nuclear test even if it was small by world standards or less than an unqualified success.

"It would not be totally surprising if it was a fizzle and they said it was a success because they learned something," he said. "We did that sometimes. We had a missile defense test not so long ago that failed, but the Pentagon said it was a success because they learned something, which I agree with. Failures can teach you a lot."

NORTH KOREA – THE NUCLEAR STATE

North Korea is a country in the Far East occupying the northern part of the peninsula of Korea. North Korea was formed in 1948 when Korea was partitioned along the 38th parallel. Its official language is Korean. Its capital is Pyongyang while its complete name is Democratic People's Republic of Korea.

In 1950, a war began between North and South Korea. North Korea attacked South Korea. United States of America dominating the UN troops countered the attack by invading North Korea from South Korea. North Korea, was however sided by China in this war. In 1951, peace negotiations started and eventually it was attained after 2 years in 1953. The previous borders were restored, thus, the war left no results.

According to recent CIA investigations, North Korea is on the verge of testing its nuclear weapons probably in a cave or mine shaft somewhere in the barren northeast of the country. It is also believed that a small amount of breakout nuclear material will fallout of the test site and drift towards Japan. This good news is really going to incite excitement in the financial markets of South Korea and Japan. Foreign investors in South Korea will move forward to decisions of pulling out their money from the market or minimizing the range of operations. This is a very bad news for the South Korean administrators since they will lose their strong economies after such a repatriation of money from their markets. Meanwhile, US will look forward to impose a blockage or other tough measures to control North Korea's nuclear tests.

It is commented that North Korea is working out on plans of testing its nuclear capabilities within a short time. Its is said that these nuclear weapons had been under preparation since last 50 years. This country has already been declared as a nuclear state as it has disclosed its nuclear weapons. The aim of North Korea behind developing nuclear weapons is believed that it wants to be a "recognized" nuclear state just like China, India and Pakistan. To attain these motives, it first needs to demonstrate its nuclear capabilities. Now lets see how was it able to develop such nuclear weapons right from the beginning through all these 50 years.

According to CIA's investigation, North Korea started its nuclear proliferation in 1956, just after 3 years of the Korean War. The programme commenced when North Korea signed a pact with USSR who agreed to train its nuclear scientists. It was with the help of USSR, with which North Korea established its first ever nuclear reactor in 1965. Then, in 1974 North Korea also signed a nuclear training agreement with China. Then North Korea built another small nuclear reactor in 1986 at Yongbyon. This time, America played its sinister role and detected the third larger nuclear reactor of North Korea in 1989. According to estimates, the nuclear proliferation ability of the nuclear reactors of North Korea was enough to enrich plutonium fuel rods to the necessary levels to make a nuclear bomb. United States considering this state of affairs predicted a future devastation and hazard within Asia. United States offered North Korea with aids and trade treaties at the cost of suspending its nuclear proliferation. In 1994, a pact was signed between North Korea and US after which North Korea put her 8000 fuel rods at Yongbyon under seal. However, they clandestinely treaded on their path, using highly enriched uranium prepared in special centrifuges allegedly supplied by Pakistan (A.Q. Khan Network).

North Korea has been openly alluding about that fact that it is going to join the Nuclear Club. United States, in 2002, found evidence of their clandestine nuclear enrichment programme and North Korea didn't decline this fact and accordingly resumed the reprocessing of Plutonium fuel rods which was suspended in 1994.

Soon after the worldwide disclosure of the fact about North Korea's nuclear enrichment programme, North Korea declared that she was willing to expose her nuclear capabilities, infact pointing to the Nuclear Test programmes. Later officials from North Korea displayed the reason of "self-defence" for retaining the Nuclear Weapons . Subsequently it was announced that North Korea had developed nuclear weapons and will retain them under any circumstances. North Korea performed some nuclear tests in 1998 using the three-stage Taedopong-I missile over Japan and the Pacific Ocean. North Korea openly announced this and its also believed that the ones that are due to take place soon will also be announced. North Korea has been alleged to have the technology to produce an actual warhead that could fit atop missiles which, by U.S. intelligence estimates, could reach parts of the United States. North Korea has not objected to this claim also.

The rivalry between North Korea and US has been since long. Bush calls Kim Jong-II, the leader of North Korea, as "tyrant and a dangerous person who starves his own people and has a high concentration of camps". North Korea, on its stance has been right. North Korea has already seen the fate of Baghdad and Kabul. Now it has two options. Either wait for America's invasion or adopt to pre-emption for its preparation to face the invasions and pressurize the Big Brother. North Korea looks inclined towards the other option much. Showing the nuclear cards is the only option to perpetuate her regime and stay unharmed. There are so less chances that North Korea will switch to negotiations regarding its Nuclear Programme any more.

North Korea, has now earned a new identity in Asia. According to it, China and South Korea should rise from their illusions and accept the reality. North Korea's nuclear capability is a tremendous threat to all the Asia. Asia needs to co-operate in this regard, with the Big Brother to explain North Korea about the repercussions and solve the problem peacefully.

8

POLITICAL DIVERSITY WITHIN DEVELOPING WORLD

Developing nations are the nations predominantly situated in the southern hemisphere. They are characterized by civil strife, political instability, hunger, high population growth, and other social misfortunes. It is however clear that they are walking away from this state towards advancement as they attain political maturity. The level of development of these countries however differs remarkably. Some are experiencing an economic boom while others are sinking deep into political oblivion, disappearing from the ladder scales. Examples include Burma and Somali which have been classified as failed states. However, there is some light at the end of the tunnel. With the current trend of globalization and the formation of political blocs, democratic governance characterized by openness in society is cropping in, all for the better of society.Political Diversity within Developing World

Politics is an aspect of social science concerned with leadership and policy making and its implementation in society. It is the exercise of power in a desired manner. Often misinterpreted as a dirty game without rules of procedure, politics is manifested in all aspects of society. Any society needs a clear political structure, lest it is a state of nature as presented by Thomas Hobbes, where life is short, brutish, disorganized and of a war of all against all. Aristotle defined it as the search for the good life. In this sense, politics is meant to bring order in society; sine man is a political animal, social in nature. Different societies have different systems of politics. The political system in application at a given time is greatly dependent on the culture of the people in the society in question. Culture may be defined as a way of life of a people. Thus the political systems of the western advanced nations would differ greatly from that of the less developed countries.

A developed nation refers to an industrialized nation, one where the major export products are finished goods. The opposite of this would therefore be a political system whose major exports are primary produce. The 'three worlds theory' attempts to classify the world into three classes: the capitalist developed world; the socialist world; and the third world, comprising newly found states resulting from independence struggles. The theory is however controversial, as the level of development is measured to the western standards, and again very many countries whose economic positions are different by far are lumped together. The theory, again, is only applicable to states, not the people or the societies in the states (Ahmad 1992). Developing nations are the countries found predominantly in Asia, Latin America and Africa. They are over 100, comprising a population of a third of the total world population.

Developing countries suffer a great deal on issues of pervasive poverty, rapid population growth, ethnic conflict, famine, disease, revolutions, and corruption. The politics of developed and developing nations has been raging for quite some time and the fact that the developed nation reached their status as a result of under-developing the developing nations is a hot debate. During colonization the developing world was the victim of the process. Inhabitants were taken as slaves to go and develop the western world, of course using resources from the developing nations. Natural resources were exploited from the third world countries at no cost to the whites. They competed in the scramble until they decided to divide the African continent among themselves as was the case during the Berlin conferences (Rosenberg). The whites brought in their education which was so basic and naked for the third world. It was education meant to make it easy for communication between natives and the foreigners as to indoctrinate the natives to think that they are lesser beings who need white supervision and guidance. Native cultures were also dismissed as archaic and demonic that they were retrogressive. All these combined had the natives developed a negative attitude against themselves.

The idea of terming some countries as under developed is totally unacceptable. There are developed and developing nations, not the other argument. Underdevelopment would indicate that the development is retrogressing which is not the case. All countries are developing and from the foregoing it is also wrong to claim that the developing world is trying to catch up with the developed world. It is ridiculous because as the third world is developing, the industrialized states are still industrializing. To get the facts right, development of the third world should be pegged on its own unique society and culture. Foreign concepts of development should not be imposed on these countries. For instance, due to the rot in the west on morality, these countries do not consider morality as an aspect of development. They are instead quick to extend indoctrination by having the less developed countries to use their language and education system. They introduce economic policies and governance principles, some of which are not compatible with the native way of living.

Developing nations are found in the southern hemisphere of the globe. They include the continent of Africa, Southern Asia and Latin America. At one time or another, these countries were under colonial administration, an era characterized by slavery and exploitation. Natural resources were exploited to Europe and America. The masters made maximum use of the available free resources to a point that they partitioned the continent of Africa among themselves for their economic gains. Australia is however exempted because it is in the Southern hemisphere but is classified among the advanced countries. The developing nations were once under a colonial rule. Latin America Africa and Asia were all being ruled at some point in time by European powers. This was the height of exploitation perpetually perpetrated by the developed countries for their political and economic gains. The United Kingdom of Great Britain and Wales dominated almost the whole world that it was once said the sun never sets in its empire. This was the depth of the imperial dominance that reflected the might of the Kingdom, and any other dominant country. The colonial administration left a legacy of use of brute force and gross violation of human rights. Divide and rule was one of the methods of containing the unrest of the native communities.

Independent struggles led to most of these countries to attain their independence after bloody struggles. They inherited the political system of former colonial masters which had some points of incompatibility with the native social systems. Poorly trained officers took over apparatus of governance, proving a disaster to some newly-found states like the Zaire. The constitutions were hurriedly amended to empower one institution in the name of national cohesion. There followed periods of coups and countercoups, with the leadership consolidating even more powers to absolute levels. Lord Acton's opinion on the absolute corruptibility of absolute power became a reality. The accumulation of power in one institution, mostly the presidency proved counterproductive, as imperial presidencies sprung up.

The economic front of developing nations is characterized by low pa capita incomes and high poverty rates. Unemployment is high due to scarcity of both jobs and skills. A concerted effort is made by some governments urging its citizens to look for jobs in other countries. These countries major in the export of raw materials both agricultural and mineral resources. They are known to be pawns of the richer nations. Patron-client relation characterized the smuggling by weaponry to sponsor wars in the developing world. Infrastructure is usually poor, complicating further the cycle of poverty.

Health wise, these countries are known to suffer from malnutrition and diseases related to this problem. The poor hygienic conditions and general state of poverty reduces the life expectancy rates. Medical care is not easily accessible as is clean water safe for consumption.

The political leadership of these nations is weak and often dictatorial. Most of governmental authority is vested in an individual who would misuse by appointing cronies to positions of influence. This would then promote corruption in the system which may turn to be an issue of political instability due to dissatisfaction by a section of society feeling neglected. It would then foment an uprising or a coup. Somali Republic is an example in Africa with Haiti in Latin America.

Civil society is not free to operate in such systems. Media censorship is practiced with some countries having the media being monopolized by the state. There is no independent media. They hold regular 'selections' in the name of upholding the rule of democracy. Such 'democratic' practices are only meant for cosmetic reasons as the electoral bodies are appointed by a player in the election.

In the international front, these countries have a lesser say. Major policy decisions are made by the major economic powers, through their manipulative abilities by use of briefcase diplomacy.

Legislative authorities of the developing world often act as rubber stamps to executive decisions. The executive overshadows the legislature and the judiciary in their operation, thus defeating the logic of having a system of checks and balances. Any discontents are treated harshly, often with impunity. Torture and political assassinations thus become a norm rather than an exception. The civil servants work at the mercies of the president, thus subjecting all state machinery at the hands of an individual.

COMPARISON WITH THE DEVELOPED WORLD

The political systems of developed countries are a product of long term experience. Distinct systems are presidential as in America, parliamentary as in the UK or a mixture of the two as in the case in France. The long tradition has made the system part of the culture of the society a reason for a strong political orientation. The developed nations as mentioned earlier owe their success to the developing world. The level they have reached allows them a variety of opportunities. They have accumulated capital and so development is not an issue. They talk of economic growth while the developing nations think of economic development.

Some of the countries in the advanced world category are welfare states. This would eliminate any talk of poverty as the state is committed to the welfare of its population. The state is in a position to take care of its entire population unlike the crippled economy of the developing world.

A robust civil society and clear separation of powers make it difficult for corruption to thrive. The high rate of literacy is a further resource. Technology grows faster due to scientific innovation. Funding is readily available for research work, a factor that remains a nightmare in the developing world.

Despite these differences, the developing world is showing some remarkable progress especially in the sphere of governance and economy. Globalization has opened the world, exposing populations to different challenges facing people in similar situations in the globe and how they got themselves out of political bondage to a free society. The Orange Revolution of Ukraine, for instance, was a clear lesson that the incumbent cannot remain in office illegitimately. The people decided to use their civil rights and had the person of their choice in the political office. This is however the opposite of what happens in Zimbabwe after President Mugabe shamelessly competed with his shadow in a run-off presidential election after unleashing terror to the opposition supporters.

On the economic front, the 'Asian Tigers' are far much ahead of other developing nations. They have reached a level almost close to that of the developed world. In this category is also included China, South Africa, Brazil, Argentina, among others, said to be the emerging markets of the world. All this is happening as Zimbabwe is reeling into a pit, with inflation rates reported by the Central Bank to be 2.2 million percent. The different developing countries practice different political systems. Some are parliamentary, while others presidential. South Korea is presidential executive system, India a Prime Ministerial system, and Kenya is a mixed system, with the executive comprising of both an executive president and prime minister.

The Kenyan system of dual executive was brought about after a disputed election in December 2007 after both the incumbent Mwai Kibaki and the leader of opposition Raila Odinga claimed victory in the election, which was later declared by the electoral commission in an enclosed place, with only the state media being allowed to air the coverage. It followed the worst political violence Kenya witnessed in its post independence history. International attention was attracted and the former United Nations Secretary General led a team that negotiated for a power sharing deal that recommended the amendment of the Constitution to provide for the office of an executive prime minister and two deputies. This is an example of political expedience in developing world. The Ugandan case involved the President taking a bill to Parliament to amend the national Constitution to allow him a further term in office. His two constitutional terms had expired but he was not ready to leave office. President Obasanjo of Nigeria attempted but was embarrassed by his vice president at the time Atiku Abubakar. This is just an indication that the leadership in the developing world is not ready to relinquish power after their constitutional terms in office. This is however contrasted by the former South African President Nelson Mandela who voluntarily retired after leading his country into black majority rule.

Political systems of the advanced world are characterized by a robust civil society movement. This aspect has begun showing prominence in the developing world as well. However, in countries like Cuba and China, the civil society is not as pronounced as in Nigeria, South Africa, India, Brazil, just to mention a few. China has been known to contain the media through censorship. Democratic space is limited by stringent legal provisions. In Cuba, it was until the retirement of the long-serving Fidel Castro that his brother Raul allowed the open use of the internet and mobile phones. The media has also been allowed some breathing space, and the civil society can speak, though still with some utmost caution.

With the current trend of globalization, promoted by the wide use of the internet, most societies are going to be opened up. The dynamism of the political play in the international level would force the conservative societies to tore the line of openness and accountability. Internationalism and transnational are fast diluting cultures which were tightly held by some societies.

From the foregoing therefore, all countries are moving the development paths, and it is the purpose of comparative politics to shed more light on the best form of political and economic leadership to embrace in order to achieve the golden Millennium Development Goals by 2015.

INTERNATIONAL RELATIONS INVOLVING A PARTICIPATORY SOCIETY

This essay seeks to explore the issues that would face a participatory democratic society when relating to other countries. It is assumed that some of the other countries the participatory society deals with are not participatory societies. It is assumed that there could exist a country whose economy was governed by participatory democratic structures as envisioned by Hahnel and Albert in their vision of "Participatory Economics" (parecon). Also, it is assumed that this country has a "Participatory Polity" (parpolity) as envisioned by Stephen Shalom. There would be other important characteristics of this society, dealing with such issues as kinship, culture, and religion, but they will not be specified here.

The purpose of this essay is not to provide vision about how a participatory society should manage its international affairs. Rather, I am seeking to address the likely scenarios a participatory nation will face, and how it will likely deal with them, given my understanding of participatory structures and institutions. Some questions along this line are: With what structures would a participatory society manage its relations with other countries? How would the institutions of a participatory society motivate it to help (or hinder) the development of other countries? Would it have an army? Would it have conscription? Would it be motivated to commit an aggressive war to conquer other nations? Would be motivated to never go to war? How would it negotiate economic deals with capitalist countries? Would it deal with capitalist countries? Would it try to "export revolution" (encourage - or force - other countries to adopt its institutions and systems)? How would foreign policy be decided? Would it have ambassadors? How would immigration be handled? How would its unique monetary system coexist with international currencies?

There are many questions to answer, and I honestly do not know how to answer them all. By interpreting the writings of parpolity and parecon, I will attempt to address some major issues.

As a bit of a preamble, I would first like to establish a basic principle of a participatory society, namely that the policy of the participatory nation, based on the wishes of the majority of its citizens, is most often fair and reasonable. I will use this idea throughout the essay. Since we are dealing with an imagined participatory society, where the opinions and beliefs of the majority of the population should reflect (for the most part) the foreign policy of the nation, it seems reasonable to think that the foreign policy will be fair minded. Evidence for this is given in polls of ordinary citizens conducted in the modern age. Polls show that most Americans think resorting to military force to promote democracy is wrong4, that the Kyoto protocols on the environment should be honored5, etc. despite what their government actually does regarding these issues. There are numerous examples of the majority of people in a democratic society (let us call representative democracies "democratic" even though it is arguable that there is very little real democracy in such societies) believing in fairly socialist values, like Medicare7, universal education, universal suffrage, etc. This is often contrary to policy delivered by elected representatives.

There are exceptions of course, Americans appear to be divided on the issue of socialized medicine8. One wonders what the result would be if the US media was not corporate owned.

However, it is possible for the majority to be irrational and nasty, for example, consider witch burning and slavery. It is probable that instances of the "tyranny of the majority" may crop up in a participatory society. Fortunately there are proposed methods for dealing with this, discussed below. Hopefully such instances where the majority of citizens want unethical things to happen to a subgroup or foreign group of people would be rare. It is of course, impossible to predict, but since there would be much debate in this society, free and non corporate media, and people would often be considering the opinions of others, one would hope and expect that the majority of people in a participatory society would be convinced by the voices of others to support ideas that are fair minded and reasonable.

I will now briefly summarize the economic system of parecon and the political system of parpolity. For more background, please see the writings of Robin Hahnel and Michael Albert on participatory economics, also see Stephen Shalom on "parpolity." People already familiar with these proposed systems are invited to skip the next bit.

Participatory Economics seeks to set up an entirely different economic system by fundamentally changing work life, and how goods and services are allocated (no markets and no central planning). By law, productive property would be owned by all citizens, no private ownership of factories of farms etc. would be allowed. Work life would be democratic, each worker would be able to vote on issues in the workplace in proportion to how much the issue effects them. Further, each worker would have a "balanced job complex." This means that each worker has a mix of tasks, some empowering, and some rote and perhaps unpleasant. Through sharing both the empowering and unempowering work, one class is established, and the economy is more fair. For instance someone might be an airplane pilot (empowering) some of the time, and a baggage handler at the airport for the rest of their work week.

Surgeons would spend some of their time sweeping floors or sorting mail. Also, if it is necessary for someone to be in charge in the workplace, then this job is rotated. For instance, if you are in charge of baggage handling at the airport, then on some other day, you are one of the baggage handlers. Finally, in a parecon one gets paid according to how much effort and sacrifice one does at work. If you work longer hours, or at a hard job, you get paid more. Balanced job complexes should have roughly the same effort and sacrifice.

Money in a participatory society is also different. A worker in a parecon gets "credits", a sort of record of how much they work. They can then use these credits to buy goods and services, but when they buy things, some of their credits disappear. They do not go into a till or a bank, they are gone. To get more, one must work more. Credits are not transferable to other people. I could not give you any of my credits no matter what you might give me. There are no banks, no stock market, and no interest rates. Investment still happens, but differently. If the parecon nation wants to invest in infrastructure, everything else gets more expensive, but no loans are given.

Allocation in a participatory society would also be very different from today. Each year, all citizens would engage in a participatory planning procedure, the goal of which would be to set prices for all goods and services for one year. At the beginning of the procedure, consumers would enter proposals on what they plan to consume for the coming year on an individual, neighborhood, city wide, provincial, and country wide basis. For instance, an individual might order a new bicycle and stereo for the new year, and a city might order a sewer system upgrade. Proposals involving more than one person would be accomplished by any citizen submitting a proposal to a facilitation board, which would be a service to help develop the proposal for approval by the rest of the population. The sum of proposals would then be approved by interested people in that region, then submitted during the participatory planning procedure. In a similar way each worker (who would also be a consumer) would propose how much they want to work in the coming year, and at what they want to work. Workplaces would also propose changes to their workplaces, such as upgrades. This proposed supply and demand will be summed up, and factors such as environmental damage involved in producing goods and the toll on workers will be added to the price of a good, making it more or less expensive. This generates prices to be reviewed for all goods and services. Since the prices incorporate information about the impact of the goods on society, it is said that the prices reflect the "social opportunity cost". After reviewing the prices, people then resubmit proposals, as prices might not be what they expected. This process is repeated several times, and less deviation is allowed each time, whittling down the proposals into something beneficial to all. After this, prices are set for a year. Note that though this might seem like a demanding process for the population, there are mechanisms to make it easy on consumers, such as getting time off work to do it.

Parecon describes how economic life would work, but this leaves out the creation and enforcement of laws. This is a job for a parpolity2. To make laws, Shalom proposes that a nested council structure be created. Each person would belong to a council of 25 to 50 other citizens. Each council would elect a representative to go to the next level council, which would then represent 625 to 2500 people, and each of these would send representatives to the next level, and so on. At five or six levels, you can represent billions of people. Each council would be deliberative, that is, capable of making independent decisions for the sum total of its constituents. Laws passed could involve new work safety standards, outlawing practices that are very harmful to the environment, etc. However, the decisions of each higher level council would be easily challengeable by a referendum. Also, the lower level councils would be asked to give general preferences for issues that come up, leaving the details to be worked out by the appropriate council. For instance people could vote that they are generally in favor of allowing stem cell research, with provisions like no babies are to be brought to maturity just to get their stem cells, but leave the exact details to a higher level council. People interested in the details could follow the deliberations of the higher level councils and comment on them as well, and perhaps petition for a general vote if many observers are unsatisfied.

Courts in parpolity would not be changed a great deal, however, there might be more juries. Presumably police would still be needed, as this is a skilled profession, and police would work in a balanced job complex. Prisons might be needed as well for seriously violent people. Hopefully the need for police and prisons would be much diminished, and prisons would focus on reform and creative ways to help people who have trouble living in a society. Courts would also be used to check tyranny of the majority. If one group tries to oppress a smaller group through voting some legislation, courts would be used to block these violations of the constitution. Courts can also assist on ruling which group of people gets to vote on what issue. It is assumed here that there would be a constitution, though Shalom has not made this explicit, since it seems to be the only way to aid court rulings. Countries like the UK, who have no constitution, rely on precedents to aid court rulings. Since there would be no precedents for many of the actions of a participatory society, it would seem a constitution is in order.

Now that each system is summarized, let us move on to international relations.

ECONOMIC RELATIONS BETWEEN COUNTRIES

Fortunately, Robin Hahnel has recently clarified how economic relations would work both between parecon countries and also parecon and non-parecon countries in his recent book "Economic Justice and Democracy"3. Previous to this, how this might work was something of a mystery.

ECONOMIC RELATIONS BETWEEN PARTICIPATORY SOCIETIES

For relations between two parecon countries, it is first important to understand a few points about parecon. In a parecon, every able worker has a balanced job complex.

In implementing the balanced job complex, though, it is proposed that not every worker work at the same place for their entire job complex. Some workers could perhaps perform their tasks all under one roof, but others will have to spend some part of their work in one place (say a coal mine) and another part somewhere else (such as a research institution). In this way, jobs are balanced amongst workplaces.

Another point to understand is that there is freedom of movement anywhere in a parecon. If you want to live somewhere within the parecon, you may live there (as long the work you can do is needed, and you can get to your workplace). If some parts of a country are much more desirable to live in, then many people will want to live there. If too many people want to live there then the resources of that region are strained, and the environment is strained.

What can be done to mitigate the undesirable (and unstoppable) effects of too much migration to more desirable parts of the country? The solution is to not develop one part of the county beyond other parts, so that each part is as desirable to live in as possible. To put it another way, if two countries go parecon at the same time, and one is less technologically advanced than another, the first priority of the more advanced former nation (now a part of a larger nation) is to help develop the less advanced region. Otherwise, too many people will move to the more advanced region and overwhelm it. Also, because jobs would be balanced across workplaces, then people from the more advanced areas of the country would be motivated to improve the less advanced regions, else they will have to work in worse conditions. The interesting (and laudable) thing is that the parecon nation is seriously motivated to aid underdeveloped regions, otherwise its own progress is hindered.

Two parecon countries geographically adjacent to each other would most likely become one country economically. The more developed country would be obligated to help the less developed country until they are on equal terms, as above. Councils would order projects that would affect both countries, effectively becoming a single entity, as there should be unrestricted trade between each. However, the farther apart each country is, the higher the price of goods would be if the good would have to be shipped all the way from one end of the country to another. Two parecon countries separated by water would presumably be able to order goods freely from each other with no restrictions, but transportation costs would factor in by raising the social opportunity cost of each item.

It is of course possible that many regions in a parecon country could be culturally and politically distinct, and might be named differently and so on. However, if both are parecon, there is no reason to assume that these differences would impede the free flow of goods between each other, and that there would be any trade restrictions. In fact any restrictions would be detrimental to the economy of each, as it would seem to hurt efficiency, and decrease the diversity of goods, and would make workers in each country work harder and longer hours. If consumer councils cannot order goods and services from other regions just because of cultural differences, then there is an unfortunate dispute between the two regions, something for the polity to resolve. In any case, restricting trade between two parecon countries would be in the economic interest of neither.

ECONOMIC RELATIONS BETWEEN PARTICIPATORY SOCIETIES AND NON-PARTICIPATORY SOCIETIES (CAPITALIST OR COMMUNIST)

Leaving aside for the moment that a participatory society would likely face hostility from non-participatory societies, there is a possibility that a "capitalist" or "communist" countries might wish to have economic relations with a participatory country. Robin Hahnel has also recently proposed how this might work as well.

Hahnel states that if a parecon country can deal with a more advanced economy (technologically speaking presumably) then it is fine to get the best deal it can get. The parecon country should sue for the most "efficiency gains" it can get, since nobody will be worse off in either country.

In physics, more efficiency means that the work or energy you get out of a device is greatest compared to how much energy or work was put into a device. A car is not very efficient if much of the energy produced by the engine goes into making heat, (typically only 10% goes into moving the car). In an economy, transposing this concept would define an efficiency gain as putting the least amount of labor and resources into producing a good for the greatest amount of the good produced and the greatest social benefits as well (including worker satisfaction, not impacting the environment etc.). If you can produce enough toothbrushes for all with 10 people in a small factory, then you shouldn't use 100 people and vast resources to do it. Also, if infrastructure is already existing to produce toothbrushes, then it is inefficient to make more infrastructure unless it will reduce use of resources and labor in the future, and maybe have social benefits. Therefore if a parecon country can get goods with less investment of labor and resources from the more developed country, then it should do so. Nobody gets hurt in either country. Also, if the parecon country can get resources to build a more efficient factory or get better job training from the advanced country, it should do so. And so on.

If however, a parecon is dealing with a *less advanced* country, the parecon country is obliged to get *less* than 50% of the efficiency gains of the trade deal. In this way the less advanced economy gets most of the benefits, but not all. The parecon country gets some efficiency gains as well, but it is morally obliged to try to benefit the less advanced economy more than itself. The parecon country does not lose anything, but it does not gain as much as it could.

Why be so nice? Hahnel proposes that to do otherwise would violate the principles of a parecon (3, p. 212-213) It seems true that violating one's ethical principles would matter to a participatory democratic society, where the fair mindedness of the population would presumably rule, as I have already discussed above.

Further, this issue relates to immigration. A principle in parecon appears to be that too much immigration is held to be "bad" for a region. Since immigration rights are an important activist topic today, it is important to clarify that advocates for a participatory society are not anti-immigration. Rather just the opposite, "freedom of association" is a fundamental right in a parecon or parpolity, and such a society could not work without it. It seems hard to have a participatory democracy without people being free to live where they want and associate with whom they want within the country.

If the principle of "freedom of association" is extended, it would imply that the international border of a participatory society would be open both ways, anyone must be free to enter, and anyone must be free to leave. Having an open border might of course lead to the problem of too many people coming into the country.

Might this motivate the parecon country to restrict immigration? If there is no internal pressure for a participatory society not to put restrictions on immigration, and the external pressures can presumably be ignored, then restrictions might very well happen. At this point, I invoke the principle (above) that the majority of citizens in a participatory society are fair minded. What would a fair minded person do? One would think that having open borders (as much as possible) is the fair thing to do. You must allow refugees into the country, it is simply the fair thing to do. It is beneficial to allow skilled workers to immigrate as is done in many "first world" countries. What about people wanting to enter the country who might not have special skills? The fair thing seems to be to let them in as well. Presumably a constitution for a participatory society would have freedom of association written into it. Thus the court system of the participatory society would uphold the constitution and keep the border open, unless the situation is very dire. Further, the parecon nation can deal with immigration issues by improving the lot of other nations it trades with. If you make life better for people in other countries, then they have less reason to immigrate to your country.

Getting back to the reason why a parecon nation would be generous (allowing them more efficiency gains) to less developed countries, the parecon nation is also motivated to be fair in economic dealings due to the above principle of freedom of association. Since the border would be presumably open, the parecon country would want to raise the standard of living in other countries, otherwise be faced with overpopulation. As well, there is motivation to be friendly to other nations and form alliances, or else be attacked or sanctioned. These reasons seem enough to motivate the participatory society to trade in a way that gives the majority of efficiency gains to another country.

It might also be possible to send workers from the parecon country to less developed, non-parecon nations, and bring workers from non-parecon countries to the parecon country, as a sort of cultural exchange (if other countries are willing). This would also be beneficial in promoting goodwill amongst nations, and beneficial to the participatory society to understand other cultures and engender goodwill from them. This raises an issue that might need discussion, "What right does a participatory society have to force workers to move?" Of course, if there is no work for their particular skill set for someone in a particular region, then it seems like they should either get retraining or move. It seems very unfair to force someone to work somewhere, though. Therefore if this cultural exchange work program is done, it might have to be voluntary.

Another point is that it may be difficult for a parecon to incorporate a trade deal with another country into its participatory planning procedure. The deal would have to be negotiated prior to the participatory planning procedure, with conditions in the deal stipulating that the parecon nation does not know exactly how much of a particular good it will want, or how much it can export until after the planning procedure is done. Other countries will have to wait for exact figures, with just estimates in the meantime. There might be other ways to do this as well.

There would also be difficulty in estimating the social opportunity cost of goods from other nations. Much less data will be available to determine the social opportunity cost. Also, workers in the other country would not be working in a balanced job complex, and would not be remunerated for effort and sacrifice. Rough estimates of the social opportunity cost would have to be made. Further, a parecon country would likely try to price products like organic food grown in a cooperative at low cost (and therefore order more of that good) and price automobiles produced in factory conditions very high (and order little or none of these things from the other country). This would be an encouragement to the other nation to develop in more equitable ways, and might be considered "exporting revolution," to be discussed below.

Currency Exchange

Other points to consider are that a parecon would not use money in the traditional sense, it would have no traditional capital to give another country for its goods. Credits in a parecon are for bookkeeping the effort and sacrifice of its workers. There are no banks.

There appear to be some options available to the participatory society, though. Presumably, the parecon nation could export goods to other countries and get foreign currency for them. It could then use its stores of currency to pay for things it wants to import.

However, this might not allow the Participatory Society to get the cash it needs. It might want to buy many goods from other countries (food, wood, metals, etc.), and if you can't pay for them, you can't get them. Presumably there are limits on any country in this day and age, you cannot produce everything internally, nor do you want to. Thus you need a loan. To pay back a loan, you need money that other nations would accept.

Another country might not accept parecon "credits." Credits, under the parecon philosophy, are a record of the effort and sacrifice a capitalist country or corporation gave to a parecon country, to be redeemed by that entity only for goods the parecon nation produces. Presumably a capitalist entity would want currency that can be exchanged on an international market so they can acquire other currency to buy things the parecon nation does not offer. Remember, parecon currency is not transferrable to someone else. Thus parecon credits might not be acceptable to other entities, and trading with a capitalist entity might be impossible.

A solution might be to have two currencies. This solution was suggested to me by Robin Hahnel in a personal communication. One currency is internal, credits to give workers that disappear, the other is a regular currency used for international trade. Other countries and corporations and people could then redeem the other currency to get things from the parecon nation. Somehow, this would have to be incorporated into the yearly planning procedure, even if some entity wants to redeem its credits right away. Would a parecon nation issue bonds to encourage foreign investment? Would it give out loans and charge interest? I'm not an economist and don't know how this might work in detail. In my opinion it deserves a detailed answer. It is probably doable, however.

One might worry about the effects of having an external trading currency and an external bank system etc. Might it undermine the principles of parecon? One can imagine a hostile entity trying to devalue the currency. Might the IMF or World Bank try to force a parecon nation to get loans and pay them back? Could trading itself (where you negotiate the best price and enter into a sort of hostile arrangement) be contrary to parecon principles and undermine the country? Presumably this danger exists and, again, I believe this issue needs serious thought. I have not seen it dealt with in any parecon literature. On the flip side, a participatory nation will presumably face military and ideological challenges from foreign powers as well. Economic hostility is just more hostility, and a participatory society must do what it can to protect itself, perhaps trying to keep trading to a minimum, and relying on its internal resources as much as possible. In the end, just because you have an external currency that mimics normal capitalist currency should not introduce mechanical difficulties so extreme as make to a participatory society impossible.

DEFENSE OF A PARTICIPATORY SOCIETY

Existence of an Army

One may question whether a participatory society would have an army, whether it would make weapons, etc. There does not seem to be any reason to have an army beyond some sort of police force if all nations are parecons and have a parpolity. However, if the example of Cuba is anything to go by, a parecon nation would most likely be ruthlessly attacked by an entity like the United States. If not militarily, then surely economically. The political situation could easily become one where the participatory nation would have to arm itself or face easy takeover by another nation. If this is not the case, then there is no need for a standing army. If the participatory nation does face takeover, what choice is there besides arming itself for defense? This assumes that it is worth lives to keep the society participatory and free. This question would have to be democratically determined by the participatory nation.

It must be noted that there are other things it can do to defend itself besides arming itself. It can form alliances with more socialist type countries (if possible). However, it would not seem fair to the allied country to expect it to do all the fighting if the alliance is attacked. The participatory country can also trade with countries by applying the above 50% rule, and will engender goodwill by doing so. Further, giving aid and support during crises will also help, particularly if aid and support is given to the population of nations who are likely to attack the participatory nation. The participatory society would also have motivation to strengthen and be an active and obedient member of an organization like the UN.

The very existence of an army might be a troubling institution for a participatory society to deal with. Soldiers must be trained to kill, other countries see a force that is trained to kill them. The socializing effects of an army seem negative. For instance, today some soldiers see being a warrior as part of being a true "man." It is this very thing that a participatory society is designed to get away from. We want to make a peaceful society. Perhaps soldiers in a participatory society will see themselves as reluctant defenders. Hopefully, the army would have a primary role as an emergency response team or a manual labor team, and a secondary role as a killing force.

Draft?

Assuming that the participatory society will arm itself for defense, who will do the fighting? An interesting answer comes from Noam Chomsky:

"One preliminary question is whether it is a democratically determined community decision that an army is necessary. Sometimes the answer is pretty clearly Yes: in World War II, for example. There were some people who refused conscription, dedicated pacifists mostly: courageous and honorable, but doesn't bear on the issue. Suppose that assumption holds. Then conscription is not a violation of basic human rights any more than parceling out other unpleasant work equitably is. Say garbage collection. In a decent society it shouldn't be "volunteer" in the sense that it's undertaken only by people who are driven to it by need. Rather, it should be equitably distributed — which one can call "conscription" if one likes. These are basic issues discussed in all thinking about decent participatory societies, within the PARECON discussions, for example."[6]

Here Chomsky is replying to a query on the Znet sustainers forum regarding conscription. He makes a good case for the idea that military service in a participatory society should be mandatory on the grounds that it is hard and very dangerous work, and thus it should be shared, like rote work is shared in a parecon. I think his point is well made, and leads us to conclude that in the event of a war, a participatory society might have to use a draft to defend itself, or perhaps make military service mandatory for all citizens when they are young, as is done in some countries. I find this a surprising conclusion, but cannot see any way around it.

Would a participatory society invade another country?

Why do countries invade one another? Traditionally, elites in one country see a chance to expand their power, or become richer by invading another country. Also there could be strong racism between the two countries, or one country might wish to terrorize another country to keep it from asserting its rights, etc. What motivation might a participatory society have to invade another country, if the participatory society does not have an elite?

The only scenario I can think of where a participatory society would have motivation to invade another country for its own benefit is if a large majority of the society voted to subjugate the other country to make the participatory society better off as a whole. Since this would need a large majority, it seems unlikely that a large percentage of any population might vote to be that cruel, again invoking the principle that the majority of the population is fair minded. However, one should that remember that early societies regularly practiced slavery on a large scale, so it is definitely not impossible. It seems particularly unlikely without a media and propaganda system to egg them on (assuming a functioning "unbiased" media). Given how the majority of people today react to the thought of war and oppression, even as their own governments carry out this oppression, it also seems unlikely. However the possibility remains. A measure against this would also be in the court system of the participatory society, where the high court would have the ability to review and block any vote to do this, just as it would block a majority decision to oppress a minority within its own borders.

It is of course possible to concoct a scenario where it would be ethical to send troops to another country. The example of the genocide in Rwanda in particular speaks to this. If it is possible to stop a horrible calamity by sending in troops, then it seems the participatory society would be morally obligated to do so. There might be a provision in the constitution where if the courts and a high majority of a population agree that something must be done, and there is good intelligence on what exactly the situation is (like Rwanda), than it is imaginable that the decision could be made to send in troops. The troops would have to be withdrawn at the earliest opportunity. Hopefully writing this stipulation into the constitution would be enough to make it enforced.

It might also be wise to stipulate that any high level council that directs the defense of the participatory society when it is invaded would have to resign once the war is over. War causes negative effects like establishing permanent hierarchies. It might even be necessary to allow a high level council to stay on longer than normal if elections are impossible. Again, measures would have to be taken to get anyone out of power once a war is over.

Hierarchy in the Military

Presumably it is possible to have a balanced job complex in an army or navy. Generals and captains can clean toilets with the best of them. However, it may be very difficult to deal with military hierarchy and have a proper democracy. Military leaders need to be few for reasons of secrecy and expertise, and people must follow orders because there may be little time to explain them. It is of course possible to rotate the captaincy of a ship between four or five people, and it is possible to explain strategy to all people in the army and vote on it. One can even rotate for expertise, when the ship is in combat, only two out of three captains (for example) might be qualified to give orders, otherwise other people can captain the ship when the ship is not in combat. The Spanish revolution provides examples where officers partied with the troops and troops voted on whether they would take a hill. According to people who fought this way, it worked. One can go beyond this and rotate the position of officer amongst those qualified. Those not fit for command can do other empowering tasks such as planning strategy or programming war games, or even have an empowering job outside the military. Even with all this to try, when it comes to fighting you want the best (nastiest?) people to be in charge and you need to follow orders. Otherwise people die and you lose. There is no getting around this. One can only hope that invasions into a participatory society can be beaten off quickly, so that the predictable negative effects of permanent hierarchy and loss of self management can be fixed.

DECIDING FOREIGN POLICY IN A PARTICIPATORY SOCIETY

High Level Councils

As described above, laws would be made by various level councils in a participatory society. It seems natural that the highest level council could represent the population in international events and decide on foreign policy. There could also be a separate high level council chosen in some manner from lower level councils for this purpose as well (if there is too much of a work load). In any case, this council would take general guidance from the population on foreign policy issues and deliberate the details of foreign policy. For instance if the lower councils send a message that it is time for increased trade with willing countries, then this council would hammer out the details (which countries, what things to trade, consult with facilitation boards for estimates on indicative pricing on non-parecon countries, etc.). The council would then inform its ambassadors with instructions on what to negotiate for and what parameters to negotiate under (bottom line for deals and so forth).

Ambassadors

There does not seem to be any reason why a participatory society would not have an ambassador(s) in other countries and an embassy. Since the job must be balanced, it would seem necessary to have a team of ambassadors and negotiators, whose other jobs would be cleaning the embassy, sorting mail and maybe taking dictation. If there is not enough rote work for the team to do at the embassy, they would go back home to do it for a few months of the year. Ambassadors would be mandated to only make statements and negotiate settlements as guided by the high level council they are answerable to.

EXPORTING REVOLUTION

How wise is it to interfere in the lives of people in other countries? Should a participatory society do what it can to export revolution, and try to convince other countries to follow its lead?

Suppose some country becomes a participatory society successfully, then a little while later, a resistance group from another country contacts the participatory society asking for military aid to overthrow their own government. What to do? Would a participatory society want to support and get involved in a bloody revolution in some other country? What if it fails and the participatory society gets attacked? What if it is successful, but only at great cost of life, and the results of the revolution turn out to be not successful?

This also bears on the issue of encouraging certain forms of work life in other countries. A parecon country would naturally encourage cooperatives that do not pollute the environment in another country and self managed workplaces, and try to buy from them. Is it right to interfere in this way? I would say yes in this case.

In any case, there are certainly no easy answers, and the right thing to do would depend on each unique case. This presumes that the majority of the population wants to do the right thing, which should hold up, as reiterated above. A general "hands off" policy (in military matters) might be wisest, simply due to the unpredictable nature of such an endeavor, even with the best of intentions.

TOURISM?

What if people from another country wanted to take a vacation in a participatory society? Of course, there is no reason to deny this, however they will have to exchange their foreign currency for parecon credits. This foreign currency can be put towards buying goods from other countries and giving it to parecon citizens that wish to travel abroad.

Why give parecon credits to someone who has not worked for the society? It is a bookkeeping system, after all. Notice though that the parecon nation benefits from these currencies, as it can use them. Since there is this benefit, it seems fair to allow the tourists credits.

There is no issue regarding tourism between two participatory societies. Since the two countries would likely order things from each other during the participatory planning process, work would be done for the benefit of each, regardless where it was done. Thus credits from one country would be redeemable in another participatory country.

ESPIONAGE?

Would a participatory society spy on other countries? Would it keep secrets from its own population? Would it spy on its own population? Would care if other countries spied on it? Let us try to address these questions in turn.

First, note that espionage is not against international law, though it is against the law of any nation who is being spied on. Whether espionage should be against international law is another question.

Is there any motivation for a participatory society to spy on other non-participatory countries? It would seem there is. Perhaps another country is planning an attack on the participatory country. My guess is that knowledge of the time and location and means used in this attack would be pretty useful information. Or perhaps the participatory society would like to know how to construct a really useful piece of technology, like a drug or a computer program, developed in a capitalist country, whose method of manufacture is a secret.

Would a participatory society respect copyright laws and patents? A reason to respect them would be to engender goodwill towards capitalist nations. If a parecon nation manufactures and sells a drug at 1/100 of the cost of the corporation that owns the patent, they are going to be upset, and there might be repercussions. If the repercussions are severe, then you don't want to do this, unless the costs are worth it. Beyond negative relations with other countries, I see no reason for a participatory society to care one whit for copyright laws or patents. Knowledge and the ability to produce what you want would be seen as something for the greater good. Respecting the right of an inventor to profits is not in the parecon philosophy.

Thus it stands to reason that there is motivation to spy on other countries. Is it worth the lives of agents to get these secrets? Perhaps there would be volunteers willing to risk their lives to steal technology or get vital intelligence on an aggressive enemy. Should they be allowed to go? Would spying be worth the risk of upsetting other countries, and fostering mistrust from other nations? Perhaps this would be best left up to a general vote by the polity, which is a funny thing to do, as you are openly announcing that you intend to spy on other countries. If allowed, then the appropriate branch of the foreign affairs council would train and send spies into other countries, and use the information gathered appropriately.

Would a participatory society care if it was being spied on? Presumably it would not care if someone was trying to steal a formula for a beneficial drug. Let them have it. However, not everything is beneficial. We don't want a foreign power to have a formula for toxic gas that researchers in a participatory society have found, either accidentally or deliberately. Therefore there would be secrets to protect in a participatory society. If a participatory society decides to have an army for defense, they should have fairly modern weapons, otherwise they pose no credible deterrent. Thus either a participatory society will have to keep up to date on cutting edge weapons by espionage, or failing that, put research and development into developing means to kill people, as distasteful as that sounds. Indeed, the socializing effects of having a military makes one wonder if it is really worth it. If research and development is going into making weapons, then do we want countries willing to attack us to know how to make them too? Presumably not, but then again it might not matter, if everyone has similar weapons technology, then attacking the participatory society would still be costly. However, maybe you don't want your enemies to know the exact capabilities of your weapons. Thus whether or not you allow people to spy on you is debatable, but might actually be allowed.

Since it is assumed that a participatory society would not have weapons of mass destruction, the method of manufacture for these weapons would be best forgotten, and knowledge of how to manufacture should be kept a secret (or destroyed?).

Finally, would a participatory society spy on its own population? There might be motivations for this if there were, for example, people committed to capitalism that for some reason conspire to commit acts of terrorism. Certainly knowledge of this sort of plot would be desirable. Of course this must be balanced by the need to not harass and monitor the countries own citizens, as this has a very negative social effect. Investigating ones own population (before any crime is committed) is routinely carried out in countries today, and is part of the work of intelligence agencies and police. One would assume that citizens of a participatory nation would have little tolerance for being investigated by their own officials, thus it seems reasonable that gathering intelligence on its own citizens would be quite limited in a participatory nation.

UNITED NATIONS?

Would a participatory society follow international law, and heed the rulings of a world court? Would it heed the rulings of the World Trade Organization, would it accept loans from the IMF and/or World Bank? What sort of member of the United Nations would it be? How would it prefer that the United Nations be organized?

There are a lot of questions. In general, one would assume that a participatory nation would want to respect the decrees of the UN, as long as it believes the structure of the UN is sound. It is important to respect the idea of an international arbiter and thus support it by obeying it, as the general idea could lead to peace around the world. Of course the democratic potential of the UN is far below the level of a participatory society. Particular problems today include the permanent members of the security council whom have veto power. Positive measures can be blocked by a powerful state with veto power. Other problems include the toothlessness of the UN, as it cannot enforce any decree that a military power like the US chooses to ignore. If the institution is compromised, why obey its decrees?

I suppose that it depends on how compromised the UN is. If it becomes a totally worthless organization, why bother supporting it? However it should be supported as long as it is somewhat functional, as I would think this is an important global principle a participatory society would want to support. Participatory societies can also form their own international organizations, with much more democratic structures if need be. One can imagine a participatory UN, where delegates from participatory societies are sent to the international body, where they deliberate on international rules and arbitrate disputes, or decree whom can attack whom and so on. Would it be logical to give such a body its own military? It might make sense that participatory nations would transfer all their military might to a proper international organization, only to be used if the member nations all agree. Then there would be no standing army in any participatory society, only on the neutral soil of the participatory UN. Whether or not this is a good idea needs discussion. It could lead to a situation where whomever is in charge of the collective army and weapons attacks and takes over the nations that donated their army.

As far as the IMF and World Bank are concerned, it is doubtful that a participatory society would have anything to do with them, as the loans given by these organizations tied to structural changes in the receiving country, benefitting the rich and not the poor. Even in a severe economic crises, it would probably be foolish for a participatory society to accept a loan from these institutions. Accepting such a loan might even make it impossible to continue as a participatory society.

SPLITTING UP OF A COUNTRY?

Shalom2 has already provided some ideas regarding the secession of a participatory society. A summary of his position as follows: Secession is not desirable, as it means you have failed to live together, but must be allowed, otherwise you encourage the tyranny of the majority.

However, secession should not be allowed if it gives more resources to one fragment of the original nation. A part of a country with vast oil reserves should not be allowed to separate from the other nation unless they would both have equal access to this wealth. Also a secession should not be allowed if it leads to some minority being oppressed by a majority. Democratic rights must also be protected in some fashion.

Shalom goes further. He argues that politically distinct subunits in a participatory society might want join another council than the one they are in. This allows for another check on the tyranny of the majority. The drawback is that less diversity is fostered.

In the end, secession must be dealt with on a case by case basis.

I personally find all this quite reasonable, and have no other issues to raise.

RESPECTING THE LAWS OF OTHER COUNTRIES?

To what extent would a participatory society respect the laws of other nations?

I suppose the short answer is "To the extent they are reasonable." I would imagine that a participatory society would not have a death penalty, and would protect people who would face a death penalty if deported from the participatory nation. Further, if a Participatory Society believes in rehabilitation rather than punishment, it is unclear to what extent it would allow any "criminal" to be deported to the nation where the crime was committed. To make this more clear, consider what might happen if we do away entirely the concept of punishment for a crime. What if someone committed a murder (say a wife kills her husband after he is abusive to her) and after being examined by a series of psychologists it is determined that there is very close to 0% chance this person would ever murder again. What point is there in locking them up? Seemingly none, the murderer is no danger to anyone. Thus a participatory society might have a different conception of justice than other nations.

Not respecting the laws of other nations leads to conflict, of course. However, countries today do not allow supposed criminals they capture to be deported if they think they will be tortured. At least that is the stated policy of countries like Canada. I don't see any particular problems beyond the international strife a participatory nation would face in any event.

9

Politics of Partial Reforms

Much of our analysis of the politics of economic reform is based on an assumption about the distribution of the costs and benefits of reform, known informally as the J-curve. Simply stated, reforms are expected to make things worse before they get better. In the short term economic reforms are believed to generate transitional costs in the form of high unemployment, price increases, and production declines as the economy adjusts to the tremendous institutional and policy changes necessary to achieve the long-term efficiency gains of an effectively functioning market. Yet the timing of the costs and benefits of reform presents politicians with a serious problem: how can they initiate and sustain reforms that demand severe sacrifices in the short run for the mere promise of future gains?

Surely losers in the short term will take revenge against reformers at the first opportunity and spark a backlash against reform. Anticipating this reaction, politicians in democratic systems are understandably reluctant to undertake radical economic reforms. The central political challenge of reform, as expressed in Adam Przeworski's apt metaphor, is therefore to traverse the "valley of transition" in order to climb the "higher hills" of the reformed system. This logic has led to a series of political prescriptions centered around the same theme—to insulate the state from the pressures of the short-term losers until the reforms have created a constituency of winners powerful enough to sustain them.

Though economic reforms in the postcommunist countries have certainly created more than their fair share of transitional costs, the expected political dynamics normally associated with these costs have been much less evident. The most radical reform programs in the region have been introduced and sustained in the most competitive political systems, where politicians have been most vulnerable to electoral backlash by the short-term losers. Although voters in many cases have rejected radical reform governments in the first postreform elections, the reform programs themselves have endured and, in some cases, even intensified. More surprisingly, the politics of postcommunist economic reforms has not been dominated by the traditional short-term losers of economic transition—striking workers, resentful former state bureaucrats, impoverished pensioners, or armies of the unemployed.

Instead, the most common obstacles to the progress of economic reform in postcommunist transitions have come from very different sources: from enterprise insiders who have become new owners only to strip their firms' assets; from commercial bankers who have opposed macroeconomic stabilization to preserve their enormously profitable arbitrage opportunities in distorted financial markets; from local officials who have prevented market entry into their regions to protect their share of local monopoly rents; and from so-called mafiosi who have undermined the creation of a stable legal foundation for the market economy. These actors can hardly be classified as short-term net losers in the overall reform process. On the contrary, they were its earliest and biggest winners. These net winners did not oppose the initiation of the reform process, nor have they sought a full-scale reversal of reform. Instead, they have frequently attempted to block specific advances in the reform process that threaten to eliminate the special advantages and market distortions upon which their own early reform gains were based. Instead of forming a constituency in support of advancing reforms, the short-term winners have often sought to stall the economy in a *partial reform equilibrium* that generates concentrated rents for themselves, while imposing high costs on the rest of society. While conventional models of the politics of economic reform are driven by the short-term incentives of the net losers, the postcommunist transitions appear to have faced far more serious obstacles to the progress of economic reforms from the net winners. Moreover, the obstacles have come less in the form of ex ante opposition to the onset of reform or ex post electoral reversals of reform than in the prolonged maintenance of partial reforms and their associated market distortions. This suggests that the prescriptions derived from conventional models about the political institutions most conducive to economic reform need to be reexamined. This paper concludes that the emphasis on insulating the state from the short-term losers—the major focus of many existing models—needs to be replaced with a recognition of the importance of restraining the winners in the early stages of reform.

The paper begins by testing the applicability to the postcommunist transitions of models based on a J-curve distribution of the costs and benefits of reform. It examines both the ex ante and ex post political constraints on reform predicted from such a model. As for the ex ante constraints, the evidence from these transitions suggests that those countries with more frequent elections and shorter executive tenures, that is, those most susceptible to electoral challenge from short-term losers, have been more likely to adopt comprehensive economic reforms than states that are more insulated from electoral pressures. As for the ex post constraints, annual rankings of the progress of economic reform are examined to demonstrate the weakness of the threat of electoral reversals of reform in the postcommunist transitions.

The paper then presents a model of the politics of economic reform in which the primary political challenge derives from the net winners in the overall reform process. Partial economic reforms are shown to produce market distortions that generate a pattern of concentrated gains and dispersed losses in the short term. Winners have an incentive to try to preserve these sources of considerable rents as long as possible by blocking any measures to eliminate these distortions. Recent evidence on changes in the concentration of incomes in the postcommunist countries is used to confirm this pattern of gains and losses. Transition economies that have introduced only partial reforms have experienced a higher redistribution of income to a narrower constituency than have those countries with either more comprehensive reforms or few reforms at all. The paper concludes with an alternative view of the political institutions most conducive to sustained progress in economic reforms given the challenge posed by the winners.

THE J CURVE

Most existing models of the politics of economic reform are based on an analysis of the costs and benefits of reform that conforms to a J-curve, depicted in Figure 1. The simple, compelling idea is that economic reforms generate transitional costs in the short term before they begin to produce their promised economic gains. The magnitude of these costs is believed to be positively correlated with the comprehensiveness (or radicalness) of the reforms adopted. Inefficient enterprises must be closed or restructured, state subsidies and social spending must be reduced, and domestic prices must be raised to world levels—a program that in the short term is expected to generate unemployment, sharp declines in production, and falling living standards. Only when the economy begins to adjust to the new structure of incentives can one expect any amelioration of the situation. Indeed, some analysts even expect the onset of reforms to increase the misallocation of resources in the short run, as poorly defined property rights, the absence of developed financial markets, the continued presence of monopolies, and insufficiently developed human capital distort the response to market incentives.

The depiction of the costs and benefits of reform as a J-curve is particularly compelling from a political standpoint, as it provides a plausible explanation for the central paradox of the political economy of reform: if reforms ultimately make all or a majority of a country's citizens better off, why are they so politically contentious, especially in democratic systems? The standard answer has been that reforms are subject to a time inconsistency problem, requiring actors to accept losses in the short term for the mere promise of future gains. If the government cannot make a credible commitment to maintain those reforms until the promised benefits arrive or to insure that those gains are not confiscated once they do arrive, then it may be rational for economic actors to reject the reforms ex ante.

The J-curve distribution of costs and benefits is also assumed to create a collective action problem that generates political obstacles to economic reform. It is commonly argued that the losses from economic reform are concentrated among specific groups—namely, those who were privileged or subsidized by the previous status quo—while the benefits of reform are more widely dispersed. Low inflation, increased availability of goods and services, a stable currency, and so forth—these nonexcludable benefits accrue to society as a whole and thus have the characteristics of public goods. If the losses are concentrated and the gains dispersed, then the losers should have greater selective incentives to engage in collective action than the winners. Thus, the losers' political opposition to economic reforms is expected to be more effective than the winners' political support of reform, even if the latter outnumber the former.

The time inconsistency and collective action problems are believed to produce both ex ante and ex post political obstacles to reform. Politicians in democratic systems will be reluctant to introduce any reforms whose benefits will not be realized before the next elections. Since radical reforms are believed to generate higher short-term costs, if they are adopted they are expected to face a high likelihood of ex post reversal as the losers react to the high costs. Politicians are therefore expected to favor more moderate reform programs.

These ex ante and ex post political constraints on reform have led many analysts and reform practitioners to emphasize the benefits of insulating reform governments from the pressures of the losers, at least in the initial stages of the reform process. In the earlier literature on the politics of reform, this was the basis for the view that authoritarian governments had an advantage in implementing economic reforms. This has largely been replaced with an emphasis on the benefits of state autonomy, the concentration of executive power, and the delegation of power to technocrats for the adoption of economic reforms. Yet the justification for both views is the same: political institutions need to be structured to shield state actors from the pressures of the short-term losers until the realization of gains from the reforms creates the necessary political constituency to sustain them.

Although the implications of the J-curve approach to the politics of economic reform have been widely accepted, they are based on a number of assumptions that have not been subjected to systematic empirical tests. This approach assumes that economic reforms will generate transitional costs prior to the realization of benefits and that these costs will be greater with the adoption of more extensive reform programs. On the political dynamics of reforms, this approach leads to a simple hypothesis: political systems in which reformers are more susceptible to the reaction of the losers are less likely to adopt extensive economic reforms and more likely to suffer reversals of reform if such measures are adopted. The postcommunist transitions provide an ideal opportunity to test these assumptions about transition costs and the behavior of reformers on a new set of cases.

The recent availability of reliable cross-national data from the postcommunist transitions allows us to test some of the economic assumptions inherent in models based on the J-curve. Though the data confirm that the introduction of economic reforms entails substantial transitional costs, they challenge the assumption linking the magnitude of these costs to the extensiveness of the reforms adopted. The transitional costs of reform as reflected in declining growth rates do appear to follow a J-curve pattern. The average growth rate for the region begins to fall in 1990 (-4.5) dropping to its lowest level in 1992 (-17.7 percent), and then beginning a gradual recovery. However, an examination of the postcommunist countries grouped by the extent of their economic reforms reveals an unexpected picture.

The World Bank has developed a set of indicators to measure the extent of liberalizing reforms adopted in three broad areas (internal prices, external prices, and private sector entry) across all the transition economies. On the basis of these indicators, the transition economies can be separated into four main groups: advanced reformers, high intermediate reformers, low intermediate reformers, and slow reformers. It is not the advanced reformers that have suffered the sharpest declines in real GDP, as the J-curve approach would predict, but the intermediate reformers. Indeed, the advanced reformers have the lowest overall output declines and the most rapid recoveries. The average ratio of real GDP in 1994 to the 1989 level in the advanced reform group was 83 percent. The average ratio declined to 65 percent for the high intermediate reformers, 57 percent for the low intermediate reformers, and 72 percent for the slow reformers. Among the postcommunist countries the preliminary evidence suggests that the deeper the economic reforms adopted, the less steep is the valley of the transition in terms of overall transitional costs. In other words, the costs of reform are not positively correlated with the extensiveness of the reforms adopted.

The pattern of unemployment among the postcommunist countries—generally seen as a critical factor shaping the politics of economic reform—conforms more closely to the expectations of the J-curve approach. The countries that have undertaken reform do exhibit considerably higher unemployment than the slowest reformers, but the relationship between the extensiveness of adopted reforms and the level of unemployment is less clear. Åslund, Boone, and Johnson find no statistically significant correlation between the extent of economic reforms and unemployment rates once some basic control variables are included in the regression. In addition, the evidence from individual cases is mixed. Despite having introduced and maintained one of the most comprehensive reform programs, the Czech Republic has kept its unemployment rates quite low. At the same time, less comprehensive reformers, such as Albania, Bulgaria, and Romania, have suffered from relatively high unemployment. States of the former Soviet Union (FSU) have generally maintained lower unemployment than those of Eastern Europe, but the most comprehensive reformers within the FSU (the Baltic states) have had the highest unemployment rates.

The political implications of the J-curve model have never been tested systematically. If ex ante political incentives are an impediment to the adoption of comprehensive economic reforms, one would expect politicians facing greater electoral pressures and having a shorter expected tenure to be less likely to initiate such reforms. As Haggard and Kaufman argue, from the politician's point of view, some degree of security of tenure "would appear to be a minimal requirement of successful reform, since a high degree of insecurity shortens time horizons and increases the discount rate to future payoffs from economic reforms."

Again, the countries are grouped by their World Bank liberalization scores. The first column indicates the number of executive turnovers that has occurred from the onset of the transition through the end of 1995. Both the advanced and the intermediate reformers have an average of just over three and half executive turnovers, while both groups of slow reformers average no more than one turnover in the same period. Poland, one of the most celebrated cases of radical reform in the region, has had seven prime ministers and three presidents between 1990 and 1997. The Baltic countries, which have been the most advanced reformers of the FSU, have all had no fewer than four prime ministerial turnovers since independence. While other advanced reformers have had more stable governments, all of them have experienced some turnover in their prime ministers since the beginning of their transitions. In contrast, among the slow reformers, Ukraine and Belarus are the only countries that have changed their chief executives since the onset of the transition.

The differences in executive turnovers are reflected from another vantage point in the evidence on the tenure of postcommunist governments. The countries of the first two reform groups had an average government tenure of approximately twenty-five months.

Six of the eleven countries in these two groups had an average government tenure of less than eighteen months. While some of the most successful reformers—the Czech Republic, Hungary, and Slovenia—have had individual governments with relatively long tenures, these governments do not necessarily fit well with the standard image of reform governments as strong, streamlined, and relatively autonomous, with the capacity to push through reforms despite bureaucratic and popular opposition. In Slovenia the Drnovsek government, which has been in office since May 1992, began as an explicitly transitional government until parliamentary elections in December 1992. Since the elections Drnovsek has headed a fragile, five-party coalition government that has been subject to frequent no-confidence votes and whose continued survival has often been tenuous. In Hungary the government of Josef Antall, though quite secure, rejected the radical approach to economic reform and pursued an explicitly gradual strategy that benefited from Hungary's prior history of communist-era reforms. The only case of radical economic reform pursued by a stable government with a high degree of security and autonomy is the Klaus government in the Czech Republic.

The slow reformers generally have political leaders with the longest and most secure tenures in the region. With the exception of Belarus and Ukraine, all of the slow reformers have been ruled continuously by the same respective presidents since the start of their transitions. Among the advanced and intermediate reformers, Romania had a similar unbroken presidential rule until the recent defeat of Ion Iliescu in the November 1997 presidential election.

The postcommunist countries with more frequent executive turnovers and shorter government tenures have generally been the most far-reaching economic reformers. Politicians with shorter expected time horizons have nevertheless been far more likely to adopt economic reforms. Those political leaders with the greatest security of tenure have tended to introduce partial economic reforms or have delayed reforms altogether, even though they would appear to have faced the weakest threat of electoral or popular challenge to more comprehensive reforms. Although this evidence cannot support a causal link between executive turnovers, government stability, and economic reform, it does challenge the notion that the threat of electoral revenge against the short-term costs of economic reform is a substantial ex ante obstacle to the adoption of reform in the postcommunist transitions.

If the political threat to economic reform is primarily ex post, then we would expect to see economic reforms reversed or otherwise moderated in the electoral cycle following their initial adoption. Przeworski argues that the high short-term costs of reform are likely to spark an electoral backlash and subsequent reversal or moderation of reforms. This creates a familiar stop-and-go pattern of economic transition in which reforms "proceed in spurts: advancing, stumbling, retreating and advancing again." The postcommunist countries have certainly experienced the pressures of electoral backlashes against reform. In three of the five countries in the advanced reform group—Hungary, Poland, and the Slovak Republic—reform governments have been voted out of office to be replaced by parties advocating more moderate reforms. Similar reversals of reform governments have occurred in three of the six countries in the high intermediate reform group—Bulgaria, Estonia, and Lithuania. However, these electoral reversals have not been accompanied by any major reversals in the course of economic reform in these countries.

The annual scores on the three categories of the World Bank's liberalization index for the six countries listed above that have had electoral backlashes against reform governments. By the end of 1994 there were only two instances in which these liberalization scores declined from year to year. In Bulgaria scores on the liberalization of internal and external prices declined slightly from 0.9 in 1993 to 0.8 in 1994 (on a 0-1 scale with 1 as fully liberalized), as the nonparty government of technocrats led by Luben Berov was replaced after a general election by the Bulgarian Socialist Party. A similarly modest decline in the liberalization score on external prices from 0.9 to 0.8 was recorded between 1992 and 1993 in the Slovak Republic following the breakup of Czechoslovakia. According to the

World Bank scores, there were no other substantial reversals of liberalizing reforms in any of the postcommunist countries that experienced electoral backlashes against reform governments. Indeed, out of the entire set of postcommunist countries the two minor declines described above were the only two reversals in reform scores from 1989 to 1994.

Electoral backlashes did occasionally slow the rate of progress in particular areas of economic reform. The speed of large-scale privatization slowed considerably in Lithuania and Poland after the electoral victories of communist successor parties in those countries. Voucher privatization was also delayed in the Slovak Republic after the breakup of Czechoslovakia. Yet there have also been cases in which electoral backlashes against reform-oriented governments were followed by an intensification of reform in some areas. Russia made the greatest progress in large-scale privatization only after the reform government of Egor Gaidar was forced out of office. Hungary and Lithuania implemented tough macroeconomic stabilization programs after electoral victories by socialist parties. Estonia has continued its rapid pace of economic reform following the replacement of the reform government of Mart Laar by the far more moderate Vahi government.

Though in most cases the introduction of comprehensive economic reform programs did spark revenge at the ballot box against reform governments, the electoral reversals did not generate the expected reform reversals. The notion that politicians would be forced to reverse reforms in response to the popular reaction against high transitional costs has to date not been evident in the postcommunist transitions.

The postcommunist countries present a paradox in the political economy of reform. In the conventional view, comprehensive reforms face ex ante and ex post political obstacles from losers who react against the short-term transitional costs of reform, despite the promise of benefits in the long term. Yet in the postcommunist transitions, more comprehensive reform programs appear to have inflicted lower transitional costs in the short term than have intermediate or slow reforms. Moreover, it has been precisely those countries in which the political leaders have been most vulnerable to the demands of the short-term losers that have adopted and sustained the highest levels of economic reform. Governments that have been insulated from electoral pressures and that have enjoyed a high level of tenure security—which traditionally have been seen as the most capable of initiating necessary, but costly economic reforms—have proven to be the laggards in the postcommunist economic transitions. Why have so many postcommunist countries chosen a course of partial reforms with higher social costs in the short term and lower expected gains in the long term? If the pressure to adopt a suboptimal course of reform does not derive from the traditional losers—unemployed workers, impoverished pensioners, superfluous state bureaucrats, and so on—what are the political dynamics driving partial reforms?

THE POLITICS OF PARTIAL REFORM

The exclusive focus on the net losers in the political economy of reform has deflected attention from analyzing the interests and incentives of the net winners. The conventional approach to the politics of economic reform is based on a simple, seemingly uncontroversial assumption, that economic reforms create winners who gain stakes in defending and extending those reforms. One of the goals of reform, therefore, is to create a constituency of winners that will support ongoing efforts to advance the transition to a market economy. The most frequently cited problem of relying on the winners in the short term is that the gains from reform are dispersed throughout the entire economy, while the losses are concentrated within particular groups. The efficiency gains normally associated with economic reform—reducing inflation, creating a stable currency, lowering fiscal deficits, and increasing the availability of goods and services—can be considered as public goods. Therefore, the beneficiaries of these policies face barriers to collective action. By contrast, the losers face concentrated costs in the short term and thus have strong selective incentives to engage in collective action against the reforms. Though the winners and potential winners are seen as the best hope of creating a constituency for reform, the pattern of gains from reform in the short term is assumed to weaken their effectiveness as a political force.

This raises a question that has not been investigated in the political economy of reform: who gains from partial economic reforms? Partial reforms entail the selected introduction of market mechanisms into an economy in which substantial spheres of economic activity still operate according to alternative mechanisms of coordination. It was recognized early in the transition that partial reforms threatened to disrupt the stability and effectiveness—however limited—of the existing economic system without necessarily generating the efficiency gains associated with fully functioning markets. As a result, partial reforms were predicted to generate higher social costs in the short term than both comprehensive reforms and maintenance of the status quo. At the same time, partial reforms were expected to generate rent-seeking opportunities arising from price differentials between the liberalized sectors of the economy and those still coordinated by nonmarket mechanisms.

Examples of such rent-seeking activities have been ubiquitous in the postcommunist transitions. Rapid foreign trade liberalization with incomplete price liberalization has allowed state enterprise managers to sell their highly subsidized natural resource inputs (for example, oil and gas) to foreign buyers at world market prices. Price liberalization without concomitant progress in opening market entry or breaking up monopolies has created opportunities for some producers to earn monopoly rents. Privatization without reform of the credit mechanism has allowed managers to divert subsidized state credits earmarked to uphold production into short-term money markets at high interest rates. In each case, these arbitrage opportunities have generated rents to those in a position to take advantage of these market distortions. Yet the redistribution of rents leads to a misallocation of resources in comparison with the more efficient rationing that might be expected from a fully functioning market. To some extent, these rent-seeking opportunities should exist regardless of the reform strategy adopted. The transition from a command economy to a market economy requires an extensive set of policy and institutional changes, many of which have different time horizons. Clearly, prices can be liberalized far more quickly than monopolies can be broken up. Interest rates can be changed more quickly than new commercial banks capable of evaluating loan requests can be created. Restrictions on foreign and domestic trade can be lifted more quickly than adequate mechanisms for contract enforcement can be put into place. These differentials in the time horizons of various components of comprehensive reform produce temporary market distortions similar to the gaps associated with the explicit introduction of partial reforms.

Both comprehensive and partial economic reforms produce winners in the short term, with gains partly or wholly determined by rents generated by the existence of distortions in the developing market economy. Moreover, these rents are highly concentrated, benefiting those in a position to arbitrage between the reformed and unreformed sectors of the economy. If economic reforms continue to progress over time, then the market distortions that produce these concentrated rents should gradually be eliminated. Further price liberalization undermines arbitrage operations between the fixed-price state sector and the free-price export sector. The progressive hardening of enterprise budget constraints eliminates the misallocation of state subsidies. Privatization coupled with the creation of an effective corporate governance structure reduces asset stripping by enterprise insiders. While these measures produce efficiency gains for the economy, they also alter the flow of private gains to the initial winners of reform. The winners give up a concentrated stream of rents generated by the initial market distortions for a share of the overall efficiency gains associated with further market reforms. As a result, progress in the implementation of market reforms could reduce the private gains to the initial winners over time, while increasing efficiency gains for the economy as a whole.

From the perspective of the winners, the traditional J-curve is reversed. Their incomes rise rapidly in the short term as the initial market distortions generate concentrated rents. Yet over time, the progress of reforms gradually eliminates those distortions, dissipating the rents from the initial stages of reform. The shape of this winner's curve would depend on the comprehensiveness of the reform at the start of the transition and the continued pace of reforms over time. The line W_p represents the winners' consumption curve in a country that began the transition with partial reforms. The line W_c denotes the winners' income curve in a country that began with a more comprehensive reform program. The flatter curve suggests that comprehensive reforms generate less concentrated rents for the winners in the short term and less steep income declines as the reforms progress.

By adding these winners' curves to the traditional J-curve, a different picture of the political economy of reform in postcommunist transitions emerges. If partial reforms generate higher social costs in the short term, then the increasing concentration of rents to the winners should entail a corresponding decrease in consumption of the losers. The losers' consumption curve in a partially reformed economy, L_p, is the mirror image of the winners' curve, W_p. As the private gains to the winners from partial reform increase, the costs to the losers increase as well. If the distortions of partial reform are gradually eliminated over time, then the winners face a reduction in their rents, while the losers share in the efficiency gains of further market reforms, thus narrowing the gap between the two curves. Countries that adopt more comprehensive reforms at the start have a narrower gap between the income curves of the winners and losers, W_c and L_c. The transitional costs of reform in the short term are lower than under partial reform and the losers begin to see gains from reform at an earlier point in the process and at a higher level.

In the standard J-curve approach, if elections are called prior to the point at which the reforms have begun to produce benefits for the majority of voters, the voters will react to the short-term costs by casting their ballots for a reversal or moderation of the reforms. Yet the addition of the winners suggests a different approach to the political obstacles to economic reform. The politics of economic reform is usually portrayed as a set of choices between omnibus reform programs (radical versus gradual) at key junctures in the political process (namely, elections) in which voters play the deciding role. Yet the process might be more realistically depicted as a sequence of many distinct choices over time on separate components of an overall reform plan—liberalization, stabilization, privatization, and many more—that do not necessarily coincide with the electoral calendar. In such a process, the winners with their concentrated gains would be expected to play a more decisive role, given their greater resources, their smaller number, and their selective incentives for collective action. Indeed, it is reasonable to assume that the winners might have an implicit veto power in the decisions over separate components of economic reform, especially those that affect their existing rent streams.

If the process of reform consists of a sequence of decisions over time, then the winners will continue to support the advance of reforms until time t_1. Beyond t_1, the winners have an incentive to veto any reform proposals that move the economy toward more comprehensive reforms, since such measures will begin to decrease the rents they gained at the earlier stage of the reform process. Thus, the winners prefer to freeze the emerging market economy in some partially reformed state that maximizes the concentration of rents to themselves, though at a significant social cost. While the political challenge of the J-curve was to maintain reforms through the valley of the transition, the challenge of partial reform is to sustain the momentum of reform past the "peak of transition," that is, the point at which further reforms threaten the rents accruing to winners from the distortions created by earlier reforms.

This highly stylized model of the politics of economic reform differs sharply from the standard approach. While the J-curve approach assumes that the costs of reform are concentrated and the benefits are dispersed, this model begins with the opposite assumption. The gains from reform are highly concentrated within a narrow group of winners in the short term and are dispersed over time only if the reform process progresses. The costs of reform, by contrast, are dispersed across the entire economy from the start. The J-curve approach assumes that the transitional costs of comprehensive reforms in the short term are greater than those accompanying more gradual reforms, while this model again assumes the opposite. The conventional approach characterizes the politics of economic reform as a choice between omnibus reform programs made by voters at key points in the political calendar. This model portrays the reform process as a sequence of decisions on separate components of reform that is continuous over time and in which the winners who gained from earlier decisions have the decisive voice. On the basis of these alternative assumptions, the partial reform model presented here suggests a very different characterization of the political obstacles to economic reform in the postcommunist transitions. The political dilemma of economic reform is not how to sustain reform in the face of opposition from the net losers in the short term, but how to advance reform in the face of efforts by the net winners to preserve the market distortions that produced their gains in the short term.

EVIDENCE

One of the key predictions of this alternative approach is that countries that have maintained partial reforms should exhibit a greater concentration of gains to the winners and a higher level of transitional costs than those countries that have pursued more comprehensive reforms. One way to gauge the degree of partial reforms is to examine different levels of progress in each of the separate components that are generally considered to constitute a comprehensive reform program. The European Bank for Reconstruction and Development (EBRD) defines nine separate dimensions of the reform process: privatization (large- and small-scale), enterprise restructuring, price liberalization, foreign trade liberalization, competition policy, banking reform, securities market reform, and legal reform. The EBRD provides a rating of cumulative progress along each dimension on a 1-4 scale. By taking the variance (that is, the dispersion around the mean) of these ratings for each of the postcommunist countries, we obtain a very rough measure of imbalances in the level of progress across the separate dimensions. Higher variances indicate more unbalanced progress across the different dimensions of economic reform and, hence, a greater degree of partial reforms. The average variances for each of the four groups of countries show a curvilinear pattern among the groups. Both the advanced and the slow reform groups have low variances across their reform scores, while the intermediate groups have considerably higher variances suggesting more uneven progress in economic reform.

If the countries of the intermediate groups have maintained the most uneven or partial economic reforms, then they should demonstrate a higher concentration of gains from reform along with higher overall social costs. Though highly incomplete, recent data on inequality and income concentration across the transition economies show some interesting trends. The transition in the postcommunist countries has sparked an extremely rapid redistribution of income. Since the beginning of the transition, the level of income inequality has risen in every postcommunist country with the exception of the Slovak Republic. The average Gini coefficient—one of the standard measures of inequality—for the entire region jumped by one-third, from 24 in 1987-88 to 32 in 1993-94, a pace virtually unprecedented in the postwar era. In a time span of five to seven years the transition economies have moved from inequality levels below those of most OECD countries to, in several cases, levels on a par with or higher than the most unequal OECD countries. The extent of the redistribution differs across the reform groups. From 1987-88 to 1993-94, Gini coefficients increased in the two intermediate reform groups by 43 percent (high intermediate) and 53 percent (low intermediate), as compared with 18 percent among the advanced reformers and 30 percent among the slow reformers. The highest Gini coefficients in the transition economies are among the low intermediate reformers, while the most advanced reformers have maintained the lowest levels of inequality. Russia stands out among the transition economies for having doubled its degree of inequality during the period.

The average changes in inequality across the reform groups to their average variances on the EBRD transition indicators. The curvilinear pattern is roughly similar. Though this evidence cannot support any causal claims, it does suggest an interesting relationship between the imbalances associated with partial reforms and increasing levels of inequality among the postcommunist countries.

The increase in inequality in the postcommunist transitions has been driven by a substantial concentration of incomes in the highest income group, though data on income concentration are less complete than for overall inequality. Table 5 reports the change (in percentage points) of total income share for the top income quintile between 1987-88 and 1993-94. The increase in income share for the top quintile in the intermediate reformers exceeds that of the advanced reformers with the exception of the Czech Republic. The top quintile in the high intermediate reformers increased its income share by an average of 7.8 points, while the average share in the advanced reform group increased by only 2.8 points. The two countries among the low intermediate group for which such data are available also show substantial increases in the concentration of income. Again, Russia stands out with a remarkable 20-point increase in the income share of the top quintile. With the exception of Hungary and the Slovak Republic, all of the postcommunist countries have experienced a highly regressive redistribution of income since the start of the transition. Yet the evidence suggests that this redistribution reached a considerably higher magnitude in those countries that have maintained partial reforms.

The variation in the pattern of inequality and concentration among reform groups is closely matched by the cumulative output declines during the transition, the standard measure of the costs of reform. The average cumulative decline in GDP for the two intermediate reform groups exceeds both the advanced and the slow reformers. By 1994 GDP had fallen by an average of 43 percent among the countries of the lower intermediate reform group and 35.2 percent among the countries of the high intermediate group. The advanced reformers suffered a much lower average GDP loss at 19.4 percent, while the slow reformers fell by an average of 28.3 percent.

The limited evidence available on changes in inequality, the concentration of incomes, and GDP across the postcommunist countries supports the predictions of the partial reform model.

Though postcommunist economic reforms have clearly generated high costs in the short term, the gains they have produced have been highly concentrated among a narrow group of winners. Countries that have adopted and maintained partial reforms have had the highest concentration of these gains, while at the same time experiencing the highest short-term costs among the transition economies. The net winners have gained more relative to the losers in partially reformed economies than have their counterparts among either the advanced or the slow reformers. Moreover, as the variances of the EBRD transition indicators demonstrate, these gains have been associated with imbalances in the adoption of reforms and the market distortions they create.

If the correction of these distortions through further market reforms threatens to reduce the rent flows to the short-term winners, then they should be expected to oppose such measures as long as their share of the efficiency gains generated by further reforms does not exceed the lost rent flows. The winners have an incentive to maintain a partial reform equilibrium in order to maximize the concentration of rents in the economy. While existing analyses of the politics of economic reform tend to assume that the net winners constitute a political constituency in favor of sustaining and advancing market reforms, the partial reform model suggests that these winners could constitute a powerful obstacle to the steady advance of the reform process.

The main political implication of the partial reform model is clear: if the winners from partial reforms have a veto power over policy, then the transition should result in a partial reform equilibrium that concentrates gains among the winners at a high social cost. Therefore, the primary political challenge of reform in this model is to restrain the net winners. Political systems that concentrate more power in the hands of the winners are more likely to preserve partial reforms over time. By contrast, political systems more open to the participation of the losers in the policy-making process should generate a greater dispersion of the gains of reform. If the initial rents in the early stages of reform are more thoroughly dissipated, then winners might find the efficiency gains from comprehensive reforms to be more attractive than the reduced rent flows from a partial reform equilibrium. It is difficult to measure with any precision the concentration of power in the hands of the short-term winners in the transition economies. One option is to try to measure the continued power of the former communist elite, since partial reforms are believed to benefit precisely those—such as state enterprise managers, collective farm chairmen, ministerial bureaucrats, and party officials—who are in a position to arbitrage between the highly regulated and subsidized state sector and the less constrained free market sector. It is possible to measure the remaining political power of the former Communist Party and its successor organizations in postcommunist political institutions. Alternatively, the extent of personnel turnover in government posts or key economic sectors from the communist era to the transition period could be surveyed. However, such measures would miss the influence of other groups benefiting from partial reforms, those whose gains are not necessarily linked to their positions in the previous communist system, such as new commercial bankers, investment fund managers, and a whole range of private entrepreneurs. In many postcommunist systems these actors have also made extraordinary short-term gains from distortions in the developing market economy and are believed to wield substantial political power.

Another possible approach to this problem is to measure the extent to which postcommunist political systems are open to pressures from the short-term losers. This assumes that the greater the participation of the losers in the political process, the more constrained will be the power of the winners. Greater participation of the losers can be expected to check the power of the winners to veto reform measures that do not coincide with the latter's short-term interests. More importantly, politicians who face regular, genuinely competitive elections may be constrained from pursuing policies that concentrate gains to a narrow segment of the electorate while generating high social costs.

The economic reform scores are based on the EBRD 's cumulative transition indicators for 1994. The measure of democracy is based on the average of each country's annual score on the

Freedom House index of political rights over the course of the transition. The Freedom House index measures individual rights to participate freely in the political process, focusing especially on the political inclusiveness of the electoral system. The scatterplot reveals a strong positive correlation between political rights and economic reform (r = 0.78). More inclusive political regimes have adopted and sustained higher levels of economic reform than those with more restrictive political rights. Given that losers outnumber winners in the short term, we can assume that a more inclusive political regime gives the losers of the economic reform process greater opportunities to influence political outcomes than a less inclusive regime.

Another more specific proxy measure of the inclusiveness of the political system focuses on the size of coalition governments. As the number of political parties in a coalition government increases, the number of actors and groups whose agreement must be coordinated for effective policymaking increases as well. This tends to weaken the concentration of power in the hands of any single political party or group. Broader coalition governments should have a lower risk of being captured exclusively by the net winners of reform than should governments dominated by a single party. One way to measure the size of coalition governments is a simple scale developed by Roubini and Sachs in their studies of coalition governments and budget deficits in OECD countries. Figure 8 shows a scatterplot of the relationship between the size of coalition governments and the sum of the 1994 EBRD transition indicators for each postcommunist country. There is a strong positive correlation (r= 0.72) between coalition governments and economic reform. As more political forces are brought into the policy-making process, governments appear to be more likely to adopt and sustain more comprehensive economic reforms.

BIBLIOGRAPHY

Ahmad, Imtiaz: *State and Foreign Policy: India's Role in South Asia*, New Delhi, Vikas, 1993.

Carl J. Friedrich: *Constitutional Government and Democracy*, Boston, Ginn, 1950.

Dikshit, D.P.: *Political History of the Chalukyas of Badami*, New Delhi, Abhinav, 1980.

English, Barbara: *The War for a Persian Lady*, Boston, Houghton Mifflin, 1971.

Hamilton, J.R.: *Alexander the Great*, Oxford, Clarendon Press, 1965.

Jack Peltason: *Federal Courts in the Political Process*, New York, Random House, 1955.

Kashyap, C.: *National Policy Studies*, New Delhi, Tata McGraw-Hill for the Lok Sabha Secretariat, 1990.

Leslie, J.: *Toward Empowerment: Women and Politics in India*, Colorado, Westview Press, 1992.

Max, Beloff: *Foreign Policy and the Democratic Process*, Baltimore, Johns Hopkins University Press, 1955.

Nevitte, Neil, and Charles H. Kennedy: *Ethnic Preference and Public Policy in Developing States*, Boulder, Lynne Rienner Publishers, 1986.

Pye, Lucian W. and Mary W.: *Asian Power and Politics: the Cultural Dimensions of Authority*, Cambridge, Mass, Belknap Press, 1985.

Robert, W.: *Public Bureaucracy and the Incentive Problem*, Washington, D.C., World Bank, 1994.

Schmidhauser, R.: *Supreme Court: Its Politics, Personalities and Procedures*, New York, Holt, 1960.

Victor G. : *Law as a Political Instrument*, New York, Random House, 1955.

INDEX

□□□